595/10
3

D0426688

WAR
and/or
SURVIVAL

WAR
and/or
SURVIVAL

William V. O'Brien

DOUBLEDAY & COMPANY, INC.
GARDEN CITY, NEW YORK
1969

UNIVERSITY LIBRARY
1818   Lethbridge, Alberta

Library of Congress Catalog Card Number 68–11769
Copyright © 1969 by William V. O'Brien
All Rights Reserved
First Edition
Printed in the United States of America

TO MADGE

Acknowledgments

I cannot adequately acknowledge all of my debts to persons and organizations who have helped me in the preparation of this book. I must, however, single out some.

My thanks for comments on the manuscript go to Professor Paul Ramsey of Princeton University, who graciously volunteered to provide an introduction to this book which I deeply appreciate; to Professor James E. Dougherty of St. Joseph's College, and to my colleagues from Georgetown, Professors Ulrich S. Allers, Paul S. Ello, and Nicholas G. Onuf.

I am particularly indebted to Lieutenant Colonel Robert L. Schweitzer, United States Army, and a number of persons in the Department of Defense who assisted him in evaluating the military and arms control portions of this book, especially Lieutenant Colonel John Granger, currently assigned to the Joint Chiefs of Staff. Naturally, their assistance involves no suggestion of U. S. Government endorsement or reference to classified information.

Dr. A. William Loos, President, Council on Religion and International Affairs (CRIA) has been a source of wisdom and encouragement to me for close to a decade and his programs have given me the opportunity to learn and to develop ideas about the interrelations between practical foreign policy and strategic dilemmas and normative values. I take this occasion to thank him personally and to thank the entire CRIA organization for their contribution to my own formation as a morally concerned student of foreign and defense policy.

I should also like to acknowledge the assistance of Mr. Jerome Spingarn of the U. S. Arms Control and Disarmament Agency, one of the first to explore the implications of the key concept of "arms control" (notably in the National Planning Association's 1958 study, *1970 Without Arms Control*), and a persevering pioneer in bringing private citizens' associations into the field of arms control discussion and action.

I could not have completed this book without the dedicated and imaginative assistance of Mr. Don Daniels, graduate fellow, Georgetown University. Nor could the book have appeared on schedule without the editorial and typing assistance of Mr. John Hébert, graduate fellow in History, Mrs. John Hébert, Secretary, Institute of World Polity, and Margaret Harrison, School of Foreign Service, of Georgetown University, and Miss Ann Yeomans, a student in the School of Foreign Service.

I gratefully acknowledge the support of Georgetown University in innumerable ways—through the Institute of World Polity, through its encouragement of special conferences on many of the subjects discussed in this book, and through its various Library services which provided accurate and prompt information and assistance when both were vital.

Finally, I appreciate permissions from the publishers for quotations from the following works:

Kenneth E. Boulding's *Conflict and Defense, A General Theory* (New York, Evanston and London, Harper and Row Torchbooks, The University Library, 1962); and

A. J. P. Taylor's *English History 1914–1945,* by permission of the Clarendon Press, Oxford, 1965.

WILLIAM V. O'BRIEN
November 1968
Washington, D.C.

Contents

Contents

Introduction

This book is about war, deterrence, revolution, and peace with justice. It is about the international system—the improbability of radically changing this system within any time-frame we can contemplate, and the consequent need to work within it for security and the good of mankind. The book is about international law resident in treaties and conventions or, more importantly, in the customary practices of states. It is about "peace research," "conflict resolution," napalm and torture; collective security, arms control, disarmament, conflict management, and the nuclear nonproliferation treaty; intervention, "assured destruction," Vietnam; "the laws of war," legitimate military necessity, and the natural right of self-defense and of revolution.

In short, this book is about most of the forces that have come upon us in the present age—the "treacherous traps" affecting the use of armed coercion by any nation or in the cause of revolutionary justice.

Above all, this book is concerned to discover the legal limits and the moral norms governing any of these activities of men or of states.

The author, William V. O'Brien, is Professor of Government and Director of the Institute of World Polity at Georgetown University in Washington, D.C. and an Associate editor of the international journal *World Justice* (Louvain). Mr. O'Brien is also the

xii   Introduction

author of an extensive list of articles in the field of international law
and international relations. He has edited, coauthored, or himself
written a number of volumes on international affairs. The most
relevant to mention, for readers of the present volume, is his
Nuclear War, Deterrence and Morality (Westminster, Maryland:
Newman Press, 1967).

An active layman in the Roman Catholic Church, Professor
O'Brien served as President of the Catholic Association for International Peace in 1961–62 and again for 1966–68. He was
Chairman of one of the sections on Peace and the World Community
at the Third World Congress of the Lay Apostolate, meeting in
Rome in October, 1967. Indeed, if the lay apostolate has *pereti*
(expert advisers), O'Brien was one of these, as he is one of those
laymen whose expertness and concern are apt to add depth to the
Church's understanding of the problems of world politics, clarity
and discipline to its ethical utterances, and sanity to us all, in a
period that seems lacking in these qualities.

The main argument of the volume is for realism and against
idealism in politics, and particularly on questions of war, deterrence, revolution, and peace with justice. To these questions the
author brings considerable learning, and his own informed and unequivocal verdicts. He is no "crackpot realist," nor does he deride
idealists in international affairs. He simply is a scholar who must
humbly conform his mind to the reality relevant to any proposed
solution or moral judgment. A morality that is out of touch with
reality is not apt to penetrate real issues in any area.

Idealists seriously advocate unlikely acts. They may describe the
world realistically, as a world wracked by dissension and conflict;
but the moral imperatives they urge are, while not immediate, for
an apparently early tomorrow. One step that relies on trust, tries
reason and reconciliation, will by a "multiplier effect" lead on to
two more such steps. And so on. This may be called a foreign
policy based on "anticipatory reconciliation." One way or another,
the idealists' vision is one of a world in which "the dynamics of

power politics are stopped in place." In this sense, idealists expect a "quantum jump" in international relations and world community.

Examples of the idealistic outlook treated at length in this volume are (1) the voluntary designing of world authority or its gradual development out of international law and organizations, (2) "peace research" or "conflict resolution," in the works of Kenneth Boulding, Anatol Rapoport, J. Galtung (Oslo), Amitai Etzioni, and David Singer, who place their confidence in the possibility of fundamental international systemic change by the imaginative and scientific use of the empirical social sciences, and (3) the most well-advertised emphases, and actually the main thrust, of the statements on war and peace issuing from the Roman Catholic Church and from the National and World Council of Churches in recent years. The author does not hesitate to disagree with the teachings of his own church where he believes them to be mistaken. That surely is to go against the stream, because today it is fashionable to disagree with one's church on everything except unearthly expectations in regard to peace. At the same time, O'Brien's mind and conscience have obviously been formed by certain of his church's teachings on political responsibility, now submerged (as Reinhold Niebuhr said of *Pacem in Terris*) by the Pelagianism of contemporary liberalism.

By realism O'Brien does not mean a view of politics closed to future possibilities. He simply means the working assumption that the present international system, at all levels, is likely to remain as it is for a very long time. One must deal with the dilemmas we face on the basis of this assumption. The moral principles with which we confront the problem of war must be relevant to what is now rather than what may be some day.

War, then, like political power, is one of the "givens" of political life in an international system that will not soon be changed. "If the world cannot survive with war, it will not survive," O'Brien writes, "for the 'elimination' of war and replacement of the present system are not in prospect." The first-order problem is to regulate, contain, and channel war, not to eliminate it, as idealists believe. This does not mean that politics is not also based on "trust and sincerity"; it is based on trust and sincerity *where they exist*. The highest task, and by far the most immediate one, is "to change men's attitudes toward war with a view to limiting war," not to change their attitudes with a view to eliminating it.

Twice—in Korea and in Vietnam—the American people nearly if not quite flunked this test of the nuclear age. This test can be flunked by warring too much or warring too little. In this connection, one should ponder O'Brien's words: ". . . A nation's obligation to negotiate . . . is inextricably linked with the attainment or protection of the purposes for which the war was fought. . . . If it is morally wrong to fight an unreasonable war, it is morally wrong to fight a reasonable one . . . and then throw away much that one has been fighting for out of a desire to end the conflict or under the always formidable pressures of public opinion."

A commendable characteristic of this volume is the author's forthrightness, after reasonable argument. It is not possible to corrupt the youth by asking pointed questions, like Socrates, and leading them to ask equally searching questions. But it is possible to corrupt others by giving them mistaken answers. This the author refuses to do. The use of napalm is certainly not illegal under international conventions, except in cases of disproportionate or indiscriminate use; and it may not be immoral, for reasons given. Our action in Vietnam falls within international law and the laws of war, though intervention in the Dominican Republic did not. The use of nonlethal gas is legally prohibited under customary international law, and this practice-rule is morally important if in a very unsafe and violent world one prefers "the defense of thresholds to situation ethics." The rule of "no first use of nuclears" and "no cities first" are to be sustained, though then one must ask what this entails for our military posture in central Europe (where we are bound to use nuclears first), and what it does to the guarantees we made in support of the nuclear nonproliferation treaty.

If the author disagrees with the stress in Church teaching on negotiations that need not fail and idealistic views of the prospects of world public authority, he also disagrees with his church's gen-

eral presumption against the revolutionary just cause. Especially
sane, poignant, and disturbing at the same time, is his discussion of
torture. "Christian advocates of violent revolution had better face the
issues of torture and who is going to do it. . . . Will the priest-
guerrillas of Latin America find 'gentle' means of torturing their
enemies to obtain the information which may be the difference between survival and annihilation by the counterinsurgents? Or will
they take a walk and say some prayers while a tough rebel does
the job?"

In general, O'Brien sets forth in these pages a legal and moral
viewpoint that must hereafter be reckoned with. Some readers will
know that I disagree with the author on a few crucial points in the
analysis of what is right in war (*jus in bello*). I know that O'Brien
distinguishes "legitimate military necessity" from "military utility,"
in that the former is subject to normative restriction by "the laws of
war" resident in treaties and in customary international law and by
a minimum natural law or considerations of humanity. Still the right
of self-defense in interstate conflicts and the right of revolution in
civil wars seem overriding. When is war right? tends to define,
What is right in war? "It is pointless," O'Brien reasons, "to concede
and condone a continued right to recourse to armed force without
authorizing the means which will render such a right meaningful."
If there is a right to violent revolution, there is an implicit right to
use the means which are all that are available to the revolutionaries.
This quickly conflicts with basic elements of "the laws of war" which
may be too much to ask of them, since if they observe these limitations they would have little or no chance of success. Torture is a
case in point. Disembowelment in the village square, too, and other
forms of what is euphemistically called "selective terror" directed
upon civilians.

In general, O'Brien believes that in all present-day forms of
warfare "the absolute immunity of noncombatants from intentional
direct attack cannot be justified as a moral imperative if the right
of legitimate recourse to armed force is conceded." This indicates
what it is that holds pride of place in the laws of war and among

the natural rights governing men and states. The right of self-defense and the right of revolution, which O'Brien describes as "one of the most fundamental human rights, ranking with that of self-defense," seem to me to have been endowed with the power rightfully to set aside any other determination of justice or humanity and also the power rightfully to set aside the laws of war insofar as those might threaten to limit military utility. This looks like a near reduction of legitimate military necessity to mere military necessity.

Yet at all points O'Brien opposes the "hardliners," the Pax-Americana approach of an Edward Teller, Robert Strauss-Hupé, or General Curtis LeMay. When I ask myself why this remaining disagreement between us on the morality of war, I can only conclude that O'Brien is a man who is concerned to elaborate moral norms in the context of the fabric of international law (*jus gentium* as an actualization of the laws of humanity) while I am a mere moralist. That, certainly, is the virtue of this book. The author penetrates to where the action is that alone can limit and contain war. This is why he is so passionately concerned to overcome those who, from two sides, effectively prevent this. "The international idealists have sabotaged and/or ignored the laws of war generally, and particularly the laws respecting the means of destruction, because they aspired to the elimination of war. The 'hardline' proponents of *Realpolitik* and military superiority have also discouraged the development of legal restraints on the means of destruction." Before O'Brien and I, or he and any other reader of this volume, come to any fundamental disagreement, there is much to be learned from his careful elaboration of "legal-moral" restraints upon war in the international system. That way alone can morality gain effectiveness in international politics.

In the final chapter of this book, O'Brien says a word to church-men and peace workers of all sorts. There he depicts two "models" that might make it meaningful for anyone to listen to moral or religious opinion on the subjects taken up in this volume. On the one hand, some moralists and theologians could specialize in war, deterrence, revolution, peace; but they would have to "make a total commitment to this problem area." On the other hand, some specialists in the empirical study of these subjects might be "willing to master sufficiently the normative subjects of theology, ethics, and legal and political theory." In my opinion, Professor O'Brien himself fulfills in a remarkable way the second of these requirements. Although he claims no competence in theology, still ethical insights and analysis as well as political theory, international law, and the behavior of nation-states in the international system are within his ambit. If I could have my "druthers," I would wish this book not only to be widely read by the public generally but to be studied and discussed in adult education groups and church circles; and in particular it should be required reading for anyone thinking of making or voting for a church pronouncement on the war-peace issues facing the world today. I hope that more scholars like O'Brien will step forward, and persons in the political and military sectors of our society, who are willing to state carefully and forthrightly their opinions about the moral decisions we face as they see them. Then might end the fashionable practice by which lay partisans pick their own preferred moralists while moralists pick their own preferred political analysts and both head, without further ado, into social arenas where the specific action is.

PAUL RAMSEY

WAR
and/or
SURVIVAL

I   The Moral Problem of War

Of all of the moral problems confronting man, war is the greatest. As an instrument of necessary change, defense of justice and as a means of survival, war has always been a wasteful, destructive, deplorable institution. War not only inflicts great, often indiscriminate, suffering on belligerents, it usually leaves pernicious effects in postwar societies that warp and hinder them in their efforts to develop normally. While it remains true that war also has a glamorous side that attracts the imagination and dedication of courageous fighting men and long-suffering "home fronts," the ravages of modern war have been such as to eliminate substantially the notion that was prevalent as recently as 1914 that war was a noble and, indeed, necessary "cleansing" institution which periodically shook up societies that had become excessively selfish, materialistic, and soft. The best that most reasonable men who are not pacifist can say today is that war may be a necessary evil. *Whether* war is, and will continue to be, "necessary" is the first principal concern of this book. The ways in which it is evil, and the ways in which reasonable men can do something to mitigate the evils of war, is the second principal concern of this book.

Men have sought for centuries to solve the material and moral problems caused by war. When I speak of "material" problems I simply mean practical human problems irrespective of their moral implications. Thus the intervention of a United Nations peace keeping force to prevent genocide might be considered morally permis-

sible but there would be material problems such as the tactics to be
employed, the best way to limit injury to the population and the
like. But these material problems, while distinguishable from moral
problems, are the stuff with which moral analyses must deal. The
"ought" is obviously not very helpful if it is substantially divorced
from the "is" or "possible."

This is no doubt the reason for the fact that most moral and legal
condemnations of restrictions on war have had little or no practical
effect. Seeing this, men have periodically decided that it is better
not to view war as a moral problem but as a material problem,
a practical predicament. Hence, efforts have been made to locate
and remove the material causes of war. These, too, have thus far
been quite unsuccessful. But, especially as modern war has become
more cruel and destructive, generation after generation resume the
perennial quest for answers to the moral and material problems of
war. The twentieth century has seen attempts to deal with the
problems of war that exist, exceed, in quantity and quality, all of
the efforts of the preceding centuries. Yet, the problems have become
more difficult and their solution seems to most to be increasingly un-
certain and distant.

In these circumstances, any approach to the moral problems of
war must begin with a recognition of their magnitude. There must be
profound humility in those who take on these problems once more.
I say this with profound awareness that I am going against the grain,
against the spirit of the time. A world torn by war and revolution,
frightened and frustrated by the threat of more and more dreadful
conflicts, *wants* to believe in an early and effective solution to the
moral and material problems of war. We *want* to believe that
Pope Paul VI was speaking prophetically when he said to the United
Nations General Assembly, "No more war, war never again." We
are profoundly moved by the words of Robert F. Kennedy, quoted
by his brother Edward in his eulogy, "Some men see things as
they are and say why. I dream things that never were and say why
not?"

One does not court popularity by critical comment on sentiments such as these. But, as both of the men quoted were profoundly aware, one must do what one must do. As I start this book I must qualify the sentiments quoted which are so responsive to the hopes of mankind. Thus, the Pope who said to the General Assembly, "No more war, war never again," and, "If you wish to be brothers, let the arms fall from your hands," also said, in the same address, "As long as man remains that weak, changeable, and even wicked being that he often shows himself to be, defensive arms will, unfortunately, be necessary," and, "you are still at the beginnings . . . in changing that selfish and bellicose mentality which, up to now, has been interwoven in so much of . . . history."

And, surely, the whole career of Robert Kennedy demonstrated a capacity to "see things as they are" and to ask himself *how* his dreams could become reality, as well as asking, "why not." We start with the facts of war, deterrence, and violent revolution. We start with the sinfulness of man. We start with the fact that *all* approaches to the problems of war have had little or no success. We should, accordingly, approach these problems, soberly, realistically, and humbly. We should, moreover, approach them with great charity toward others who approach these problems differently. We should, finally, recognize that all approaches to the moral problems of war begin with optimism about some things and pessimism about others. Very generally, approaches to the moral problems of war fall into one of the two broad categories:

1. Eliminate war, or the world will not survive. War must be eliminated by legal and moral prohibitions, by the growth of international law and organizations, and by great feats of global social engineering that will eliminate any rational necessity for war and virtually exclude the practical possibility of war.

2. Regulate, contain, channel war, which, in some form, is "given" in the international society in order to survive. This involves the twofold enterprise of diminishing the frequency of recourse to armed conflict and the mitigation of the destruction incident to such conflicts as do occur.

Each approach tends to discount the realism and utility of the other. Each approach tends to rest upon premises which, if true, make the other appear as an attempt to accomplish the impossible. Moreover, each approach tends to consider the other as mischievous or pernicious, as well as futile, since, it is believed, the other approach is encouraging faith in the impossible. Finally, each approach is inclined to view the other as verging either on hypocrisy or immorality.

The reaction of those holding the second position to the "world without war" concept is rather like that of the Duke of Wellington who, when approached by a stranger who said, "Mr. Brown, I believe," replied, "If you can believe that you can believe anything." The "world without war" school of thought, for its part, is inclined to believe that the war regulators *want* wars and want to have moral excuses to justify them.

This century has provided ample occasions and incentives to test all variants of both approaches. There have been more and more serious efforts to replace the so-called "war system" with collective security and a world governed by international law and organization in this century than in all previous centuries combined. Yet ever more terrible wars continue to occur.

On the other hand, there have been extremely comprehensive efforts to regulate war and mitigate its horrors. The success of these efforts is somewhat more difficult to judge than those seeking elimination of war, since they are more complex and relative in character. Certainly regulation of the means of destruction has been a dreadful failure with very few exceptions. On the other hand, one could argue that efforts to ameliorate the lots of prisoners of war and of the sick and wounded have been comparatively successful. But the judgment is relative and subjective and based ultimately on the point of view that "it could have been worse," an essential notion underlying the war-regulation approach.

With this historical background in mind, the two broad approaches to war and morality may be further distinguished. Before doing so, however, I would like to clarify the *sources* of these moral positions. As a Catholic I take the traditional Just War Doctrine and the contemporary teaching of the Church on war-peace problems as my starting point. As will be seen, my own views differ from many of the positions taken in Catholic teaching, especially some of the more recent. But the discussion of issues is more important than the analysis of Catholic thought on war. Were I a Protestant, I might use the pronouncements to the World Council of Churches or the U. S. National Council of Churches as my starting point. For the issues that emerge from a critical analysis of Catholic Just War Doctrine and contemporary Catholic teaching on war are issues that all men of all faiths must confront. Indeed, they are issues which everyone who deals systematically and normatively with war must face whether he be a Christian, Jew, Moslem, Hindu, secular humanist, or Communist. Moreover, many of the practical questions that will be discussed in this book are questions of political, legal, military, scientific policy with which all nations, statesmen, and citizens must grapple. This includes the Communists who have their own ideological equivalents of religious morality as, for example, the Sino-Soviet rift over such issues as nuclear war and deterrence and revolution in the Third World demonstrate.

A more pretentious book, which could qualify for the designation "treatise," written by one or more persons considerably more erudite than I, could usefully chart the points of convergence and disagreement within the different religious traditions and ideologies with respect to the moral problems of war. Since my background is that of the Catholic tradition and since this tradition has very often served as a kind of common meeting place—and battleground—for normative discussions of war and peace, I choose to restrict my sources to Catholic sources but trust that the issues will be drawn in such a way as to be of interest and benefit to anyone who is concerned about the moral dilemmas and practical predicaments of modern conflict.

As I view theories and policies regarding war, I can discern five basic moral approaches: *pacifism, idealism, realism, religious* and *ideological crusades,* and, finally, a position which I term, *"keep politics out of the church."*

Pacifism takes a number of forms, and, like all of the approaches distinguished, can be broken down into a number of positions and any subdivision of this or any of the other categories. Absolute pacifism denies the possibility of the state engaging in a just, or morally permissible, war. It also denies the individual the right to take the life of another human being, for any reason, even self-defense or the defense of an innocent person. This position is generally coupled with a commitment to nonviolence as a means of asserting rights, as in the thought and practice of Dr. Martin Luther King. There are also nuclear or partial pacifists who assert that some wars in the past were morally permissible, at some point in the evolution of modern total war: particularly with the advent of nuclear war, war ceased to be morally permissible. Presumably those who take such positions concede some possibility of moral resort to armed force, for example, in individual self-defense or in police internal security measures. This is the point with which I shall be concerned in Chapter VII on revolutionary warfare and intervention, and in Chapter VIII on the laws of war, since some such wars often do not assume the characteristic of modern "conventional" total war and do not involve the use of nuclear weapons.

The position of the contemporary official teaching of the Catholic church is one of *idealism*. And, indeed, when one thinks about moral, or for that matter legal or normative, approaches to war and to international relations generally, one tends to think of an idealist approach. Together with other moral and humanist approaches to the problem of war, contemporary Catholic teaching may be summed up in the following propositions: Defensive war is still conceded, very reluctantly, to be necessary and morally permissible as a last resort after every peaceful means of dealing with an aggressor have been exhausted. Modern "total war," even "conventional war" in which nuclear and other means of mass destruction are not employed, is condemned. Nuclear war and deterrence, especially "countercity" warfare, i.e., attacks on large population centers, is condemned. The arms race is condemned, and early, substantial progress toward its discontinuation and toward virtually total disarmament are demanded. The church proclaims as a moral imperative—others assert as a moral, legal, normative, human imperative, or as a fundamental requirement for survival—the duty of nations, statesmen, and citizens in all nations to work for world law, order, and justice, ultimately assured by some kind of world authority that would preside over a world in which war would have been eliminated. In short, we must *eliminate* war in order to survive.

It should be noted that the official Catholic teaching on war-peace issues tends to pass over or treat vaguely an important point which greatly concerns other international idealist schools of thought: peace-keeping during phased moves toward world law, order, and disarmament and enforcement of this order once achieved, i.e., the problem of an international police force.

Realism, associated in America with Reinhold Niebuhr and his disciples, as well as with Hans Morgenthau, considers war, like political power, part of the perennial "given" of political life. Realism insists that morality must deal with—not, as it were, wish out of existence—power politics, no matter how terrible and intractable the moral dilemmas that result. This includes the greatest political and moral dilemma of all, that of war.

For many morally motivated people, the principal moral problem of war is not how to avoid or limit it but how to ensure that the "right" side defeated the "wrong" side. This is what I call the *religious and ideological crusade* approach to war. From the Emperor Constantine's victory in the battle of Milvian Bridge (A.D. 312) which led directly to the proclamation of Christianity as the official religion of the Roman Empire by the Emperor Theodosius I in A.D. 380 through the Crusades against the Saracens and other assorted heretics in the Middle Ages down to the calls for anti-Communist crusades in our time, there have been popes, bishops, clergy, and laity who linked secular political and ideological interests with the institutional Church and with morality. With varying degrees of legitimacy, it has often been the case that the principal moral problem of war was not how to eliminate it or even to mitigate it but how to initiate and win it against forces which were thought to be vital threats to the welfare of a regional world or area in which a particular religion and/or ideology prevailed or in which even a divided pluralistic society was deeply committed to particular values.

The disagreements between pacifists, idealists, and realists are disagreements over moral and material analyses of the problems of war, all looking either to its elimination or curtailment. In these disagreements it is all too often forgotten that there has always been a substantial, frequently a preponderant, number of morally moti-vated persons for whom the only moral issue has been, "Who are the angels and who are the devils, who are the just and who are the wicked?" For them, obviously, the end justifies the means. For that reason I omitted reference to this viewpoint in my initial division of approaches to the moral problems of war. I will return to the problems created by this viewpoint in my chapter on arms control and disarmament because of the influential role that is played by persons with a morally motivated propensity for Christian Crusades. Otherwise, this viewpoint will be excluded from the book, since it is not, in my view, morally defensible or politically prudent.

There is finally, a point of view that could be summed up in the admonition "keep politics out of the Church." It is held by some of the most devout, informed, and thoughtful members of the Christian and other religions, as well as by some of the most apathetic, nar-row-minded, or prejudiced persons professing moral beliefs and loyalties. This is the view that politics, including the problems of war, is not a proper subject for moral analysis, teaching, and action. Many with deep commitments to standards of personal morality simply do not believe that morality extends into international rela-tions. The more sophisticated are often content to say that personal and even domestic social morality are not transferable to interna-tional relations. When pressed with the question whether it is not in-admissible that this enormous, critical area of human relationships should be utterly free from moral constraints, they say, in effect, no one has found a persuasive formulation for bringing international relations under moral principles.

I reiterate that this kind of view prevails among people who have tried very hard to make a connection between the moral principles to which they adhere and international problems and failed. It also prevails among people who seek comfort, solace, "peace and quiet" in their moral commitments and who resent the intrusion of teachings or actions related to the questions with which this book is concerned into their moral tranquillity. This, of course, is especially true when, as is often the case, the teaching or activity runs counter to the individual's own political and other views. Obviously this book is not directed to most of the people in this category. Perhaps, given the sometimes truly moral and sometimes moralistic character of contemporary foreign policy debated, it is appropriate to say that this book *is* intended for the kinds of people who seek moral judgments on war-peace issues and also seek to impose them, sometimes with a rather heavy hand, on people who in some cases are incorrigible and in others are decent souls who should be left alone.

In concluding this brief appraisal of moral approaches to war, it is important to underscore one basic dividing line between the approaches. The decisive point is the extent to which each approach evaluates the possibilities for change in the international system. By "international system" I do not mean a particular definition of this currently "in" term in international-relations theory. I could as well refer to the "international society" or the "international community"—more traditional, and also equally elusive, terms. By international system I simply mean the world as it is now.

The pacifist does not like the world as it is now, either domestically or internationally. He rejects the existing system. Apparently the total and consistent pacifist assumes that he must and can live outside of the system in the sense that active participation in it would involve support of it. (I leave it to adherents to such positions to work out the intricate and agonizing problems of defining "participation" in the system, e.g., paying income tax, registering for the draft, voting, accepting any kind of benefit from the government.) Presumably the genuine pacifist could only support the domestic

political system if the international political system were changed
from the present "war system" to the one in which war no longer
existed. I gather that individual pacifists differ on the prospects for
international systemic change. Some do not expect it and liken
themselves to the early Christian pacifists who were outcasts in
Roman society. Others, like Gordon Zahn and Kenneth Boulding[1]
who, in addition to being pacifists, are themselves competent and
possessed of great faith in modern empirical social science, argue
that international, as well as domestic, systemic change is practically
possible as well as morally imperative. Presumably partial and nuclear pacifists would split on the prospects for systemic change eliminating war, much as do the total pacifists.

   The idealists clearly see both domestic and international systemic
change as possible. Accordingly, at least in the Catholic version of
idealist thought, such systemic change is made a moral imperative,
not just a hope, wish, or prayer (or, in traditional diplomatic
language at conferences that cannot resolve a problem, a *voeu*)
or "wish." Since it is the position I will take, I will now treat
separately the realist view with respect to systemic change. It is
hardly necessary to note that the Christian Crusade approach
favors systemic change by such programs as "rolling back the Iron
Curtain," an undertaking that receded in probability on a grand
scale, just as "return to the Mainland" of the forces of Chiang Kai-
shek did in the years after the Eisenhower administration "unleashed" him. As for those who would "keep the Church out of
politics," systemic change may or may not occur but it will have
nothing to do with morality.

   This book takes a *realist* approach to war. That does not mean
that it contends that it is self-evidently more "realistic" in the
sense that it is objective, true, and likely to be borne out by events.
Naturally these characterizations represent goals for the realist,
but, *especially,* because he is a realist, he is skeptical, cautious, and
aware of his vulnerabilities. Not the least of these is vulnerability to

[1] See pp. 95–102.

being tabbed in the C. Wright Mills manner a "crackpot realist"[2] or confronted with the foreign policy mistakes of all the well-known realists who make U.S. foreign policy. This, of course, is fair enough, since the idealist has to become accustomed to being labeled a "fuzzy one-worlder," and the pacifist a "peacenik."

All that is intended by the characterization realist is that one works on the assumption that the present international system, at all levels, will remain as it has for a very long time and that one must deal with the dilemmas of international wars, revolutions, and interventions in them on the basis of this assumption.

Both national and international systemic change are quite conceivable. The present international system was made possible by the gradual emergence of sovereign state, most of which were "nation-states." These states are the actors, members, players— one wishes to call them—in the international system, together with many other entities ranging from international organizations to international corporations. In terms of politics, law, security, economic and social policy, states remain the principal, typical components in the international system. Efforts to treat supranational and international institutions have had varying success but the system is still a decentralized one wherein war and revolution are familiar instruments of resolving disputes and bringing about change.

This system, in both its national and international aspects, is only about five centuries old and it will probably change. Whether changes will be beneficial and whether they will run in the direction of more rather than less unity, security, justice, and welfare remains to be seen. But, at the moment, the international system looks as though it would continue for the indefinite future along its present lines, perhaps with some improvements *within* the system.

---

[2] C. Wright Mills was a competent but overambitious sociologist who produced popularized, simplified, and sweeping verdicts on a broad range of contemporary problems, including "A Pagan Sermon" to would-be Christian realists, in *The Causes of World War Three* (New York: Simon and Schuster, 1958), pp. 145 ff. His views on war are, in my view, adequately dealt with in a brief footnote in Paul Ramsey's *War and the Christian Conscience* (Durham, N.C.: Duke University Press, 1961) p. 195, n. 4.

Since the international system is far from satisfactory and since fundamental systemic change *might* (again, not necessarily *would*) be desirable, efforts to effect such a change should be studied and encouraged. I will say a few words on that subject in Chapter IV. But, here and now, the presumption must be that the international system will continue to be plagued with recourse to war and *the* moral problem of war is to confront this central fact of international political life with moral principles relevant to what is new rather than what might be someday.

However, as important as it is to confront the present moral problems of war, there is a sense in which it is even more important to confront the future problems of security which will exist as long as government, whether world or regional or whatever, exists. Even if the international political system is changed, the moral problem of war, i.e., recourse to armed force at all levels of society, will remain—except that it may have a different name and/or formulation, such as the moral problem of world security. *All* political societies (to use a traditional term) or political systems (to use contemporary political science terminology) require coercion of some kind, including that armed coercion which we call "war" whether we are referring to Vietnam, or the Congo or racial disturbances in American cities. What is at issue, then, between the realist position taken in this book and the various idealist positions is whether progress toward changing and improving the international system will automatically mean solving the moral problems of war or whether such progress may only shift the identities and locations of the decision makers who, in the first instance, deal with the problem of war, e.g., from an American President such as Lyndon B. Johnson to a UN Secretary General such as U Thant, or from an American general such as Westmoreland to a senior UN military adviser to the Secretary General such as the Indian General Rikhye.

The thrust of the book is not, therefore, so much in the direction of opposition to international systemic change as it is toward a responsible consideration of the problem of recourse to armed force under the present system, during transitions if they occur, and under a future system if it becomes possible and seems desirable.

In undertaking this study, a moral perspective is explicitly taken and promised. Two points should be made in this regard. First, one of the basic assumptions of virtually all pacifist and of many idealist approaches to war is rejected. This is the assumption that there exists, or ought to, a code of moral principles above and divorced from the facts, problems, and attitudes of empirical reality, which, once determined, resolve all problems of social mobility. I believe that valid and meaningful moral principles regulating social questions are hammered out by, modified, and sometimes eliminated through a dialectical process between the material facts and issues of a morally significant subject and the normative principles, rules, or guidelines which relate to that subject matter.

This is not to say that there are no basic moral principles governing war and related subjects. But these principles (such as the right of legitimate self-defense, the principle of proportionality between permissible ends and means) only become meaningful when they are discussed in terms of the political and technical problems central to the phenomenon of armed conflict.

To give a concrete example from Catholic experience, throughout the later years of the Second Vatican Council, when the document which finally was issued as the Pastoral Constitution on the Church in the Modern World was being prepared, there were numerous appeals to the Council Fathers to produce "moral judgments" (presumably condemnations) with respect to war and deterrence. The Bishops and their experts were told that they should not be influenced by complicated technical arguments that served only as excuses for continued tolerance of immoral behavior. Rather, it was argued, a purely moral judgment should be made about modern war and deterrence.

I argued then, and I continue to believe, that this was nonsense. One ought not to discuss human social problems—and war is one—in purely abstract terms. Supposedly enlightened persons no longer do this about the population problem or domestic social and eco-

nomic problems. We agree here that there has to be interaction
between human social facts and realities and doctrine. The recent
encyclical *Humanae Vitae* of Pope Paul VI on birth control, sad to
say, flies in the face of this trend. It threatens not only the authority
of the Church in general and its teaching on birth control but the
authority and relevance of the entire body of social teaching on
practical issues of the contemporary world. This is also eminently
true in the area of political morality which includes the moral problems of war. When the hard core of principles is established and
when provisional indication is given as to the relative importance
and priority of these principles in various contexts, I will attempt
to apply them to the practical problems of modern war, deterrence,
and revolution.

The theme of this book, therefore, is that man must accept the
reality of armed force as a fact and as a necessity at every level
of society. Man must learn how to limit the occasions of recourse to
armed force. He must learn how to best mitigate the effects of
armed force in conflicts when they occur. He must attempt to
channel the resources of a decentralized international community
so that, more often than not, armed force prevails in the interests of
the community, not against it. Man, in other words, must learn to
live with and regulate armed force in order to survive.

There are a number of ways in which one could organize a book
of this kind. The overlapping character of many of the central
subjects makes organization difficult. For example, an examination
of the war-peace sections of Vatican II's *Pastoral Constitution
on the Church in the Modern World* reveals the difficulty which
the Council Fathers experienced, even after prolonged study, discussion, and editorial revision, in ordering their subject matter.

This book begins with a summary of contemporary official Catholic teaching on war, deterrence, and revolution. I begin with this
summary, because Catholic thought on war has tended to attract
attention from many other traditions and perspectives and because
it is the tradition with which I am most familiar. I will then offer
an alternative view, one that is realist rather than idealist as is the

present "official" Catholic teaching on these subjects. The other three views briefly identified in this chapter will be treated only in the event that they become relevant to the issues examined.

I will then assess practical and theoretical efforts to eliminate or, as some put it, "find a substitute for," war. This is done to give some perspective to the insistence in the book on the need for extensive moral rights to wage war and revolution. It is fair to raise the question which, in international law, is "exhaustion of peaceful remedies." To the extent that it would be thought that adequate peaceful solutions to international and domestic disputes and conflicts existed or that some less lethal "substitute for war" could be devised, some of the ground would be cut out from underneath those who insist on the necessity and permissibility of war and revolution. It should be clear from the orientation of the book that I do not find the peaceful alternatives to war adequate. But I have to explain why I reached this conclusion in order to justify my continued tolerance of armed conflict. It should not be necessary to say so, but experience has taught me that it is: If I am wrong about the alternatives to war I will rejoice.

Turning to the delicate balance of terror, I will devote a chapter to the moral issues of nuclear war and deterrence. The emphasis will be on the uniqueness of the moral issues which fundamentally involve threats to do things which are "unthinkable." The practical problems of assessing and responding to these threats will be treated and moral guidelines suggested, with a reiteration of the admonitions of the Church, which I think can be characterized as typical of morally responsible contemporary analyses of the subject, that the *price* for *any* continued reliance on nuclear deterrence is a really serious effort to progress in the area of arms control and disarmament.

Concurrent with the quest for alternatives to war is that for arms control and disarmament. I will undertake to summarize briefly the progress that has been made in this quest and the outstanding issues facing us. This analysis will bring us back to the interesting question of the requirements for security *after* "peace breaks out,"

General and Complete Disarmament is achieved, and everyone lives happily after, or do they?

Turning from the frightening threats of nuclear deterrence and the efforts to curtail the state of affairs that seems to require them, I will turn to an equally disturbing problem area, that of revolutionary war. These are the wars that are "happening." They raise moral and material questions as difficult as those of nuclear war and deterrence. Since modern revolutions usually involve covert or overt foreign intervention, the moral aspects of this subject will also be explored.

The penultimate chapter will attempt to summarize the laws of war as they stand today. Many discussions of the morality of war are confused in their assumptions about the laws of war. For example, many controversial means of war such as the use of napalm, which produce enormous moral indignation, are not clearly illegal under positive international law. On the other hand, torture is clearly prohibited by conventional international law to which virtually all nations are parties, yet it is notorious that torture as a part of interrogation, especially in revolutionary wars, is standard practice. What does this practice do to the conventional law? After wrestling with this problem, which understandably does not attract many commentators, I will speculate on possible unwritten rules of customary law which may be emerging.

Finally, the concluding chapter, "War and the Christian Conscience," will attempt to sum up the implications of the book for different types of individuals—clergymen, teachers, experts in the communications media, statesmen, leaders of civic and peace organizations, and responsible citizens. To this end, I undertake to reconcile the technical vocabulary, methodologies, and scholarly standards of the various disciplines with which a book such as this must deal, about which so much is said, often very emotionally, and about which much more must be thought, said, and done if we are to have real progress in answering the challenge War and/or Survival.

II War Deterrence, and Revolution
in Contemporary Catholic Teaching

I begin with contemporary Catholic teaching on war-peace issues
for several reasons. First, I am more familar with it and prefer not
to undertake to interpret the teachings of other traditions on these
issues. Second, it is a historical fact that Catholic Just War theories
have been and remain central to analyses of the moral problems of
recourse to armed force. Third, papal diplomacy, pronouncements,
and the documents of Vatican II have increasingly commanded
broad international interest. Finally, Catholic influence in government, on public opinion, and in moral debates on foreign policy
is conspicuous in the United States, the United Kingdom, and
France, the three Western nuclear powers, and in the Federal
Republic of West Germany, which is the key to satisfactory resolution of many of the dilemmas that confront mankind with respect to war-peace issues.

I hope, therefore, that the reader, whatever his moral identifications, will find the current state of official Catholic thought on
this subject interesting and significant. I also hope that Catholics
who have not had the occasion to think through recent pronouncements of the Church on these matters, or who are desirous of an
interpretation which is sympathetic but critical, will find this chapter
worthwhile.

Finally, it is my hope that those concerned with the moral
problems of war will be interested in the *ways* in which the

Catholic Church at the highest level has approached these problems. As will be seen, I sharply question the substance of contemporary Catholic thought on war and remain deeply concerned over the habits of thought and procedure that produced modern Catholic teaching on this subject.

Whatever new concepts and approaches may have penetrated Catholic social teaching, those which deal with political theory and international relations remain eminently within the Scholastic natural-law tradition. This is adequately demonstrated in the two most influential documents concerning international problems that have emanated from Rome in recent years. Seldom has a papal encyclical had the impact of Pope John XXIII's *Pacem in Terris*. It has been hailed and discussed throughout the world as a landmark of "fresh, optimistic thinking" about war-peace problems. But the basis of his approach is extremely traditional, which may only prove that Catholic Scholasticism has been a haven for "fuzzy oneworlders" for longer than anyone, especially some Catholics, cares to admit. Pope John's natural-law position appears in the Introduction to the Encyclical. Under the rubric *Order in human beings* he says:

5. But the creator of the world has imprinted in man's heart an order which his conscience reveals to him and enjoins him to obey; *this shows that the obligations of the law are written in their hearts; their conscience utters its own testimony . . .*

6. But fickleness of opinion often produces this error, that many think that the relationships between men and States can be governed by the same laws as the forces and irrational elements of the universe, whereas the law governing them are quite a different kind and are to be sought elsewhere, namely where the Father of all things wrote them, that is, in the nature of man.

7. By these laws men are most admirably taught, first of all how they should conduct their mutual dealings among themselves, then how relationships between the citizens and the public authorities of each State should be regulated, then how States should deal with one another, and finally how, on the one hand individual men and States, and

on the other hand the community of all peoples, should act towards each other, the establishment of such a community being urgently demanded today by the requirements of universal common good.[1]

In a similar vein, Vatican II's *Pastoral Constitution on the Church in the Modern World,* addressing itself specifically to war-peace issues speaks of "the permanent binding force of universal natural law and its all-embracing principles." It is stated that "actions which deliberately conflict with these same principles, as well as orders commanding such actions, are criminal . . ."[2]

Brave words! But all that follows from them is a condemnation of genocide which is about as evidently violative of any minimal natural law as anything could be. And genocide is not at all an issue of the morality of war. It is precisely because genocide undertakes the extermination of or discrimination against a particular category of human beings *as such,* regardless of any reasonable military necessity, that it has been universally accepted as "criminal." But aside from countercity warfare, the threat of which in a deterrent situation is not clearly condemned by Vatican II, this impressive invocation of a "universal natural law" is not applied in the war-peace sections of the *Pastoral Constitution on the Church and the Modern World.*

One begins, therefore, a critique on official Catholic teaching on international relations with a disquieting concern over the emphasis on a "universal natural law," violation of which is "criminal," which somehow does not seem to produce very many practical issues concerning morality of war. As will be seen, the approach taken in this study is *one* very limited natural law—a law of nations approach to war-peace issues. But the formulations of *Pacem in Terris* and *Pastoral Constitution* (hereinafter substituted for the unwieldy *Pastoral Constitution on the Church in the Modern World*)

---

[1] National Catholic Welfare Conference, *Encyclical Letter of Pope John XXIII, April 11, 1963* (Washington, D.C.: 1963), p. 4.
[2] Walter M. Abbott, S.J., General Editor, *The Documents of Vatican II* (New York: Guild Press/America Press/Association Press, 1966), Chapter 5, Section 1, Paragraph 79, p. 292.

have both a theological and metaphysical note to them that sounds to an interested but nonexpert observer very different from prevailing emphases in contemporary Catholic theology and philosophy —much less to the theological, ethical, jurisprudential, and political theory perspectives of other normative bases for analysis of the problems of war.

It would seem to me that the combination of emphasis on the *concept* of a "universal natural law," the lack of application of such a law to the crucial questions of war, revolution, and deterrence, and the singling out of genocide as a principal example of the kind of behavior "condemned" by the universal natural law, suggests that there is a great, and proper, impulse within the Catholic Church to retain the general idea of an immutable natural law while leaving open its application to detailed and expert analysis of specific problems. I am not in a position to prove this on the basis of a kind of "legislative history" of the drafting of *Pacem in Terris* and other papal documents or of the *Pastoral Constitution* but a reflective reading of these documents suggests something of the kind.

On the basis of the natural law, written in the hearts, minds, and consciences of men, the prevailing view of man, the state, and international society is as follows:

First, Man, by poper use of his reason, can discover the best form of life to pursue, the most appropriate political and other social institutions, and the most just laws to live by. *Second,* he is by nature a political and social animal; political society is natural, not artificial. Further, the ultimate purposes of political society are to maximize the extension of natural rights (social, economic, and racial, as well as legal and political) and to produce that condition which will be most conducive to the good life. To the extent that these purposes are achieved, man's earthly state will enhance his efforts to attain eternal salvation.

As to war, armed force is an exceptional, relatively abnormal phenomenon. It should be employed only when all possible efforts have been made to resolve conflicts in a peaceful way. Moreover, it is man's experience that reliance on armed force does not truly settle conflicts and that the seeds of future conflicts are present in the apparent successes of contemporary wars.

This viewpoint goes back to the very way in which St. Thomas formulated the question of the just war. His formulation was not "When is war just?" but, rather, "Is war *ever* morally justified?" Thus the presumption was against killing, which is sinful, but, St. Thomas concluded, this presumption of sinfulness could exceptionally be overridden by the existence of certain conditions, namely, competent authority to decide to have recourse to war, a just cause, and right intention.

Finally, the key to good and effective government, as well as to the adoption and observance of just laws, is reason. Good rulers and good laws will recommend themselves to reasonable men who will co-operate with the government and obey the law. This is true at all levels of political society and would be true in the event, which is to be desired, that the inchoate international society is unified.

In summary, the official Catholic teaching on war assumes the reasonableness of man, the feasibility of achieving the good society based on reason and general acceptance of enlightened authority and laws as the normal human condition. It considers war, or any armed violence, to be abnormal and difficult to justify morally or in terms of sound policy. War is only condoned in exceptional cases. As we come to modern wars, this point of view is strengthened and the limits of morally permissible recourse to force are restricted further.

The Church, with obvious reluctance, still permits recourse to armed force in international relations, but, as we have said, major restrictions have been imposed in recent years in papal pronouncements and by Vatican II.

First, the Church has put increasing emphasis on the obligation of parties to international disputes to exhaust pacific remedies before resorting to war as an instrument of foreign policy. Pope Pius XII was a strong supporter of efforts to improve and apply international law and organization. Pope John XXIII's specific support for the United Nations in *Pacem in Terris* (143) was widely noted and appreciated by internationalists. Pope Paul VI has greatly advanced this endorsement, not only by his appearance before the General Assembly, October 4, 1965, but in his very active diplomatic interventions, at times almost in tandem with Secretary General U Thant, on the Vietnam War and other recent conflicts.

Second, one of the traditionally permissible just causes for war, "defence of justice," has been restricted to defensive wars. Offensive wars, that is, first resort to armed force, are morally condemned. Thus the Church strongly supports a rule of international law that has been developing since the establishment of the League of Nations and which is authoritatively stated in Article 2 (4) of the UN Charter:

> All members shall refrain in their international relations from the threat or use of force against the territorial integrity or political independence of any state, or in any other manner inconsistent with the Purposes of the United Nations.

Continued treatment of defensive wars as morally permissible likewise is in accord with the Charter which provides in Article 51:

> Nothing in the present Charter shall impair the inherent right of individual or collective "self-defense" if an armed attack occurs against a Member of the United Nations, until the Security Council has taken measures necessary to maintain international peace and security. Measures taken by Members in the exercise of this self-defense shall be immediately reported to the Security Council and shall not in any way affect the authority and responsibility of the Security Council under the present Charter *to take at any time such action as it deems necessary in order to maintain or restore international peace and security.*

The italicized portion of Article 51 raises a question on which Catholic teaching has been strangely silent or ambiguous. Whenever morally permissible war is discussed it is referred to as defensive war. But if the United Nations system, or the kind of more powerful "world authority," so often discussed by the popes and

Vatican II, were ever to function as the UN system was designed to function, offensive actions, including the use of armed force, would be taken on behalf of the UN as "enforcement" action to deal with a "threat to the peace." Chapter VII of the Charter specifies that the Security Council may call upon the member nations to contribute armed forces to such enforcement actions and provides for the establishment of a UN Military Staff Committee.

As we know, ideological and political rifts in the Security Council have prevented the operation of these collective security arrangements. The closest that the UN has come to an enforcement action was in the Korean War. Fortuitously, the Soviets were boycotting the Security Council over the issue of exclusion of Red China from the UN when the North Koreans launched their invasion. The Security Council did make a finding that the attack was a breach of the peace and ordered its cessation. But before the Council could proceed to order enforcement action the Soviets hurried back with their veto, and no such action was ever ordered. However, the General Assembly did pass resolutions urging (not ordering) members to go to the assistance of South Korea. A number did, and although the overwhelming bulk of the forces engaged in the collective defense of South Korea were South Korean and U.S., the allied force was called a "United Nations" force.

Presumably, if a majority of the Security Council, including the Five Great Powers, were ever to order enforcement action in the sense of Chapter VII, such an action would be supported by Catholic teaching, even if it took an offensive form. It may be that the practical unlikelihood of such an eventuality explains the silence of the principal recent pronouncements on this point. But if the Church is serious about the concept of a "world authority" it must address the issue of recourse to armed force by such an authority in the common interest.

Third, there have been a number of condemnations of certain forms and means of war. There have been frequent condemnations of "total war." Since they occurred both before and after Hiroshima, it is difficult to know what is meant—general war including nuclear war, general "conventional" war not including nuclear war but similar in magnitude and destruction to World War II, or a war such as the war in Vietnam. "Total" presumably has some relation to capability. Although the United States has waged a very destructive war in North and South Vietnam it has been far from total in terms of U.S. capabilities, even if the option of nuclear war is excluded.

Pope Pius XII condemned weapons of mass destruction, specifically "atomic, bacteriological, and chemical warfare . . . When . . . putting this method to use involves such an extension of the evil that it entirely escapes from the control of man . . ."[3] This condemnation has not proved particularly helpful since it invites debate over the meaning of the words "entirely escapes from the control of man." Many reputable technical authorities consider this to be an incorrect way of stating the problem. They argue that it is not so much the lack of control—there is control—but that the problem is what is done by those who have control.

Much more to the point, the *Pastoral Constitution* of Vatican II states that warfare conducted with modern weapons, which have "immeasurably magnified the horrors and wickedness of war," and, which "can inflict immense and indiscriminate destruction," goes "far beyond the bounds of legitimate defense . . ." The Council therefore called for "a completely fresh reappraisal of war." But none is given. Instead the Council endorses "the condemnation of total warfare [undefined] issued by recent popes . . ." In a seemingly clearcut judgment, the *Pastoral Constitution* then states:

> Every act of war directed to the indiscriminate destruction of whole cities or vast areas with their inhabitants is a crime against God and man, which merits firm and unequivocal condemnation.[4]

Earlier in 1965, on August 8, the twentieth anniversary of the dropping of the atomic bomb on Hiroshima, Pope Paul VI charac-

[3] Address to Delegates of the Eighth Congress of the World Medical Association, Rome, September 30, 1954.
[4] All quotations are from Article 80, Abbott, *op. cit.*, pp. 293–94.

terized the act as an "outrage against civilization" which must never be repeated. His words present the strongest and most unequivocal official Catholic statement on the subject.[5]

One point that puzzles those who follow Catholic teaching on war is the fact that the various condemnations cited all involve large-scale destruction. The rationale could be primarily one of disproportionality. The traditional absolute principle of noncombatant immunity from direct, intentional attack is not explicitly mentioned in these condemnations. I believe that the traditional principle of noncombatant immunity is incompatible with the legitimate necessities of morally permissible, limited wars. Many disagree. Pacifists in particular hold out the principle as absolute and immutable. The failure of key Church statements to address the issue explicitly leaves the field open for several interpretations.

Even more troublesome is the ambiguous and potentially contradictory relationship between the treatment by Pope John XXIII, Pope Paul VI, and Vatican II of nuclear war and their treatment of nuclear deterrence. Logically, a condemnation of nuclear war leads to a condemnation of a continuing credible threat to wage nuclear war as retaliation in kind or response to some massive aggression. In *Pacem in Terris* (Articles 126–29) Pope John did not actually condemn nuclear weapons. He said, "it is hardly possible to imagine in the atomic-era war could be used as an instrument of justice." But, he continued:

Nevertheless, unfortunately, the law of fear still reigns among peoples, and it forces them to spend fabulous sums for armaments; not for aggression they affirm—and is no reason for not believing them— but to dissuade others from aggression.

Pope John met the problem not by condemning as immoral both nuclear war and deterrence but by pleading for negotiations whereby

[5] "Let us pray that the world may never again see a disgraceful day such as that of Hiroshima, that men may never again place their trust, their calculations, and their prestige in such nefarious and dishonorable weapons."

"men may come to discover better the bonds that unite them together" and dismantle the nuclear deterrence system.

The dilemma, what to do about the fact of nuclear deterrence, is
even more clearly manifested in its treatment by Vatican II. As we
have seen, the *Pastoral Constitution* appears to be adamant in
Article 80 when it condemns as "a crime against God and man,
'acts of war' directed to the indiscriminate destruction of whole
cities or vast areas with their inhabitants . . ." This, of course, is
exactly what a credible nuclear deterrent threatens. Logically, then,
such nuclear deterrents are immoral. That is what many wanted
the Council to say. But the Council Father chose to follow the line
of Pope John by treating the nuclear deterrence system and the
arms race as a predicament, a treacherous trap, "rather than a sin
or crime."

Speaking of the fact of nuclear deterrence, the *Pastoral Constitution* says in Article 81: "Many people look upon this as the
most effective way known at the present time for maintaining some
sort of peace among nations." The next paragraph continues:

> Whatever one may think of this form of deterrent, people are con-
> vinced that the arms race, which quite a few countries have entered,
> is no infallible way for maintaining real peace and that the resulting
> so-called balance of power is no sure path to achieving it. Rather than
> eliminate the causes of war, the arms race serves only to aggravate the
> position. As long as extravagant sums of money are poured into the
> development of new weapons, it is impossible to devote adequate aid to
> tackling the misery which prevails at the present day in the world.
> *Instead of eradicating international conflict once and for all, the con-
> tagion is spreading* to other parts of the world. New approaches, based
> on a renewal of mentality, will have to be chosen in order to remove
> this stumbling block, to free the earth from its pressing anxieties, and
> give back to the world a genuine peace. [Emphasis added]

The first sentence of this paragraph is careful and tentative. With
Pope John the Council Father acknowledged that the nuclear powers
are not headed by maniacs who are itching to start World War

III. Sentiments very close to those in the pronouncements we have reviewed have come from every American President since Truman and from all of the Soviet successors of Stalin. But the italicized sentence puts its finger on the vital issue with which I began this book, the possibility of fundamental international systemic change leading to "eradicating international conflict once and for all."

We have noted that genocide was condemned by Vatican II although not mentioned explicitly. The condemnation, given as an example of the kinds of actions prohibited by the universal natural law, was of "actions designed for the methodical extermination of an entire people, nation, or ethnic minority." (Article 79.)

Finally, in the category of Catholic teaching forms and means of war, there is the question of guerrilla war. Since this form of warfare is almost always found in modern revolutionary wars we can profitably discuss them together in a preliminary fashion here.

Contemporary Catholic teaching on violent revolution is sparse and negative. Vatican II avoided the subject. In *Populorum Progressio,* Pope Paul VI insists that the only hope for peace with justice is development in the poor nations of the Third World. In paragraph 30 of that encyclical, headed appropriately, "Temptation to violence," Paul observes that when men are denied their rights, the necessities of life, and any share in the determination of their destinies "recourse to violence as a means to right these wrongs to human dignity is a grave temptation."

Pope Paul continues, then in paragraph 31, "Revolution":

> We know, however, that a revolutionary uprising—save where there is manifest, long-standing tyranny which would do great damage to fundamental personal rights and dangerous harm to the common good of the country—produces new injustices, throws more elements out of balance, and brings on new disasters. A real evil should not be fought against at the cost of great misery.[6]

In his August 1968 visit to Latin America, Pope Paul specifically rejected violent revolution, while continuing to demand peaceful change, reform, and social justice. He said: "Let us exhort you not

[6] United States Catholic Conference (Washington, D.C., 1967, pp. 22–23).

to place your trust in violence and revolution. That is contrary to the Christian spirit and it can also delay instead of advancing the social uplifting to which you lawfully aspire."[7]

From this we gather that injustice within a society is a temptation to bring about change by violence but that, apparently, violent revolution tends to cause more damage than is proportionate to whatever justice, deserved punishment of oppressors, and social good is likely to achieve. So, it appears, as with the problem of war, the presumption is against resort to armed force. But in every discussion of war, the right of legitimate self-defense is reaffirmed, no matter how much stress is placed on the presumptions against the necessity and moral permissibility of war. Pope Paul's treatment of violent revolution does not even accord that moral basis for violent revolution. If I were one of those people deprived of their rights as defined in the encyclical and if it made a difference to me what the Church held on the right, or at least the option, to engage in violent revolution against entrenched tyranny, I would certainly not be satisfied with paragraphs 30 and 31 of *Populorum Progressio.*

In all fairness, one must recognize that popes long for peace and deplore violence. But they also long for justice, and sometimes one must fight for justice or there will be none. If the affluent and powerful nations who want rights of self-defense and deterrence are in a "treacherous trap," I suggest that the Church which wants development and justice in endemically underdeveloped unjust societies without violent revolution is in a "treacherous trap" of its own. We will return to these dilemmas in Chapter VII.

When we take up the decision to resort to violent revolution we will be further handicapped in efforts to sort out the moral issues by recent denunciation of "guerrilla warfare" in general, irrespective of its causes.[8]

---

[7] *On the Development of Peoples,* March 26, 1967 (edition of the Association for International Development, Paterson, New Jersey) pp. 22–23.
[8] In his encyclical *Mense Maio* Pope Paul said:
  Today, as if no lesson had been learned from the tragic experiences of the two conflicts which shed blood in the first half of our century, we have the dreadful spectacle in certain parts of the world of antagonism on the increase

Vatican II likewise deplored guerrilla warfare in Article 79 of the *Pastoral Constitution,* noting with alarm that, "in many cases the use of terrorism is regarded as a new way to wage war."[9]

If *Populorum Progressio* is enigmatic on the rights of victims of oppression to have recourse to violent revolution, *Mense Maio* and the *Pastoral Constitution* seem to deny such victims the only known form of violent resistance against an entrenched, oppressive regime namely, guerrilla warfare, with external assistance whenever available.

In summary, the papal and conciliar pronouncements of the Catholic Church:

1. Confirm a restricted right of self-defense;

2. Avoid the question on international peace-keeping or enforcement involving recourse to armed force;

3. Condemn total war, weapons of mass destruction, nuclear war and countercity war, genocide, and guerrilla warfare;

4. Tolerate the continued existence of nuclear deterrent pending prompt and decisive progress toward arms control and disarmament and international law and organization;

5. Offer virtually no guidelines on the question of recourse to violent revolution and condemn the principal if not sole form of warfare available to contemporary revolutionaries.

We have seen that the Church, particularly in Pope John's *Pacem in Terris* and in Vatican II's *Pastoral Constitution,* has chosen to emphasize the position challenges enjoining us to change the present system, to escape the "treacherous trap" of the arms race, and to progress toward arms control and disarmament and improved international law and organization, rather than to condemn the existing balance of terror system as a sin or a crime. For the realist

---

between peoples, and see repeated the dangerous phenomenon of recourse to arms instead of negotiation to settle the disputes in the opposing parties. *This means that populations of entire nations are subjected to unspeakable sufferings, caused by agitation, guerrilla warfare, acts of war, ever growing in extent and intensity, which could at any moment produce the spark for a terrible fresh conflict.* [Emphasis added] Pope Paul VI, *Mense Maio,* from *The Pope Speaks,* Vol. 10, Spring 1965, p. 222.

[9] Abbott, *op. cit.,* pp. 291–92.

this is heartening, for he would wonder what would have happened if the Church had heeded all of the demands of pure idealists and pacifists and simply denounced the state of affairs for which virtually every nation peopled by Christians is responsible in some way as immoral. It would be ironic indeed if the Vatican were the source of a condemnation of those deterrence and defense measures which permit the Vatican to operate unimpeded by Communist secret police, a possibility which cannot lightly be discounted if Christians all embark on a dash for instant peace and repentance. But the Church does not ask instant peace, although it rightly asks repentance for some of the things that have been done or threatened in the name of defense and deterrence and some of the things that have not been done in pursuit of arms control and disarmament, support for international law and organization.

So, as a realist, I must speak respectfully and reasonably to those in my Church whose teaching authority I respect. In this spirit I thank those who have produced the "official" teaching of the Church for not demanding the impossible or remotely conceivable goals urged by some as the only goals, immediately. But, as a realist, I must point out that what are demanded or urged as goals to be seriously pursued in an apparently imminent future must be very carefully and, indeed, skeptically, considered. The specifics of these issues will be dealt with in Chapters VI and VIII, and a preliminary characterization of and comment on the approaches taken by the Church on these subjects is appropriate here.

As I read the papal and conciliar sources, the Church, having recognized that nuclear deterrence, however, terrible and dangerous, is in fact the basis for whatever contemporary international order exists. But the Church insists that there is a moral imperative to change this state of affairs by effective arms control and disarmament and by the improvement of international law and organization. Let us examine the specific recommendations of the two most comprehensive treatments of the subject, *Pacem in Terris* and Vatican II's *Pastoral Constitution*.

The first recommendation of the Church is that all nations obey international law and respect the international common good. The formulations of this recommendation could have been made by, say, Francisco Suarez in the seventeenth century. Pope John says in *Pacem in Terris,* "the same natural law, which governs relations between individual human beings, serves also to regulate the relations of nations with one another" (80) . . . "Lastly it is to be borne in mind also in the regulating of relations between states, authority is to be exercised for the achievement of the common good, which constitutes the reason for its existence" (84). The *Pastoral Constitution* asserts: "Peace results from the harmony built into human society by its divine Founder, and actualized by men as they thirst after even greater justice" (78).

One is tempted to drop the matter there. How can there be peace, reason, justice, harmony, agreement on an international common good in a world deeply divided by religious, ideological, racial, national, economic, social, and other differences, grievances, and conflicts? Impossible. But the stern moral imperative is thrown back to the despairing Christian or any other person who attributes some significance to the teachings and advice of the Catholic Church. Try! Try reason. Try discussion. Try requests for common interests among enemies. Try.

This, then, is the second recommendation of the Church. It is made with progress from the nuclear balance of terror to disarmament specifically in mind. Pope John says:

> In the highest and most authoritative assemblies, let men give serious thought to the problem of a peaceful adjustment of relations between political communities on a world level: an adjustment founded on *mutual trust,* or *sincerity* in negotiations, on faithful fulfillment of obligations assumed. Let them study the problem until they find that point of agreement from which it will be possible to commence to go forward toward accords that will be sincere, lasting and fruitful. (118.)

The latter portions of Article 82 of the *Pastoral Constitution* recognizes that such efforts have already begun and encourages their continuance.

The third recommendation of the Church is to stop the arms race now and to start reducing armaments. Since a number of recommendations accompany this one I will enumerate them first and then provide representative quotations which include several of them. The fourth recommendation is to ban nuclear weapons and the fifth to abolish war altogether. Recognizing that this will take some time, how much neither we nor the Church knows, a sixth recommendation calls for interim measures of symmetrical, fair disarmament. The seventh and final recommendation calls for establishment of a world authority to preside over a world without war or arms.

Thus, *Pacem in Terris* calls for an end to the arms race, reduction of existing nuclear stockpiles "equally and simultaneously," a ban on nuclear weapons, "and finally that all come to a fitting program of disarmament, employing mutual and effective control . . ." (112).

A similar program is endorsed by Vatican II in a section headed, "The Total Banning of War, and International Action for Avoiding War" (82).

One need not proclaim oneself a realist to ask whether this is all well-intentioned nonsense. Who ever thought of such a series of events. Why do popes and bishops seriously advocate such unlikely acts?

There are several answers. The first is, quite properly, religious. The Church thinks that this is right and just. Vatican II, in a passage quoted earlier, called for an "entirely new attitude" toward war. Acknowledging that "enmities and hatred" exist, the *Pastoral Constitution* insists that they must be "put away and firm, honest agreements concerning world peace reached in the future." While this admonition is first supported with the suggestion that failure in this matter may bring the "dreadful peace of death," the *Pastoral Constitution* ends its treatment of this subject with an explicitly religious "reason why." Over and above the argument based on fear of destruction, "the Church of Christ takes her stand in the midst of the anxiety of this age, and does not cease to hope with the utmost confidence. She intends to propose to our age over and over again, in season and out of season, this apostolic message: 'Behold, now is the acceptable time' for a change of heart; behold, now is the day of salvation" (82).

The second reason has already been made apparent in quotations from *Pacem in Terris* and the *Pastoral Constitution*. The measures advocated are, in Pope John's words, "demanded by reason." Everyone is expected to see this, regardless of his viewpoint or aspirations. Nations and statesmen will start the process recommended because they will have the common sense to see their predicament and take reasonable measures to escape from it.

The third reason for the Church's seriously advancing the sweeping proposals discussed is a belief shared with many secular experts in or supporters of arms control and disarmament. To borrow from the economists, this is a belief in the "multiplier effect."[10] That is to say, some co-operation and trust will induce greater mutual confidence and produce more co-operation and trust.[11]

One of the benefits which the Church thinks will clearly result from implementation of its proposed disarmament program is the transfer of more human and material resources from the arms race to positive works of reform and development. *Pacem in Terris* decries the "heavy burdens" that the cost of armaments places on

[10] The noted economist Paul A. Samuelson describes the multiplier effect in economics as follows: "Modern income analysis shows that an increase in net investment will increase national income by a multiplied amount—by an amount greater than itself! Investment dollars—like any independent shifts in governmental, foreign, or family dollar spending—are high powered, double-duty dollars, so to speak." *Economics: An Introductory Analysis* (6th ed. rev.; New York: McGraw-Hill, 1963), p. 232.

I discern a similar rationale and set of expectations in theories that envisage a multiplier effect for what might be termed "investment initiatives" toward peace, international law and order, arms control and disarmament.

[11] Thus, Pope John argues:

There is reason to hope, however, that by meeting and negotiating, men may come to discover better the bonds that unite them together, deriving from the human nature which they have in common; and that they may also come to discover that one of the most profound requirements of their common nature is this: that between them and their respective peoples it is not fear which should reign but love, a love which tends to express itself in collaboration that is loyal, manifold in form, and productive of many benefits (129).

the powerful nations, while "other countries as a result are deprived of the collaboration they need in order to make economic and social progress" (109). Vatican II, in the *Pastoral Constitution* made the same point: "While extravagant sums are being spent for the furnishing of ever new weapons, an adequate remedy cannot be provided for the multiple miseries afflicting the whole modern world." (Article 81.) This, of course, is another point in common between Catholic idealists and others who think along the same lines.

CATHOLIC TEACHING ON WAR, DETERRENCE, AND REVOLUTION—
A CRITICAL ANALYSIS

Some of the problems raised by the official Catholic teaching on war, deterrence, and revolution are based on the assumptions underlying this body of teaching and some on the content of this teaching.

First, there are a number of troublesome questions to be asked about the assumptions behind the contemporary teaching of the Catholic Church on war, deterrence, and revolution. Some of them are really general questions applicable to most idealist approaches, some are shared by other religious denominations, some are peculiar to the Catholic Church. My questions are the following:

1. Is traditional Catholic natural law a valid, sufficient, relevant basis for ethical doctrine on this subject? Obviously there is mounting disagreement on this point among theologians and philosophers. At best, theologians of the stature of Father Robert Johann, S.J., are saying that natural law must be understood and applied in very different ways from those found in textbooks which were standard in Catholic institutions just a few years ago. Yet, as I have noted, some of the "fresh views" of *Pacem in Terris* and the *Pastoral Constitution* sound very much like those of the Late Scholastics of the sixteenth and seventeenth century. Are they reliable bases for normative analyses and practical initiatives in the difficult fields of war, deterrence, and revolution? Or, to change tack, does it make any difference? Is it not the case that most of the proposals of the Church's

social teaching on international relations are to be found in numerous other places?

These are profound questions which I am utterly unable to answer and, I gather, they are questions that are troubling people with much more training and background in theology and philosophy than I. It may be recalled that *Pacem in Terris* referred to three sources of human responsibility: reason, heart, conscience. If a particular proposition of the Church's official teaching on war, deterrence, and revolution does not persuade my reason, my heart, or my conscience, what am I to do? As will be seen in the next chapter, I place great value on the natural law tradition, especially as it relates to the law of nations. But I am troubled by the traditional, uncomplicated, "everything will be quite clear to all reasonable men" tone of the recent teaching of the Catholic Church on war, deterrence, and revolution.

2. This leads to a question which apparently greatly troubles professional moralists, the authority of the social teaching of the Catholic Church for Catholics. If I am not persuaded by a point of view or a specific prescription about international affairs, this will seldom if ever be a question of faith and morals requiring a presumption of obedience. On the other hand, one respects and welcomes the social teaching of the Church and one does not lightly ignore or oppose it. As will be seen in the last chapter, my only suggestion with regards to this problem area is to work for better research and policy processes within the Church so that its social teaching is as technically competent and worthy of consideration by all men of good will as possible.

3. How adequate is the command of technical methodologies and data among those who prepare papal and conciliar statements on issues of war, deterrence, and revolution? I would venture to say that it was not until the revised version of the *Pastoral Constitution* was prepared that the literature on arms control and disarmament and on contemporary military science were seriously scrutinized before a pronouncement on these subjects was issued. After years of avoiding the hard issue of birth control and of confronting the popula-

tion explosion, the Church finally called in experts from a great
variety of empirical disciplines and, equally important, it had to
broaden greatly the range of viewpoints solicited among moralists.
The results of this effort remain unclear. But it is clear that positions
based on extremely dogmatic principles which were, until quite
recently, held to be unshakable, are now being abandoned, modified,
or discredited. If the Church wants to speak to the moral problems
of war, deterrence, and morality, it must consult the people who deal
with the subjects the way medical doctors and demographers deal
with birth control and population problems.

To take another example that is directly related to this book because of the correct contention that international development
is a key issue regarding both war and revolution, a more subtle
manifestation of the problem marshaling expertise may be perceived.
As in its approach to war, deterrence, and revolution, the Church has
strong and presumably informed views which may be summarized
as follows:

1. Development is a practical necessity and a moral imperative
which must be immediately dealt with on an unprecedented, global
scale.

2. The expertise to make international development a reality
exists, all that is needed is moral responsibility, and the will and
resources necessary to help the experts do what must and can be
done.

Here, we have a problem, not in sufficient consultation of experts
but of evaluating their expertise. Certainly in the United States,
which has more experience in foreign aid than any country in the
world, experts, including Catholic experts, on aid and development,
are increasingly disillusioned and divided about the feasability of
producing the drastic changes demanded by the Church's social
teaching and the rising expectations that have risen to some degree
in reliance on that teaching. In this instance, the problem is not a
failure to consult experts from the relevant empirical disciplines, it is,
rather, a twofold problem of determining the reliability of the experts
and of the empirical disciplines from which they come and of

weighing the claims of optimistic experts against the informed doubts of the pessimistic experts.

As will be discussed in the last chapter, the Catholic Church, like its parallel religious organizations, is increasingly aware of and addressing this kind of problem. My point here is that much of the teaching of the Church on war, deterrence, and revolution is based on relatively modest empirical analyses and assessments of data and could profit considerably from more informed analyses.

There are problems with the content of contemporary Catholic teaching on war deterrence and revolution. The reader undoubtedly has his own list of issues, this is mine:

There is the propensity to press the adequacy of pacific settlement of disputes, and the corollary that war is an outmoded means of settling them. This is true, it is argued, in part because of the nature of modern war, and in part, because of the supposed development of international law and organizations. But we find some disquieting facts:

Even when deep-rooted ideological forces engendering war or some form of conflict, e.g., Naziism, Communism—or anti-Naziism or anti-Communism—are not present, major differences between states have not been submitted either to international arbitration or adjudication or, to the appropriate organs of international organizations. Conflicts such as those between Israel and the Arab states, India and Pakistan, Indonesia and Malaysia come to mind. But, we also have limited and sometimes discontinuous conflicts, or the threat thereof, between nations such as Algeria and Morocco, Somalia and practically all of her neighbors, the U.A.R. and Saudi Arabia, Greece and Turkey over Cyprus, and Venezuela and Guyana.

If a dispute has deep ideological roots, if the parties to the dispute remain true to their ideological convictions and derivative responsibilities, and particularly if a global or regional balance of power is at stake, one does not have a mere political-legal dispute, one has a showdown over the spheres of influence of the Great Powers and alliances, all of which represent basically antagonistic world views and strategic considerations. Berlin, the Cuban Missile Crisis, Vietnam, are examples of such collisions. It appears to be impossible or at least uncommonly difficult to find anything other than power political solutions to such problems. Such solutions involve the threat or use of force.

It is also well known that the international institutions themselves reflect a divided world of conflict. The agonies and near disasters of efforts to resolve serious international problems are well illustrated by the cliff-hanging UN intervention in the Congo, the trials of UNEF in the Middle East, the continuing problems of peace-keeping in Cyprus, the impasses with respect to the statues of the People's Republic of China and the United Nations, and the impotence of the United Nations with regard to the Vietnam conflict.

Moreover, the present teaching of the Catholic Church on war fails to deal at all, or in a meaningful way, with war and deterrence as UN enforcement or police action or deterrence and "internal security" in a world under partial or general disarmaments by forces of an international authority. All of the problems will still be there. Nuclear energy will be increasingly available. The means of delivering weapons on targets will be constantly improved. The possibility of violations and revolutions within a world state will remain. In short, whether world security problems are called "war" or not, war, recourse to armed force, in this sense cannot be "banned" or abolished or eliminated.

Related to the problem of a world police force is the credibility of the demand for and projection of an advance toward a "world authority" which modern Catholic teaching in harmony with international idealist thought generally, appears to consider indispensable. Some of the key questions to be examined are the following:

How reasonable is the admonition to work for co-operation based on "mutual trust and sincerity"? Granted that recent history has shown that positions can alter and conflicts abate, is it reasonable at this stage of the world's history to say in effect, "Stop all conflict, sit down and reason, trust each other, and world peace and order is within your grasp?" I question the reasonableness of this approach not only because of the profound ideological, national, social, and racial rifts in the world but because it is an approach that disregards ordinary political experience.

Politics, whether in the United States, the Soviet Union, Italy or even within the Catholic Church is not based on "mutual trust and sincerity." It is based on trust and sincerity where they exist. Otherwise politics is based on the management of competing interests to obtain the best possible results for the common good. Surely it is too much to expect statesmen and responsible citizens to take greater risks with their nations' independence and security in dealing with foreign nations, some of the avowed enemies, that they would be willing and entitled to take with competing groups within their own national societies.

Does the theory that co-operation breeds more co-operation stand examination? Certainly the proposition is plausible and is one that is frequently advanced by very hard-headed arms control negotiators. But, it seems to me, it is a theory which is all too uncritically accepted in the Church's teaching on war and deterrence. Wartime co-operation between the West and the Soviet Union was followed by a vicious Cold War. Or, to look at the other side of the coin, the Cold War experience of constant confrontation, negotiation, espionage, intelligence assessments, elaborate research, on all sides would at least have taught the parties to the Cold War a great deal about each other. But it now appears, for example, that the West entertained greatly exaggerated fears of Soviet aggression in Europe in the 1950s while obviously underestimating completely the willingness of the Soviets to risk the Cuban missile adventure.

Moreover, the literature on the history of arms control and disarmament efforts reveals many instances where supposed understanding and co-operation, particularly among scientific, allegedly nonpolitical experts, was abruptly terminated or altered for patently political reasons. This point is made, not to reject the concept of progress through technical discussions and co-operation, or to discount entirely the multiplier effect that may arise out of discussions, but to inject a strong cautionary note into analyses of the prospects for arms control and peace based on "mutual trust and sincerity."

Is the assumption that reasources withdrawn from the arms race will be transferred into internal and foreign development valid? A detailed answer is beyond the scope of this book. But a perusal of the literature on the economic consequences of disarmament, which is naturally comparatively speculative, would probably show many differences of opinion about the economic and social implications of "peace breaking out."

Finally, it is important to note that there is a serious problem in defining "progress" toward the goals set in the Church's teaching on this subject. The difficulty is twofold: definition of the goals themselves and assessment of their feasibility; vagueness with respect to the time frame in which these goals ought to be substantially achieved.

III   A Realist Approach to War

The characterization "realist" explicitly accorded this book is made with some reluctance and great awareness of the vulnerabilities, past and especially present, of the concept of political realism. Let us therefore confine the terms "idealism" and "realism" to differing approaches to the theory and practice of international politics, beginning, as is quite common in the United States, with the theories and policies of Woodrow Wilson. President Wilson's idealistic policies failed, but among international practitioners and theorists there was a great idealist vogue in the interwar years supporting his approach to international relations.

By and large, those who had any normative approach to war and to international relations generally took idealist, legalist, pro League of Nations positions during the interwar period. The Kellogg-Briand Pact "outlawing" war was perhaps the high point of internationalist attitudes and activities during these years. War was a thing of the past, so much in disrepute that the international law of war was neglected and, indeed, excluded from courses in international law and organization in the universities.

World War II brought about a reaction. The United Nations, taken literally in terms of the Charter, was first of all to be a security organization that would deal with the problem of war through effective enforcement action (Chapter VII), i.e., war to prevent or halt war. Moreover, the moral permissibility and, indeed, necessity, of community-oriented wars was seemingly vindicated by the most prestigious moralists and scholars concerned with the morality of war, such as Reinhold Niebuhr, John C. Bennett, Hans Morgenthau, and George Kennan. Against the idealist approach of the interwar period, these men argued for more realistic "power political" approaches to war which emphasized the political and moral responsibilities of the decision maker to use power, but with due appreciation of normative restraints. This was thought to be both practically and morally more effective and responsible than the drive for comprehensive codes and bans that had characterized the interwar period.

The events that followed World War II seemed to vindicate the realists. Moreover, for whatever reasons, those prestigious in terms of normative and philosophic interest in the nature of international relations, for example, Niebuhr, Bennett, Morgenthau, and Kennan, seemed clearly to have established political and normative theories on war that were not met with persuasive rebuttals from equally prestigious idealists. Idealism was largely discounted as an approach to international relations.

And so it came to pass that the tough-minded intellectual realists moved back and forth from their institutions and centers of study to the Departments of State and Defense. Dissenting idealists were lectured sternly on their lack of knowledge or of facts. And, often the "insiders" among the realist ranks were quite correct in deploring uninformed and/or hopelessly simplistic suggestions and criticisms from the idealists, or anyone else.

But the problem of being a realist is akin to that of being an economist, that is to say, how do you answer questions such as, "If you know so much about money why aren't you rich?" and "If you are so realistic why do you make mistakes?"

With the deepening concern, especially among élite individuals and organizations which had prided themselves on being realistic and morally sensitive over the prudence and morality of U.S. policy in Vietnam, all else pales in comparison—the reaction set in. Today the kind of "morally perceptive but realistic decision makers" who were held up as models of political realism in discussions of morality and foreign policy, men such as Dean Rusk and Paul Nitze, are the targets for graduation ceremony walk-outs, teach-ins, pickets from the nearest seminaries, and some of the most prestigious realist thinkers.

The case of Professor Hans Morgenthau is perhaps the most striking. Morgenthau takes a pessimistic view of human nature and of the propensity of man to sin. He is convinced that politics is based on the pursuit of power, not on the happy reasonableness and unity envisaged and enjoined by the idealists. He was and remains of the opinion that the moral dimension of politics consists not in eliminating but in mitigating the interplay of power politics. He was one of the first and most prominent commentators to be critical of the "new diplomacy" centered around the United Nations "goldfish bowl" rather than in the quiet, private negotiations and exchanges of views of professional diplomats and foreign offices. Morgenthau was particularly skeptical about the role that domestic and world public opinion plays, or ought to play, in politics. His key concept, which, it must be remembered, is normative as well as selfish or nationalistic, is that of the "national interest."[1]

But in the debates on Vietnam, Morgenthau found himself appealing to public opinion in order to oppose policies made by "professionals," who, however, declined to follow his advice. The ideologue of power politics found himself sharing platforms with people whom he clearly considered naïve if not positively dangerous and demented, speaking to crowds of emotionally indignant students, professors and clergymen—not to mention women striking for peace and demanding instant world government. He apparently felt it necessary to do and endure all of this because, as a *realist,* Morgenthau opposed the American involvement in Vietnam because he thought it to be contrary to the American national interest.

Or consider the predicament of another morally perceptive realist, Vice-President Hubert H. Humphrey, addressing a banquet honoring the twenty-fifth anniversary of the founding of *Christianity and Crisis,*

[1] Hans J. Morgenthau, *Politics Among Nations* (4th ed. rev.; New York: Knopf, 1967).

the leading American Protestant realist journal of opinion, from a podium which seated, among others, the editor of the journal, John C. Bennett, one of the most effective critics of the Johnson-Humphrey administration's foreign policy, and Mrs. John C. Bennett dressed in black with a large white dove across her bosom.

For realists, it has been civil war, brother against brother. It is increasingly difficult to tell the "good guys from the bad guys."

The idealists, on the other hand, have been prospering. A great identification of millions of people around the world with John F. Kennedy's ideals, continues to exist notwithstanding the record of his almost constant (and to my mind necessary) warlike preparations and activities. There is the unprecedented impact of John XXIII's *Pacem in Terris* which, after more than five years, is still the best subject around which a conference on international problems can be organized almost anywhere in the world. We witnessed the startling success of "peace candidates" in the 1968 U.S. primaries, the sudden outbreak of enthusiasm for arms control and disarmament measures registered in polls. All of these things point very clearly to a swing of the pendulum in the direction of a return to international idealism, perhaps, as in the twenties and thirties, accompanied by a return to some form of isolationism.

But, just as idealists pride themselves on sticking to their viewpoint "in season and out of season," so a convinced realist must do the same. It is certainly not a propitious moment to espouse a realist line on war and peace. But if that is the line that one believes to be most responsible, that is the line to take. The temper of the times may change, but I must say what I believe, after years of thought, study, and prayer concerning the material and moral problems of war. *Man must accept the reality and necessity of armed coercion as a fact at every level of society. Man must learn how to limit and channel armed coercion insofar as possible in the interests of the community, at every level, in order to survive.*

Accordingly, recognizing all of the substantive, psychological, and historic problems of writing on war, especially today, from a realist position, I choose to label my approach to war, deterrence, and revolution *realist*. This approach is at odds with official Catholic teaching in some respects—mostly with regard to issues which, in the official teaching, are shrouded with ambiguities and flawed by serious omissions. However, the Catholic Church has never denied the right, duty, and necessity of recourse to armed coercion, and Catholic tradition of moral restraints on war overlaps the Catholic tradition of the law of nations, which in turn is central to the development of positive international law and is of considerable relevance today.

Much of what I will have to say about war will not be distinctively "Catholic." I hope that it will be morally responsible, politically and militarily relevant, and responsive to the pleas that come, not only from the Catholic Church, but from all men of good will, to study the question of war.

In taking a realist approach, I endorse the proposition that all political systems that have existed or are likely to exist rest, in part, on the operation of power politics. Ultimately, this involves the use of armed force, sometimes rightly or wrongly in the pursuit of individual interests, sometimes in defense of law, order, and justice. Any blueprint or model for a political society, at any level from local to provincial to national to regional to global, which tends to discount or wish away this need for force is unrealistic and invalid on its face "as long as man remains that weak, changeable, and even wicked being that he often shows himself to be." Please remember, those are the words of Paul VI at the UN, not John Calvin, General Karl von Clausewitz, or Hans Morgenthau. However, all of this is held without prejudice to the possibilities that the normative and/or empirical sciences, or the hand of God, may move men of good will in directions that will change the present system, one characterized by almost unremitting threat or use of force, at every level from the village to the world arena.

There is a natural law, but the ways and implications of defining that natural law remain, and probably will always be, controversial and challenging. This has been strikingly and tragically demonstrated by the deep-rooted and negative reactions to Pope Paul's encyclical

Humanae Vitae on birth control. The problems confronting an attempt to gain acceptance for *one* "universal natural law," i.e., as a philosophic rather than theological source of normative principles, are manifest. Moreover, I wonder whether they are necessary. It will be recalled that after placing great stress on the obligation to conform to "the universal natural law" Vatican II linked only one specific crime with that law, genocide, a crime so self-evidently monstrous that it has been condemned by positive international law created by states of every conceivable philosophy and ideological world view. The other pronouncements on modern war and deterrence, their horrors and dangers, are not of necessity based on the contention that they are contrary to "the universal natural law" but are, rather, common-sense statements that many would agree with who would not for one moment admit either that the Roman Catholic Church had a monoply on "the universal natural law" or even that such a natural law exists.

As a realist, I maintain the following positions, on which this book is based: There is a natural law, implanted in the minds, hearts, consciences, and aspirations of men, and man's perennial quest for such a law is sometimes successful. This natural law gives normative guidance with respect to practical human problems. The content of natural law—and I would not use the term *"the* universal natural law"—is determined by a comparison between principles and rules deductively derived from fundamental concepts of men and societies and the actual principles and rules inductively identified in the patterns of behavior of men and societies.

The value of the concept of natural law, the reason for my insisting on reference to it, notwithstanding the ancient wounds and suspicions reopened by the mere mention of the notion—as well as the present bitter reaction to its application by Pope Paul to the birth-control issue—is, in my view, threefold. It provides a needed body of normative imperatives. It suggests a mode of normative analysis. Finally, it encourages application of lessons learned by men and societies in addressing difficult material and moral problems.

Natural law lays down morally binding imperatives insisting that certain problems must be confronted and dealt with. This is an important function, especially with respect to recourse to armed force, a subject about which men and nations are not given to honest, realistic thinking.

Natural law suggests ways of formulating the issues which the moral imperative of that law insists must be confronted. The key to such a formulation is the imaginative application of rationally conceived ends, purposes, or goals of men, societies, and their institutions. One could quote Plato, Aristotle, or St. Thomas Aquinas on this point. But I prefer not to, partly to avoid the implication that I share their optimism about the possibility of ascertaining more or less accurately and objectively the "true" end or "nature" of men and society and partly because a less ambitious, as well as apposite, formulation is available in a question much quoted by students of military history and science. It is General Ferdinand Foch's question regarding the end of war, *"De quoi s'agit-il?"* What is war about? What is its end, its nature? A natural-law approach, in this sense, helps to structure—or, at least it helps me—responses to that question.

Finally, since men are rational, what they have thought and done, however misguided or imperfect, is, at least in its finer moments, instructive with respect to what men ought to do. Not everything that men do is in accordance with the natural law. Man, alone, is not the measure of man, but, in the lonely areas of social morality wherein, God-given guidance is sparse. What men have thought and done, or tried to do, again and again, is of normative significance and is responsive to the moral imperative that certain problems must be confronted and dealt with.

This means, then, that there are few if any immutable principles of natural law and few rules that are not subject to change. But the moral discipline of the natural law is always at work: Men must seek moral solutions to human dilemmas. Men must shape formulations of those dilemmas in terms of ultimate ends to the extent that they can be perceived after honest examination. Men must consult the opinion of society as to the acceptability of the answers that are being given to these dilemmas, and, judge, in conscience, between what the natural law appears to demand and what men are doing with a sense of moral rectitude, or at least, no sense of moral wrong.

The need for some kind of higher law approach to war-peace problems is perennial. This is demonstrated by the evolution of the Roman *jus gentium* as a positive law application of the *jus naturale* (natural law) from a private international law for non-Roman citizens to, over many centuries, the modern law of nations, the *jus inter gentes*. The need for such a natural-law approach was most fortunately perceived by Hugo Grotius, rightly considered the father of the modern law of nations, whose *De Jure Bellis ac Pacis* appeared in 1625, early in the Thirty Years' War, a war whose ideological roots and savage conduct were all too similar to modern international conflicts. Following the approach taken in this book of comparing principles deduced from basic concepts and the behavior of men and nations Grotius wrote:

> In two ways men are wont to prove that something is according to the law of nature . . . Proof a priori consists in demonstrating the necessary agreement or disagreeement of anything with a rational and social nature; proof a posteriori in concluding, if not with absolute assurance, at least with every probability, that that is according to the law of nature which is believed to be such among nations, or among all those that are more advanced in civilization . . .

Natural law is, of course, central to the development of the American and other forms of constitutional democracy. It is the basis for the Nuremberg principles and the Human Rights Convention adopted by the UN General Assembly in 1948, the common preambles to the conventions on war, of the Hague, 1899 and 1907, of Geneva 1949, and of such decisions of the International Court of Justice as the Corfu Channel and Reservation to the Genocide Convention cases. Here are some relevant examples of the language and the normative resources of the natural law in positive international law:

Until a more complete code of laws of war has been issued, the high Contracting Parties deem it expedient to declare that, in cases not included in the Regulations adopted by them, the inhabitants and the belligerents remain under the protection and the rule of the principles of the law of nations, as they result from the usages established among civilized peoples, from the laws of humanity, and the dictates of the public conscience [in the 1899 version: "as they result from the usages established between civilized nations from the laws of humanity, and the requirements of the public conscience."].[2]

The denunciation [of one or more of the Conventions] shall have effect only in respect of the denouncing Power. It shall in no way impair the obligations by which the Parties to the conflict shall remain bound to fulfill by virtue of the principles of the law of nations, as they result from the usages established among civilized peoples, from the laws of humanity and the dictates of the public conscience.[3]

We have already mentioned genocide, the principal "crime against humanity," to emerge from the Nuremberg and other war-crime trials. It is instructive to note the words of the International Court of Justice, representing all major areas of the world and most important viewpoints, in the Reservations to the Genocide Convention Case:

The origins of the Convention show that it was the intention of the United Nations to condemn and punish genocide as a "crime under international law" involving a denial of the right of existence of entire human groups, a denial which shocks the conscience of mankind and results in great losses to humanity . . . The first consequence arising

[2] Hague Convention No. IV Respecting the Laws and Customs of War on Land, 18 October 1907; Hague Convention No. II, on the same subject, of 1899.
[3] Geneva Convention for the Amelioration of the Condition of the Wounded and Sick in Armed Forces in the Field, Art. 62, par. 4; Geneva Convention for the Amelioration of the Condition of Wounded, Sick and Shipwrecked Members of Armed Forces at Sea, Art. 62, par. 4; Geneva Convention Relative to the Treatment of Prisoners of War, Art. 142, par. 4; Geneva Convention Relative to the Protection of Civilian Persons in Time of War, Art. 158, par. 4.

from this conception is that the principles underlying the Convention
are principles which are recognized by civilized nations as binding on
States, even without any conventional obligation.[4]

The same World Court, in the Corfu Channel Case, referred to
"elementary considerations of humanity, even more exacting in peace
than in war."[5]

In my view, one need not become enmeshed in metaphysical,
ideological, theological, or behavioral debates regarding the sources
and content of higher or natural law or about the impact of the
empirical natural and social sciences on traditional natural law and
law of nations principles and perspectives. There is a natural law
there somewhere, operating in the minds of men, Mr. Justice Holmes's
pronouncement that there is "no brooding omnipotence in the sky"
to the contrary notwithstanding. Men act as though there was a higher
law. They make judgment about right and wrong in international and
other political, social, economic, racial matters. The standards employed and the manner of applying them are often vague, illusive,
and controverted. These judgments are often subjective, self-serving,
and inconsistent.

But while it is not possible for most scholars to reaffirm the existence and relevance with respect to detailed, specific problems, single
"universal natural law" in quite the traditional, sweeping formulation
of *Pacem in Terris* and the *Pastoral Constitution,* belief in some kind
of fundamental natural law appears to be a recurring need and
propensity of men and nation. For, whenever one or another version
of natural law is demolished, some other version, sometimes only a
restatement with modest modifications of the earlier epochs, seems
to rise from the ashes.

The relevance of the persistence of natural law thinking to war
should be clear. In a primitive, decentralized society, such as the
present international society or system, lacking institutions backed
by adequate authority and coercive power, states and other interna-

[4] I.C.J. Reports, 1951.
[5] I.C.J. Reports, 1949.

tional entities must place great reliance on mutual respect for natural rights. They must also shape their policies concerning war, deterrence, and revolution in the light of their convictions concerning the character and interrelationship of these rights.

In these circumstances there is an important job of work to be done in order to reconcile the kind of traditional thinking that underlies modern Catholic teaching on war, based on a single "universal natural law" and the more relativistic concepts of *jus gentium,* the principles of the law of nations, and the other formulations quoted from modern international agreements and judicial opinions. Perhaps the principal thrust of contemporary Catholic natural law analyses has been in the direction of distinguishing the *jus naturale,* that which by metaphysical and/or theological standards man ought to do, from the *jus gentium,* that which empirical observation establishes as standards by which men, in a particular historical, geographical, and/or cultural context, have in fact considered themselves to be morally or legally obligated to observe.

This distinction, emphasized by scholars such as Jacques Maritain and Heinrich Rommen, was pressed as a corrective to nineteenth and early twentieth century indifference to natural law theories based, in part, on the mistaken idea that there had been only *one* natural law tradition, namely, the "state of nature-natural rights" tradition of Grotius, Locke, Pufendorf, Rousseau, and others, closely related to the Enlightenment and to the American and French Revolutions, as well as to the development of the law of nations. But despite the fact that this particular strand of natural law thinking provided the doctrinal basis both for the law of nations and for modern constitutional government, it was discarded as archaic by the more "scientific" world views of modern positivism. In the process, the Aristotelian-Scholastic strand of natural-law thinking, which had great perennial potentialities, was not so much discredited as ignored, forgotten, or never heard of. Thus modern neo-Scholasticism worked hard at the twofold task of reviving interest in its own natural law antecedents and of distinguishing those antecedents from "the" discredited natural law. (It is, thus, all the more interesting, if not ironic, that modern official Catholic teaching on war and peace insist on the formulation *"the* universal natural law.")

Whatever the validity of this corrective emphasis in Catholic neo-Scholastic thought and the need, as it were, to set the record straight, it seems clear that modern man is not well served by emphasis or insistence on a distinction between an allegedly objective basis for natural law and natural rights and the necessarily subjective bases of inductive natural law approaches. This is particularly the case in view of the fact that it is now increasingly possible to develop inductive natural-law norms on the bases of comparatively scientific and reliable studies of man rather than on the creative but scientifically primitive constructs that the "state of nature-natural rights" naturalists employed to build their theories of international law, constitutional law, and the right of revolution.

A realist natural-law approach for our times will not seek to dominate jurisprudence and political thought with immutable principles of deductive natural law from the perspective of which the inductive principles of the *jus gentium* are somewhat suspiciously inspected. It should instead, seek dialectical interaction between: (1) reductions from first principles—whether taken from theology, philosophy, or human experience (as in the law of nations, the *jus gentium*); and (2) inductively derived insights drawn from observation of recurring convictions and patterns of behavior in men and social institutions, obtained by intensive empirical observation and analysis—and, let it be remembered, also, by human experience and personal insights, wisdom, and hunches.

For example, the right of legitimate self-defense is established in all the normative disciplines. It is also the case that individuals, groups, political societies, hold observable beliefs, on which they act, with respect to the right of self-defense. It is not necessary to contend that there is a universal natural law in order to uphold the "inherent" (to use the language of Article 51 of the UN Charter) right of self-defense. It is reassuring to find that many versions of natural and positive law and the expectations and behavior of men and nations all combine to demonstrate the validity and reasonableness of this right. At least, it is reassuring to realists like myself.

Some idealist may find this expectation pernicious. They have a long way to go if they are to change it.

At this point I would like to emphasize the importance of the concept of "expectations" about the operation of normative rules as distinguished from more traditional formulations of "rules of law" and "moral principles." I am indebted to Professor Myres McDougal for this concept and term. Before turning to the application of natural law-law of nations perspectives and principles to war I would like to quote a typical passage from McDougal's principal work on war to elaborate on the concept of "expectation" which figures importantly in my own thinking. Under the rubric, "The Role of Rules," McDougal and Florentino P. Feliciano observe:

Observers have too often assumed that it is the function of inherited legal rules to point definitely and precisely to certain preordained conclusions. The difficulty with this assumption is that it seeks to impose too great a burden upon man's frail tools of thought and communication and an impossible rigidity upon the processes of both decision and social change. The fact is that the rules of the law of war, like other legal rules, are commonly formulated in pairs of complementary opposites and are composed of a relatively few basic terms of highly variable reference. The complementarity in form and comprehensiveness of reference of such rules are indispensable to the rational search for and application of policy to a world of acts and events which presents itself to the decision-maker, not in terms of neat symmetrical dichotomies or trichotomies, but in terms of innumerable gradations and alternations from one end of a continuum to the other; the spectrum makes available to a decision-maker not on inevitable doom but multiple alternative choices. The realistic function of those rules, considered as a whole, is accordingly, not mechanically to dictate specific decision but to guide the attention of decision-makers to significant variable factors in typical recurring contexts of decision, to serve as summary indices to *relevant cyrstallized community expectations,* and, hence, to permit creative and adaptive, instead of arbitrary and irrational, decisions.[6]

[6] *Law and Minimum World Public Order* (New Haven and London: Yale University Press, 1961) pp. 56–57.

All natural law approaches as well as the modern law of nations recognize the right of men to form political societies. All of these normative sources recognize the rights of these societies by endowing them with juridical equality and other fundamental rights well summarized in the United Nations Charter.

All of these natural law theories, and the modern law of nations, recognize that there are three sources of limitation of political societies:

First, there are the rights of their citizens, as established by their own domestic law, which is increasingly under the scrutiny of international law, and authoritative expressions of world opinion such as the Human Rights Declaration. Second, there are the rights of other states, as defined by international law, and, where gaps occur, theories of natural or higher law. Third, there are the rights of the global world society, summed up in the "international common good," as the scholastic tradition of the law of nations termed it, or in McDougal's language, "the world public order."

Insofar as the rights of individuals, groups, states, and the world public order are concerned all theories of natural law, and, especially, that followed in this book, recognize the need of coercion, including the use of armed force. It is in this respect that my approach parts company from the idealist formulation of issues characteristic of the modern teaching of the Catholic Church on international relations summarized in Chapter II, and of international idealism generally.

I contend that the following forms of military coercion are morally permissible, given the proper conditions: (1) collective security or other collective measures carried out under an international authority (see Chapter VII of the UN Charter); (2) measures of individual or collective self-defense, a right reiterated in Article 51 of the UN Charter as we have seen.

Given the well-known condition of our world of conflict and the presumption of the realist against early and radical changes in this international political system in which we live, it is my contention that the task of defining and regulating the forms and occasions, as well as the means, of armed coercion employed in defense of the natural and positive-law rights of men, groups, states, and the world public order, is the highest task, and by all odds the most immediate confronting us today. The elimination of war, "No more war, war never again," is a great but all-too-distant goal that must be pursued with a sense not only of the distance between such a condition and the present state of affairs but also with a realization that elimination of "war," may very well *not* mean elimination of armed coercion of some kind.

Thus, whereas the modern social teaching of the Church on war and peace starts at the top—or at the end—of an a priori assumption that man is and ought to be inevitably involved in a process leading to unity under a world authority, I, in effect, respectively table that assumption, reject the implication that nations are in fact presently progressing in this direction, and urge immediate, concentrated attention to the material and problems of war here and now in the world as it is. Most important, the problem is not the elimination of war; it is conflict management.

This involves a triangular analytical matrix: (1) moral imperatives (derived from many sources, according to the beliefs of concerned men of good will); (2) human positive laws and institutions; (3) human practice and belief, to the extent that we can observe, record, and interpret them.

For example, there is a moral imperative which I believe is readily evident to reasonable men everywhere, that there should be greater and more rapid progress toward strengthening international law and organization and toward the goals of arms control and disarmament. Nations have, in fact, made some progress, particularly on paper. Volumes can be filled with solemn international agreements pledging such progress. But the expectation of war, including nuclear war, is so great that statesmen and nations take attitudes and actions which they would not take if they thought those paper commitments meant a great deal.

Judgment of "progress" then, ultimately turns on an analysis of practice which reflects a concern for normatively derived values or, lacking that, plain fear of the consequences of aberrant practice, but also on the expectation that these values will hold up under the stresses on international politics and war itself. This judgment leads to one of the oldest and most profound of problems, that of evaluating the "sources" of international law, that is to say, the sources of principles and rules regulating international intercourse.

In addition to hundreds of text writers, the framers of the basic statutes for the Permanent Court of International Justice and its present successor, the International Court of Justice, have answered this question implicitly in the manner in which they have framed their definition of the sources of international law, or, as I have been referring to it under its older and more traditional title, the law of nations. Article 38 of the Statute of the International Court of Justice, which is an integral part of the United Nations system provides:

The Court, whose function is to decide in accordance with international law such disputes as are submitted to it, shall apply:

1. international conventions, whether general or particular, establishing rules expressly recognized by the contesting states;
2. international custom, as evidence of a general practice accepted as law;
3. the general principles of law recognized by civilized nations;
4. subject to the provisions of Article 59, judicial decisions and the teachings of the most highly qualified publicists of the various nations, as subsidiary means for the determination of rules of law.[7]

Particularly because I take the approach that the limitation of war is not most effectively accomplished by broad moral and legal codes

[7] This provision shall not prejudice the power of the Court to decide a case *ex aequo et bono,* if the parties agree thereto. [Article 59 of the Statute provides "The decision of the Court has no binding force except between the parties and in respect of that particular case." In other words there is no international law rule of *stare decisis* in the sense of the Common Law and U. S. Constitutional Law wherein precedents are to be rather strictly followed. This is not to say that the relatively rare decisions of international tribunals, international arbital tribunals as well as the World Court, are not extremely influential in international law and diplomacy.]

and rules, it is important to dwell on the sources of that law of nations which presently provides what little explicitly legal limitation exists with respect to the preparation for and recourse to war.

The order of the sources listed in the I.C.J. Statute is interesting and important. First, it is widely accepted that the first two sources, conventions and custom, are qualitatively more important than the last two categories, general principles, judicial decisions, and the opinions of the most highly qualified publicists. It is, moreover, generally assumed that as between the two primary sources of international law, international conventions are superior evidence of the law, while custom is inferior and less reliable. It is important to the approach of this book to emphasize that I am skeptical about the first assumption and reject the second.

As a matter of fact, general principles of law, judicial precedents, and the opinions of publicists often play a major role in shaping the formulation of claims and counterclaims concerning international issues. This is especially the case when conventional law is either lacking, or (more of a problem) existent but not observed and when the state of customary international law is controverted. Sometimes, very much in the way that "judicial activists" operate in the U.S. constitutional system, someone has to proclaim boldly that a certain principle, judicial precedent, or body of authority is or ought to be the law and, in effect, "sell" the argument. Moreover, one should never underestimate the practical propensity of judges and statesmen to reach for established authority, literally, to reach up on the shelf and pull down a book containing a legal argument supportive of a position they wish to take as a matter of policy.

As to the widely held preference for conventional (treaty) law over "vague" customary law, I dissent. The most important thing in international law and relations, especially concerning conflict regulation, is realism, contact with reality. The law must actually reach and affect the parties it purports to regulate. If the law is far removed from the habitual behavior of its subjects, particularly in the absence of a higher authority and the expectation of community sanctions, the law may be a snare and delusion. If a treaty is viable it is because it is declaratory of the past and projected customary international law. No matter how "clear" and "solemn" its commitments, a treaty is not viable if it is at variance with the intents and habitual behavior of the parties supposedly regulated by it. But there is always a price for realism. I believe that it is realistic in assessing the sources of international law not to be overimpressed by clear-cut conventions and to look to resources of customary law, general principles, judicial decisions, and the opinions of publicists. But there is no question that these other sources are less readily identified and interpreted. The very flexibility and closeness to reality that tend to recommend customary law, general principles, judicial decisions, and the writings of publicists also make them more subjective and subject to controversy. So, at one extreme we can have very clear law about war, which is not too related to reality, or we can have very flexible and controversial law about war which is subjective, changeable, and always vulnerable to the charge that it is being bent by practitioners of power politics. In a primitive legal system such as the world public legal order, it seems clear to me that, as concerns the most vital interests of nations and their security, the risks of the latter approach have to be accepted in the interests of relevancy, for the advantages of emphasis on conventional law are all too often outweighed by the disadvantages of irrelevance. This, of course, is not an iron-clad rule. Whatever source of international law promises to produce the best results should be used, and it is obviously possible to approach problems from several sources, giving differing emphases to the sources, in the pursuit of the difficult goals of war limitation.

The state, then, requires military coercion to defend itself and also to work for security, law, and order in the international society to the extent that it's possible. The state also requires military and other coercion to maintain law and order within its jurisdiction. Both idealist approaches to politics and the law of nations tend to avoid the question as to two occasions for recourse to force within the state. How far may the state go in maintaining "law and order?" And, supposing that the state denies its subjects their fundamental human rights, when and how may its citizens rise in violent revolution and seek to protect their rights by violent revolution?

It is perhaps understandable that the eminently idealist view expressed in the official social teachings of the Catholic Church almost literally *flee* from the issue of violent revolution. One can appreciate the horror of human suffering which moves popes and Councils to abhor "guerrilla warfare" and "terrorism," virtually the only effective forms of violent revolution. But the realist understanding of natural law leads him to conclusions about the "inherent" right of self-defense of individuals, groups, and oppressed societies similar to those he holds about organized states. True, the presumption is greater against the use of armed force against a constituted political society than is the case in the international order (rescinding here from the very important fact that the quality of international conflict may be so much greater, at least in the case of nuclear war, than in the case of civil strife) because there is an "authority," there is some kind of a public order, and one does not lightly overthrow even very unsatisfactory public orders. But one *does* sometimes overthrow them and rightly so. Moreover, if there is a right to violent revolution—and this is accorded by all natural-law approaches—there are implicit rights to use whatever means are available to the revolutionaries.

Meanwhile, in emphasizing the importance I attach to the moral right of revolution I ask the reader's indulgence for a personal reference which is apposite to me. My professor of international law was Ernst H. Feilchenfeld, a Berlin Jew, who, having acquired a Doctor of Law at Berlin, left his native land, for which he had fought as an infantrymen in World War I, and went to Britain and finally to America. He left Germany in the twenties, perhaps the first refugee from Hitler, because he could see the beginnings of trends that ended with war, concentration camps, and an abortive revolution that showed that at least some Germans knew that revolution is sometimes a duty as well as a right. Whenever Professor Feilchenfeld discussed a situation wherein human rights were obviously being denied on a massive and brutal scale, he would say: "Pretty soon, some local Jefferson is going to start writing—'When, in the course of human events . . .'" I think that Professor Feilchenfeld was right in his analysis and in his insistence that revolution, like war, has to be faced as a phenomenon that not only can happen but that sometimes ought to happen. It, like war, is a terrible thing. We should study the question, as to when it is justified, what the alternatives to it may be, and how it can be mitigated. But violent revolution must be confronted as a rational and often unjust option that sometimes raises questions virtually undistinguishable from those raised by war itself. Having plumbed the depths of the unpleasant picture of the world that confronts the realist, let us move directly to the heart of the matter of war, deterrence, and revolution, the definition of legitimate military necessity.

Military necessity is a term that evokes emotion. To many it means the cynical explanation that is not an explanation of the excesses of military action. To some it means the unquestionable prerogative of "the commander" to do whatever needs to be done for the accomplishment of "the mission" and the defense of the nation. To international lawyers and diplomats it is the "elastic clause" conditioning virtually all international agreements about the conduct of war, the open escape hatch which permits apparent adhesion to moral and legal principles regulating war while providing for release from those principles when the going gets tough.

I use the term *legitimate military necessity* with the conviction that there are things that are necessary in war and that it is pointless to concede or condemn a continued right to recourse to armed force without authorizing the means which will render such a right meaningful. My concept of legitimate military necessity is based on the following propositions:

1. "Military necessity" as a term of military art and science, properly conceived, does not mean unlimited violence. Rather, it means genuine military utility in consonance with the classic military principle of force.

2. *Legitimate* military necessity is true military utility which is, moreover, limited by the laws of war and the natural law. Thus,

there are three tests that an act must pass to qualify as legitimate military necessity:

a. It must be truly necessary. That is to say, it must be necessary for and proportionate to a valid military objective.

b. It must not be violative of the positive international law of war.

c. Given the gaps in the positive international law of war, especially as concerns the means of destruction, it must not violate basic principles of natural law and, indeed, of the positive international law of war.

This is all very interesting, but the question remains, "Who decides and who judges the determination of the one who decides?" The answer is that the responsible commander decides what is "military necessity," subject to review. The review may take many forms. It may take the form of a war-crimes proceeding. Given the chancy prospects for war-crimes trials in contemporary conflicts this is a comparatively secondary consideration. More to the point, states and alliances have agreed positions on what military policies should be pursued. Violation of such policies may result in personal and official condemnation, denigration, or disavowal. The fact is that, in modern conflict, "rules of the game" emerge. Those who break the rules may not be prosecuted as war criminals, but they will be disciplined or disavowed in such a way as to disassociate a state from measures allegedly taken as "militarily necessary" acts of state. In the final analysis, the decision makers and citizens of each state decide what is "legitimate military necessity," and have to stand by the practical, legal, and moral, consequences.

The political-military counterpart of this ambitious and precarious concept of legitimate military necessity is clearly the concept of "limited war." The political-military model for war fought with full consideration of the principle of legitimate military necessity is what has been widely and popularly characterized as "limited war."

"Limited war," is not a panacea. To say that war ought to be "limited" rather than "total" is nice but not overly instructive. The efforts to define limited war represent a quest for a reasoned, limited commitment to seemingly necessary armed coercion. The war in Vietnam is evidence of the controversial character of the concept of "limited war." For some, the war in Vietnam has been a classical model of limited war; for others, it has been an atrocity of "total war."

Limited war developed as a reaction to attitudes such as the massive retaliation postures of the early 1950s. The Korean War and the recurring threats of war in Europe sparked by the several Berlin crises, as well as the endless succession of threats and outbreaks of lesser "brush-fire" wars all over the world compelled professional military men to develop new strategic and tactical concepts and new organizational and command arrangement to meet these new and varied challenges. Moreover, the magnitude of the threat of nuclear war moved men from the natural and social science, as well as the normative disciplines, to try their hand at developing new theories, or to recover and dust off old theories, about the conduct of war on a limited basis, not on the basis of a spasm-of-violence reaction to the threat or use of armed force by an adversary.

We are now in a period of critical re-examination of the concept of limited war. The concept is attacked from those who deny the moral permissibility and rationality of war or who deplore almost any recourse to armed force even when they cannot provide a plausible alternative. It is also attacked by the hard-line seekers of victory who scorn cowardly no-win policies and who want to return complete control over the formulation of national-defense policy—which, in effect, means most of the critical aspects of foreign policy—as well as the strategies, tactics, force compositions, and budgetary requirements of the nation to the trustworthy hands of the professionals. To be sure the hard-liners are not adverse to all limited war concepts in all situations. But they would retain the option of unlimited war concepts as well as the option of unlimited preparation for war and research and development designed to increase the effectiveness of the armed forces.

The realist position of this book is that the condition precedent to acceptance of the proposition that war remains a rational and morally permissible necessity in an international system that is not likely to undergo fundamental systemic change is acceptance of the proposition that all recourse to armed coercion must be limited in ends and means in every way possible. The pernicious spirit of the crusading United Nations of World War II that applauded every form of destruction visited upon the "dirty Nazis and Japs" (who "started it") was wrong at the time and would be monstrously wrong in a conflict involving the threat or use of nuclear weapons. Such a spirit is also clearly wrong in a revolutionary war or intervention into such a war, whatever the side and whatever the values which the party to the conflict claims to defend.

Having taken this position I am all too aware that the prerequisites for limited wars are extremely difficult to meet and maintain. I see five such prerequisites.

First, limited war requires the material means necessary to provide flexibility in the disposition of forces, their co-ordination with diplomacy, their strategic and tactical deployment, and, extremely important, their redeployment or withdrawal. Arms, weapons system, organizations, command structures, transportation, communications, and logistical capabilities, must all be of such a nature that war can be, in effect, turned off as well as on, de-escalated as well as escalated, and, if need be, left with its motor idling, depending on policy considerations.

Second, limited war requires at times the subordination of perfectly legitimate military necessities to the necessities of political policy. Clausewitz was right when he said that war was a continuation of politics by other means. He was wrong to the extent that he can be interpreted as contending that once war is unleashed it has its own built-in logic and necessities which must be pursued relentlessly. This reading of Clausewitz's dictum is inadmissible to the proponent of limited war. Equally inadmissible is the nasty shot that General MacArthur took at President Truman and the Joint Chiefs of Staff when he told the Joint Session of Congress that greeted him on his return to Washington from Korea that he had always thought the object of war was "victory." The object of war is to obtain legitimate political and military ends and the definition of those ends, as well as of the means, is ultimately the responsibility of the political authorities.

This is especially true in the messy conflicts of our times. The classic example of this principle of limited war was the decision of the Truman administration not to bomb north of the Yalu River. Bombing halts, limitations of areas and targets to be bombed, and insistence of approval of targets by the White House, with respect to the Vietnam War are likewise prime examples of the principle of subordination of military to political necessities or considerations.

Third, limited war requires an effective and loyal command structure which accepts the general concept of limited war and accepts the political restrictions that are placed on the conduct of such a war. This imposed a terrible burden on military commanders. This was dramatically brought home by the agonies imposed by U.S. and other UN commanders during the period of fighting and negotiating that marked the last years of the Korean conflict. Battles such as those for Pork Chop Hill during the endless Panmunjom talks imposed restrictions on troop deployments and tactics right down to the company level. A number of commanders had to order units to conduct operations necessary to maintain the political-military position of the United Nations in ways which predictably made very little military sense and which, equally predictably, ensured dangers and casualties that could otherwise have been avoided. This is very hard on commanders and troops but it is essential to the limited war concept of armed force as an instrument of policy, not an end in itself.

Fourth, in addition to loyal and disciplined commanders limited war also obviously requires obedient and courageous military forces which will endure restrictions on their fighting capabilities and will cope with the potential disillusion of seeing what they have won on the battlefield bartered and perhaps surrendered in international politics.

Fifth, limited war requires a home front that will support such a war, even when it is protracted and costly. Indeed, this is probably the most difficult prerequisite for limited war. The very essence of limited war is that it is resorted to rationally, not emotionally, that it is waged with all possible moderation and a minimum of what Secretary Rusk calls a "war spirit," and that it tries to focus on the sufficient reasons for engaging in conflict rather than on the natural tendency of a nation and its armed forces to "win and bring the boys home." As the Vietnam War has shown, such a war places strain on a society that can become almost literally intolerable. One element of public opinion wants to go all out and get it over with, another wants to pull out, and the moderates, both supporters and critics of the war, soon find themselves the targets of extremists of both sides, and, indeed, increasingly they begin to snap and snarl at each other. It may well be that the need for home-front support, patience, and civility among those who disagree with the government and among themselves places a requirement on the state that would wage long but limited wars that is more difficult to meet than any of the other prerequisite identified. To the extent that this may be the case, it is as well that this problem be squarely confronted. For there will be more wars and they ought to be as limited as possible. There are, to be sure, approaches to war contending that fundamental change in the international system is not only desirable but possible. Some talk of changing men's attitudes toward war with a view to eliminating war. I am interested in changing men's attitudes toward war with a view to limiting war. Both viewpoints advocate approaches that are considered necessary and possible. I think the idealists are overoptimistic and that the approach of the realist is called for on its merits and, in addition, is positively related to the efforts of the idealists to change the system, for, if the realist approach is relatively successful now, it may take time for the idealist approaches to work out the enormous feats of social engineering that they seem to have in mind. In any event, in my view, all of us are best served by candor with respect to the possibilities and defects of his approach to war. It is not easy to keep a limited war limited. But this is the first order of business for those concerned with the problem of war. For the realist the relationship between war and survival is limited war in order to survive, not the "elimination" of war in order to survive.

Both of these positions—political realism and limited war—are vulnerable. Perhaps one of the most recurring of these vulnerabilities is the charge that the realists take refuge in Pentagon-Rand jargon in order to cover up their otherwise morally, politically, and humanly outrageous arguments. Since many of the principal criticisms of realism and the limited war approach recur constantly, a specialized vocabulary often becomes necessary.

There are three basic criticisms that are usually directed to the realist, the proponent of limited war, who professes some degree of moral concern over these subjects.

First, Vatican II and its idealist counterparts demanded an "entirely new approach" to the problem of war. The realist, limited-war approach is certainly not "an entirely new approach"; it is an old one. But new and old are very relative terms. There have been ages of "total war," in terms of capabilities and intentions of parties to conflict, but there have also been long periods of comparatively limited war, as in the period between the end of the Thirty Years' War in the Treaties of Westphalia of 1648 and the beginning of the troubled epoch triggered by the French Revolution in 1789. Highly respected authorities have suggested that contemporary dilemmas, such as the East-West confrontations, may usefully be viewed in terms of other historic religious-ideological confrontations which did not end up in Armageddon such as that between Christendom and Islam. It is my belief that it is at least equally valid to recall that the alternative choices are not, or at least have not been, "no war or total" but "total war or limited war." To take such an approach, in our present circumstances, may not meet the requirement to take an entirely new approach to the problem of war. But it certainly represents an attempt to take a *different,* and humanly extremely difficult, approach to war. Consistent adhesion to the concept of limited war would represent a change in modern approaches to war. It might not be "an entirely new approach," but it would represent a necessary change. Meanwhile, it remains to be seen whether the entirely new approaches do, in fact, produce systemic change. If they do, so much the better. Meanwhile, some of us think it most relevant to try to regulate the dangerous system in which we operate.

Second, it is frequently alleged that it is not the idealists but the realists, the crackpot realists, who are hopelessly ingenuous in their reliance on rationality surviving in preparations, threats, and the conduct of war.

This is a respectable and, indeed, a prestigious position. I suppose that it found its classic exposition in Tolstoy's *War and Peace*. But it is not a position that is conspicuously represented by the present rulers of Russia or any other state with which I am familiar. It may be overly optimistic to expect rationality and limitation in preparations, threats, and recourses to armed force. But it is not also optimistic to expect rationality and limitation in the governance of peoples in most parts of the world wherein the policies and institutions vary so greatly. Perhaps the answer is all to be found in some literature, drama, or art of the "absurd," but that does not sound very much like the extremely rational and reasonable idealist approach to war-peace problems. In short, there is, and can be, no answer to the charge that realism is really unrealistic. The same can be said of all approaches to—and retreats from—the basic dilemmas of war in a divided world.

Third, it is often charged, realists are uncompassionate, clinical merchants of death, "cold Warriors, who discuss without feeling a subject that concerns human death and suffering, blood and guts, scorched children, terrified mothers, smashed homes, and the release of brutal instincts under spurious claims of "military necessity."

This is the lot of the realist. If he sees some satisfaction in the conviction that his approach to war is more helpful and less productive of false hopes which will predictably be dashed than the idealist or the extreme bellicist, he must accustom himself to the charge of clinical inhumanity.

For the humanity of the realist, especially for the Christian realist or any other proponent of realism and/or limited war, is shown by his commitment to grapple with a very unpleasant and difficult subject, which, he fears, cannot be wished away or eliminated by legal bans or social engineering. Once the realist has made that decision, he has to maintain a certain calm. He has to try to control his emotions so that his reason may operate with, he hopes, some salutary effects as regards the mitigation of the suffering and horrors of war. Yes, he should remind himself that he is dealing with human flesh and blood and not with words or symbols or extras dying in war movies. But the subject is war and war is hell. Moreover, the subject is modern war, which is refined hell. The victims of war will not be helped if the realist proponent of limited war turns from the subject in disgust, despair, or nausea—as well he might. For then it will be in the hands of the people who enjoy wars or who are insensitive to the suffering of war. War, which is at best a very bad and tragic business, will then be left to the direction and control of those for whom it is not bad and tragic. The realists and the proponents of limited war care about the human dimension of war. That is why they seek a balance between the extremist approaches to war and bear the brunt of attacks from all directions. It is not a very comfortable position, but then no honest position on War and/or Survival is comfortable.

IV Alternatives to War:
State of the Question

As just stated, the critic of internationalist idealism who adopts a realist view has an obligation to review seriously developments to which the idealist looks as indicative of possible fundamental change in the international system making possible the elimination of war. This brief review of such developments is not meant to denigrate such hopes and efforts. Nor is it an attempt to set up straw men to be easily toppled so that the grim business of justifying war can be taken up, as it were, with clean but hypocritical hands. A sensible realist does not take satisfaction in his view of war nor does he wish anything but the best for those who seek to eliminate or drastically reduce its incidence and destructive character. But a responsible realist believes that it is his duty to maintain a critical attitude toward efforts at international systemic change, which have thus far generally failed, with dreadful consequences for the human condition. This chapter, then, represents a look at the status of alternative approaches to war as an instrument of resolving international conflicts. Two approaches are briefly appraised:

1. The international law and organization approach, which seeks evolutionary change in the international system, supported by progress in arms control and disarmament;

2. The "peace research" approach which seeks to demonstrate the theoretical possibility of fundamental international systemic change

by the application of concepts and techniques developed by the natural and social sciences.

As to the first approach, the men of good will of the late nineteenth and early twentieth century were very optimistic about the prospects for the development of international law and organization. The concept of "the machinery for peace" prevailed among them. Peace would come about if the procedural means—good offices, mediation, arbitration, adjudication—were more readily available to nations.

Well, today we have the "machinery for peace" at the global and regional levels, but there is not nearly as much peace as there ought to be. International law, especially in the natural law of nations sense I have stressed, is inadequate, particularly with respect to the issues that engender war. There are few encouraging signs pointing to a broadening and deepening of international law, even as concern those interests which are normally discussed under the international law of peace. For example, the legal problems raised by the practical possibilities of exploitation of the continental shelf and of fisheries either adjacent to or historically used by particular nations were debated from the time of the Truman declarations in 1945 through international conferences and in the International Law Commission of the UN for thirteen years. In 1958 a majority of the participants in a conference on this and related subjects thrashed these problems out in Geneva. Several conventions were produced, but ratification, much less observance, of these conventions remains problematical, particularly as concerns many of the most important states especially sensitive about the subjects covered by the conventions. The machinery for peace, the codified law, are there. Real consensus and willingness to use the machinery and abide by the law are inadequate.

Now it would take a very hard sell to one of the Latin American or other holdouts from the 1958 Geneva Conventions to persuade an open-minded third party that their socioeconomic interests were not superior to the obvious need to regularize exploitation of the continental shelf and fishing areas of the world in the common good and, indeed, in the interests of the resisting states concerned. Yet such conventions and arguments, as well as policies supporting them, languish. On the other hand, much advertised treaties about outer space and Antarctica flourish, since the consideration relinquished is often nebulous or unknown. But when the "national interest" rears its head, progress toward international law and organization becomes slow and painful.

Curiously enough, there has been more progress in the development of international law on paper in the realms of collective security and regulation of the conduct of international war than in virtually any other field close to the vital interests of states. This progress is both encouraging and a source of concern. The nations of the world have shown, since 1918, their great and continued interest in outlawing war as an instrument of foreign policy. Moreover, both before and after two world wars states have shown, in the Hague Conventions on Land warfare of 1899 and 1907 and in the four Geneva Conventions of 1949, their desire to mitigate the sufferings of international conflict. For those who think of law primarily in terms of international agreements, there is more, and more detailed, law regarding the legal permissibility of recourse to armed force and the means that are permissible in wartime, than exist with respect to almost any other problem area of international law.

But it certainly cannot be argued that the international law and organization approach to war has remotely approached the achievement of fundamental change in the international system. The key concept in this regard has been collective security and collective security, as distinguished from collective defense, has not matured into a reliable international institution in our times.

The Wilsonian concept of collective security, central to the League of Nations Charter and essential to the meaningful operation of the United Nations system, has these components:

1. An attack or threat to the peace against any member of the collective security system is an attack or threat against all members of the system and against the system itself.

2. On the finding, in the case of Chapter VII of the UN Charter, of the Security Council, that aggression or a threat to the peace had occurred, international community enforcement actions to meet the aggression or threat to the peace are authorized.

3. Forces are available, whether national forces designated for international community service or permanently organized peace-keeping forces of an integrated nature. Knowledge of the existence of such forces would presumably have some deterrent effect on potential aggressors. Otherwise collective security calls for a war against war wherein the overwhelming resources of the majority of the members of the international community are expected to suppress the minority aggressor or aggressors, no matter how powerful they may be vis-à-vis individual victims of aggression.

Let us examine these three components of collective security in the light of present realities and prospects. The only body that is legally competent to make a determination that a threat to the peace, i.e., to the security and order of the international community, is the Security Council. In order for the Security Council to make such a determination it must not only secure a substantial majority of votes from the membership, it must secure all of the votes of the five permanent members of the Council (unless one or more of the permanent members abstain). This creates the problem of the veto power of the permanent members. The U.S. and the U.K. are more or less together on most issues. The U.S.S.R. holds the record for vetoes. France has increasingly played "wild cards" in the Council.

Finally China (Taiwan) presents many problems. Among these is the fact that it has a veto over any matter concerning its very peculiar position in Asia. Moreover, Taiwan is in no sense a Great Power. It holds a seat that logically should be held by the People's Republic of China and presumably would be, if the profound freeze in its relations with the United States, the Soviet Union, and the UN itself could ever be broken. But even leaving the enormous problem of Red China aside, and assuming growing U.S.-Soviet co-operation on at least some problems in at least some parts of the world, and further assuming a co-operative attitude on the part of France, acquiescence of China (Taiwan), and the assent of a majority of the nonpermanent members of the Council, all to the end that the Council, could under the provisions of Article 39, "determine the existence of [a] threat to the peace, breach of the peace, or act of aggression," what would happen? Acting under Article 39, the Security Council could then "make recommendations or decide what measures shall be taken in accordance with Articles 41 and 42, to maintain or restore international peace and security."

"The first form of collective security sanction available to the Security Council is nonmilitary coercion." Were the Security Council to begin with its options under Article 41 it might be able to forge an alternative to war. Article 41 provides:

> The Security Council may decide what measures not involving the use of armed force are to be employed to give effect to its decisions, and it may call upon the Members of the United Nations to apply such measures. These may include complete or partial interruption of economic relations and of rail, sea, air, postal, telegraphic, radio, and other means of communication, and the severance of diplomatic relations.

The concepts of economic sanctions and nonintercourse, as alternatives to war are hardly new. Thomas Jefferson applied these concepts with results more deleterious to the United States than to Britain and France during the Napoleonic wars. But his sad experience might be waved aside as irrelevant since the United States was acting alone at a time when it was not a great power. But we do have some representative experiments in the kind of nonmilitary coercion envisaged in Article 41 of the Charter. The League of Nations toyed with the idea of invoking economic sanctions against Japan because of her recourse to armed force in the "Manchurian incident" which began in September 1931 and ended with the conquest of Manchuria and the erection of the puppet state of Manchukuo in January 1932, sealed by the truce of Tangku in May 1933. Although the League adopted the Lytton Commission report in 1932 and censured Japan for resorting to force before all peaceful means of settling her differences with China had been exhausted, it did not invoke sanctions under Article XVI. Nor was there any widespread enthusiasm for U. S. Secretary of State Stimson's "doctrine" and practice of nonrecognition of conquest resulting from illegal aggression, much less than for his initiatives to have the United States join the League in economic sanctions against Japan. This was the background for the first major effort at nonmilitary coercion on behalf of international law and order by an international organization, economic sanctions against Italy after that nation invaded Ethiopia (or Abyssinia as it was then more commonly called).

On August 3, 1935, Italy invaded Abyssinia. There were various pretexts given, mainly related to the inevitable "incidents" between Abyssinian tribesmen and Italian troops and police along the desert borders separating Abyssinia from neighboring Italian colonies. Italy went through the motions of attempting peaceful settlement in the so-called "Wal Wal Arbitrations" in which Abyssinia was represented by some of the most outstanding French and American international lawyers. The only problem was that the Italian negotiators never seemed to remember when and where meetings were to be held, they stalled outrageously, and the whole exercise became one of the most ludicrous and bald-faced examples of a "fight and negotiate" policy to be found in modern history, the more so because time and fighting were on the side of the Italians.

The situation cried for application of the concept of collective security through League of Nations sanctions, starting with nonmilitary coercion but, if all else failed, involving joint military enforcement action. Moreover, it cried for leadership by Britain and France. They were the great powers who dominated the League. They had the means to employ both nonmilitary and military coercion. Nazi Germany was a growing threat but, in 1935–36, very far from a clear and present threat. Nobody knew what to think of the Soviet Union. Japan walked out of the League when the Lytton Commission report was accepted. The United States was increasingly cooperative with various League activities but was not a member of the League and certainly could not lead a serious League move to bring sanctions to bear against Italy. France had its own endemic domestic problems and a growing uneasiness about Nazi Germany. In short, the first trial test for nonmilitary sanctions required British leadership and action.

International idealists, when they talk about concepts such as collective security and other alternatives to traditional international war, are prone to talk in abstract terms, for example, "States must relinquish some of their sovereignty to form a world authority which will enforce law and order through collective security." Or, according to the epoch, idealists like to talk about "taking it to the League" or the UN, or about "collective action," by an organization such as the League or the UN. But just as a government is made up of people, an international organization is made up of national units which in turn are dependent upon their respective governments and peoples. Generalities are all very well, but Mr. Truman's proclamation that "the buck ends here" applies to international as well as to national government. Some nation, some organization, some individual or group—with the support of their constituencies, whatever they may be, has to terminate the buck passing which is especially characteristic of collective-security measures. In the case of Italian aggression against Abyssinia, the buck appears to have ended with Britain.

To repeat, this buck was not an outlandish challenge. It had nothing in common with the potential risks that would face a contemporary actor in a collective-security situation in the nuclear age. But it is instructive to see how the British reacted to the challenge of 1935. I trust that the reader will not be offended if I quote the version of events of that time given us by A. J. P. Taylor, whose erudition and wisdom may be equaled by the controversial character of his writing but who seems to me to have put his finger on the heart of the whole problem of collective security, with or without armed force, in his treatment of the domestic and international reaction of Britain to Mussolini's imperial adventure in Abyssinia.

Taylor unfolds the story, in part, as follows:

> The advocates of disarmament, too, had not been inactive while the plans for rearmament and the White Paper [on defence of March 4, 1935, which despaired of the reliability of collective security and advocated an independent national defence policy] were being prepared. They, too, appealed to public opinion, and more skillfully than the civil servants. The League of Nations Union organized a house-to-house canvass, on the model of the Gallup polls which were coming into fashion. Householders were asked five questions, phrased, of course, to elicit a favorable response. In October, 1934, when the questions were framed, disarmament still seemed the burning issue. Only question 5, thrown in as an afterthought, asked whether an aggressor should be stopped by economic measures and, if necessary, by war. This was not, as it was abusively called, a Peace Ballot, if by this was meant a ballot for pacifism. It was a ballot for international disarmament and collective security, though no doubt pacifist sentiment was mixed in with it . . .[1]

Here we have an extremely instructive test case of the feasibility of collective security in general and of economic sanctions in particular. Taylor tells us:

> Those who conducted [The Peace Ballot] were not pacifists. Most of them were non-party men or former Liberals. All were from the middle class, and the ballot was actually opposed by the Left wing of the Labour party. The response was formidable. Over 11½ million replied—a substantial majority of all householders. More than ten million answered Yes to every question except to the second half of the last— whether the aggressor should be stopped by war. Here six and three

[1] A. J. P. Taylor, *English History, 1914–1945* (New York and Oxford: Oxford University Press, 1965), p. 379.

quarter million said Yes; over two million said No; another two million did not answer. The answers were announced on 28 June 1935. By then international disarmament was a dead cause. Only the answers to question 5 mattered. The Peace Ballot had become undesignedly a ringing assertion of support for collective security by all means short of war, and a more hesitant support even for war.[2]

Taylor contends that his Peace Ballot created "a conundrum for the national government," which was edging toward a rearmament policy (actually of very modest dimensions). "Pious and abstract phrases of loyalty to the League of Nations in Stanley Baldwin's best manner," were not sufficient for:

A concrete case of aggression was in the offing, Mussolini had resolved to attack Abyssinia, a member of the League of Nations. The national government had not the slighest wish to go against Italy. They had none of the Labour's hostility to Mussolini as a "fascist" . . . The service chiefs, with the problems of Japan and Germany on their hands, were insistent that Italy should not be added to the list of possible enemies. Eden, the supposed champion of collective security, went to Rome and attempted to butt Mussolini off. Italy could have the lowlands of Abyssinia without war; Great Britain would secure Abyssinia's agreement by surrendering part of British Somaliland to her. Mussolini rejected the offer: Italy, he insisted, must have the position in Abyssinia which Great Britain had in Egypt—an awkward analogy for a British government to reject.[3]

According to Taylor, the nationalist government tried to finesse the situation by announcing its wholehearted support for collective security, "on condition that all other members of the League were as wholehearted as she was."[4] As it happened, the Manchurian crisis had put the League to work on the prospects of applying sanctions and detailed planning had been accomplished. Economic sanctions

2 *Ibid.*, p. 379.
3 *Ibid.*, p. 380.
4 *Ibid.*, p. 380.

"were applied after 3 October when the Italian armies attacked
Abyssinia. Italian credits were cut off; all imports from Italy and
some exports to her were banned by virtually all members of the
League."[5] Although the U.S. and Germany were outside of the
League, their appraisal of Italy's predicament seems to have reduced
their trade with that nation and, on the whole, Italy did experience
grave economic difficulties because of the sanctions.[6]

In the end, however, the economic sanctions were not effective.
The national government was able to slip through modest rearmament measures and to take credit for loyalty to the League and
collective security. Efforts to include oil in the list of commodities
excluded from Italy were more than overcome by slippery U.K.-
French-Italian diplomatic maneuvers to get everybody off the hook.
These were blown up by press coverage of the Hoare-Laval Plan,
which was the final sellout of Abyssinia and the concept of collective security. The unhappy denouement is thus described by the
acerbic Taylor:

. . . The Hoare-Laval Plan was dead.
The League died with it. The outcry in England against the Hoare-
Laval Plan was the greatest explosion over foreign affairs for many
years . . . [but] it was effective only in negation. It subsided once the
Hoare-Laval Plan was withdrawn. *The problem remained just what it
had been before: how to stop Mussolini without war. No answer was
found.* The oil sanction was repeatedly proposed and as repeatedly
put off when Mussolini objected to it. Compromise was still in the
air: another version of the Hoare-Laval Plan waiting to be produced
when rain closed the campaigning season in Abyssinia. Instead Mussolini whipped his armies on and won the war in a hurry. On 1 May 1936
the Emperor Haile Selassie left Abyssinia. A week later Mussolini pro-
claimed the foundation of a new Roman empire. Haile Selassie appeared at Geneva to protest in person; was welcomed at Victoria
station by Anthony Eden and settled as an exile in Bath [until he was

[5] *Ibid.*, p. 380.
[6] *Ibid.*, pp. 380–81.

restored to his throne in 1941]. On 10 June Neville *Chamberlain acting on his own in foreign affairs for the first time, condemned the continuance of sanctions as "the very midsummer of madness." On 18 June they were withdrawn.*[7]

A major effort, as seen from the perspectives of some not altogether cynical and inept statesmen and citizens, to find a nonmilitary alternative to war and sanction for collective security ended up as a failure. As Taylor observes, "The League died with it." And what of the United Nations?

The United Nations has had one major occasion to apply the nonmilitary coercion authorized by Article 41 of the Charter. Just about everyone is able to agree on the illegal and unjust character of the apartheid policies of the Republic of South Africa. But for a number of reasons, there is very little that the UN or its members have been able or willing to do about South Africa and its mandated territory, South West Africa. It is with the frustrations of the unsuccessful attempts that have been made to bring international pressure to bear on South Africa that one should view the unique and indeed bizarre efforts of the United Nations to prevent the entrenchment of another white racist regime in Rhodesia.

Rhodesia, after years of commission reports and negotiations, cut loose its bonds with Britain and declared its independence. It established a white racist regime similar to that existing in the Republic of South Africa. Efforts at an *inter se* commonwealth settlement failed, and the United Kingdom was obliged to brand Rhodesia as a rebellious, outlaw state, dedicated to principles violative of international law and international human rights. Once again, the buck-passing on collective security and enforcement of international law ended with the beleaguered British. But, unlike the situation in the thirties, a large number of states have been willing to support non-military sanctions, and so a second great experiment in this method of community coercion on behalf of peace and justice has been tried.

[7] *Ibid.,* p. 385.

The form and progress of his second great attempt at nonmilitary sanctions is authoritatively and concisely described by a Report of the Secretary-General:

On 16 December 1966, the Security Council, acting in accordance with Articles 39 and 41 of the United Nations Charter, determined that the present situation in Southern Rhodesia constitutes a threat to international peace and security. It called on States to take a number of measures which were laid down in operative paragraphs 2 and 5 of resolution 232 (1966), which read as follows:

2. *Decides* that all States Members of the United Nations shall prevent:

a. the import into their territories of asbestos, iron ore, chrome, pig iron, sugar, tobacco, copper, meat and meat products and hides, skins and leather originating in Southern Rhodesia and exported therefrom after the date of this resolution;

b. any activities by their nationals or in their territories which promote or are calculated to promote the export of these commodities from Southern Rhodesia and any dealings by their nationals or in their territories in any of these commodities originating in Southern Rhodesia and exported therefrom after the date of this resolution, including in particular any transfer of funds to Southern Rhodesia for the purposes of such activities or dealings;

c. shipment in vessels or aircraft of their registration of any of these commodities originating in Southern Rhodesia and exported therefrom after the date of this resolution;

d. any activities by their nationals or in their territories which promote or are calculated to promote the sale or shipment to Southern Rhodesia of arms, ammunition of all types, military aircraft, military vehicles, and equipment and materials for the manufacture and maintenance of arms and ammunition in Southern Rhodesia.

e. any activities by their nationals or in their territories which promote or are calculated to promote the supply to Southern Rhodesia of all other aircraft and motor vehicles and of equipment and materials for the manufacture, assembly, or maintenance of aircraft and motor vehicles in Southern Rhodesia: the shipment in vessels and aircraft of their registration of any such goods destined for Southern Rhodesia:

and any activities by their nationals or in their territories which promote or are calculated to promote the manufacture or assembly of aircraft or motor vehicles in Southern Rhodesia;

f. participation in their territories or territories under their administration or in land or air transport facilities or by their nationals or vessels of their registration *in the supply of oil products to Southern Rhodesia;* notwithstanding any contracts entered into licences granted before the date of this resolution;

5. *Calls upon* all States not to render financial or other economic aid to the illegal racist regime in Southern Rhodesia.[8]

The same Report of the Secretary-General states that, "up to 21 February 1967, he has received replies to his notes referred to above from seventy-two States Members of the United Nations or of the specialized agencies."[9] Without going into the details, then, it is clear that a very large number of states have participated in economic sanctions against Rhodesia, including France, the Federal Republic of Germany, India, Japan, the United Kingdom, the Soviet Union, and the United States. Yet Rhodesia has survived. She has survived because of indirect importations through the Republic of South Africa. She has survived because of indirect and illegal exportations through adjacent weak African states, as well as South Africa, which are accepted without serious objection by some of the seventy-two states formally committed to participation in the economic sanctions as mandatory enforcement actions under Articles 39 and 41 of the UN Charter. More than two years after the Security Council invoked articles 39 and 41, the "threat to international peace and security" posed by the rebellious state of Rhodesia remains. This does not encourage confidence in economic and other nonmilitary sanctions as an alternative to war.

If Article 41 measures do not succeed in suppressing a threat to or breach of the peace, or if they appear insufficient from the

[8] United Nations Security Council, S/7781/21 February 1967, *Report of the Secretary-General in Pursuance of Resolution 232 (1966) Adopted by the Security Council at its 1340 Meeting on 16 December 1966.*
[9] *Ibid.,* p. 3.

outset of a crisis, the Security Council—again assuming it has
the votes of nine of its fifteen members, including all five permanent
members—may invoke Article 42 which states:

> Should the Security Council consider that measures provided for in
> Article 41 would be inadequate or have proved to be inadequate, it
> may take such action by air, sea, or land forces as may be necessary
> to maintain or restore international peace and security. Such action
> may include demonstrations, blockade and other operations by air, sea,
> or land forces of Members of the United Nations.

Two observations about Article 42 are in order. The first is that
it has never been invoked in the twenty-four-year-old history of the
United Nations. It was designed to be the cornerstone of the United
Nations, but that organization finds it possible to stand without a
cornerstone. When it comes to anything like international police
actions or peacekeeping, the United Nations has been obliged to rely
on the Article 51 right of collective defense (Korea) reinforced by
the "Uniting for Peace Resolution" of November 3, 1950. The
essence of the Uniting for Peace Resolution is the following: If the
Security Council is unable to act "because of lack of unanimity of
the permanent members," with respect to threats to and breaches
of the peace, or acts of aggression:

> . . . the General Assembly shall consider the matter immediately with
> a view to making appropriate recommendations to Members for Col-
> lective measures, including in the case of a breach of the peace or act
> of aggression, the use of armed force when necessary, to maintain or
> restore international peace and security. If not in session at the time,
> the General Assembly may meet in emergency special session within
> twenty-four hours of the request therefor. Such emergency special ses-
> sion shall be called if requested by the Security Council on the vote
> of any seven members, or by a majority of the Members of the United
> Nations.[10]

[10] U. N. Gen. Ass. Off. Rec. 5th Sess., Supp. No. 20, at 10 (A1775) as quoted
in William W. Bishop, Jr., *International Law, Cases and Materials* (2nd ed.;
Boston and Toronto: Little, Brown, 1962).

There are a number of limiting factors which restrict the usefulness of the "Uniting for Peace Resolution's" attempt to fill the gap in the field of collective security created by divisions within the Security Council's permanent members.

First, the General Assembly can only "recommend" that UN members participate in a so-called international police action. The quantity and quality of UN members' participation in the "United Nations" defense of South Korea was sparse and spotty. Second, the very nature of the Assembly's approach to collective security precludes the kind of precrisis planning and marshaling of forces which the Security Council was supposed to accomplish under Articles 43–50 under the direction of the Military Staff Committee, which has never become a reality. Third, with the expansion of the General Assembly to more than twice its 1950 size, largely as the result of the acceptance of militarily weak, underdeveloped states, one of the most basic of the assumptions of the United Nations system is flaunted, necessarily but unfortunately. The whole point of giving the veto to the five permanent members of the Security Council was to link real power with responsibility for collective security. Now a large number of very weak states can recommend that some of the stronger states engage in "United Nations" police action involving either nonmilitary or armed coercion, but dissenting strong nations can ignore the recommendation.

As a matter of fact, since the one time when the Uniting for Peace formula produced some results, namely, in the "United Nations" defense of South Korea, it has seldom been used. The concept was raised in respect to the 1956 crises in Hungary and in the Middle East, in the 1958 Middle East Crisis. The Assembly condemned the use of force by Israel, the United Kingdom, France, and the Soviet Union in 1956, but did not recommend any sanctions. In the other instance the Assembly did not even condemn any of the parties to the disputes, much less recommend sanctions. The future of collective security involving armed coercion recommended by the General Assembly is, then, not very promising. Nor does the future of collective security based on U.S.-Soviet *détente* look very bright.

For one thing, such *détente* as has been achieved is highly selective and contradictory with other policies of the two superpowers, e.g., the Americans and Russians cheerfully sign test-ban and nonproliferation treaties, while Americans are shot down by Russian weapons supplied to North Vietnam in a war which the Russians characterize as imperialist aggression. For another, it must be remembered that the reason for the failure of the Security Council to act on the Suez Crisis was the vetoes of the United Kingdom and France; for once the U.S. and U.S.S.R. were in agreement on a conflict situation. France's recent behavior holds out prospects for obstructionism in the Council, underscoring the fact that the problem of the veto is not simply the problem of U.S.-Soviet Cold War opposition. At present, the prospects for UN global collective security are nil.

Recognition that UN global security does not and will not foreseeably exist has led to attempts to achieve at least *regional collective security*. The most notable of these attempts have been the Organization of American States, NATO, and the Warsaw Pact. It is extremely important that these attempts be carefully scrutinized precisely because they seem to offer the best hope for partial collective security and, to that extent, an alternative to war in the sense of indvidual recourse to armed force.

The key issue in appraising these attempts is this: Many regional organizations which purport to operate within the bounds established by the United Nations Charter (and they all do claim to) take enforcement action in the sense of Articles 41 and 42 of the Charter on the basis of *their* determination, *not* the Security Council's that a "threat to the peace, breach of the peace, or act of aggression" in the sense of Article 39, has occurred.

It is quite clear to me that the answer is "yes" insofar as Article 41 is concerned and "no" with respect to the measures authorized for the Security Council in Article 42. Absent a particular treaty obligation on the subject, breach of which might or might not be justified depending on the circumstances, there is no problem if a regional organization uses nonmilitary measures of coercion such as "complete or partial interruption of economic relations and of rail, sea, air, postal, telegraphic, radio, and other means of communication, and the severance of diplomatic relations." This is within the competence of individual states and collections of states and can be properly used as nonmilitary coercion, especially if taken in pursuance of the law and public order of a regional which has organized as has the inter-American system. Thus the determination that Castro's Cuba is a threat to the security of the hemisphere because of its highly publicized program of organizing and training revolutionaries and subversives and the nonmilitary sanctions levied on Cuba by the OAS are perfectly justified under international law.

But, as previously stated, the *only* alternative military coercion to a Security-Council enforcement action under Article 42 is an Article 51 war of individual or collective self-defense. There can be collective action on an *ad hoc* basis, as in the defense of South Korea, if there is an antecedent attack by an aggressor. There could be highly organized resistance by NATO to an armed attack under Article 51, pending a highly unlikely intervention by the Security Council. There can also be collective defense against indirect aggression, a universally recognized form of war, in which a foreign state intervenes decisively in a civil war. In Vietnam, the U.S. claims this to be the case with respect to North Vietnam, and, if the U.S. version of the facts is substantially accurate, the U.S. is fighting in an Article 51 war of collective self-defense with South Vietnam. (I will abstain from extended comment on the belated discovery by the Administration of obligations to assist South Vietnam under protocols to the SEATO treaty which add nothing to the basic legal position of the U.S., which I happen to agree with, and which would *not* justify U.S. intervention if the U.S. claim that there was "aggression from the North" was not sufficiently substantiated.) If the Communist version of the facts is the more accurate, the Soviet Union, People's Republic of China, and the various other Communist states are quite justified in assisting the Vietcong and the Republic of North Vietnam and, indeed, would be acting legally if they sent their own armed forces into the conflict.

Thus, there must be an armed attack, or a very imminent threat of an armed attack such as seemed to have faced Israel in the Spring of 1967, to justify self-defense, individual or collective. But to have collective security there must be more than the last-ditch right of self-defense. Article 39 quite properly authorizes enforcement action under Articles 41 and 42 of the Charter if "The Security Council shall determine the existence of any threat to the peace," as well as in cases of "breach of the peace, or act of aggression." Obviously there can be "threats to the peace" of a serious character which do not constitute recourse to armed force sufficient to justify Article 51 individual and collective self-defense.

So the advocate of a regional approach to collective security has a dilemma. If a state which threatens the peace of the region will oblige with something that can be plausibly termed an armed attack, even if it be "indirect aggression," in the sense of Article 51, regional collective security can operate within the UN Charter. However, if a situation arises which, in the opinion of the majority of the members of a regional organization, constitutes a threat to the peace, but cannot be called a breach of the peace or an act of armed aggression, the regional organization is powerless—unless it plays fast and loose with international law, or simply opts to change the existing law.

This brings us back to the point made in connection with Britain's role in the unsuccessful attempt to coerce Italy with economic sanctions. Regional organizations like global organizations have precious little flesh and fiber in and of themselves. Some nations must lead and sustain them, just as some groups and individuals must lead and sustain a nation. In the OAS, by all odds the most advanced regional organization if one looks at all the possible functions of such an organization, the United States is *the* leader. It is also a world power which frequently feels compelled to act as a "world police-man." One should not for a moment try to sweep this vital fact of American and international life under the carpet.

The United States sees many security responsibilities that are beyond its "national interest" by all but the most ridiculously imperialistic, ambitious standards. This is good, for had the "Great Powers" of the twenties and thirties displayed any comparable inclination to police the world there would have been no World War II. Power may, indeed, breed "arrogance," but it also engenders responsibility and no collective security system, regional or global, will operate successfully without great powers willing to live up to their responsibilities.

The difficulty is that the United States, and, for that matter, the Soviet Union, were it more given to expending its resources and blood for international community or other nations' rights, have painted themselves into a corner in terms of international law and organization. Legally, there is only one authority to give marching orders to take enforcement action involving armed force on behalf of international law and order, that is the Security Council, which, as we know, is one of the last sources of such marching orders that one can think of.

Confronted with this fact, the United States has tried to finesse the problem, and that is a pity. The United States has decided:

1. It will do what it must do for world and regional order.

2. It will always try to involve other nations in its acts—which it considers valid on their merits—on the theory that collective action is better than individual action.

3. It has endeavored to justify its wide-ranging interventions not only on the basis of collective consultation and participation with other states but of mandates from regional organizations, such as the OAS and SEATO.

The origin of the American drive to lend collegiality and the blessings of regional organizations to policies, which it was to adopt in any case, goes back at least to the 1939–40 proclamations of the inter-American system about the supposed immunity of the Western Hemisphere from the evil effects of the European beginnings of World War II. An interesting period in 1944–45 saw some maneuvering between U.S. defenders of the inter-American system and proponents of the new United Nations, resulting in the 1945

Treaty of Chapultepec and in Chapter VIII of the UN Charter to which we will shortly refer. Perhaps the trial balloon of the exercise was the 1954 U.S. attempt to get a serious anti-Communist sanction with teeth out of the OAS which was "overtaken by events" in Guatemala, where the U.S. had to stick with tried-and-true individual initiatives through the CIA in order to oust a left-leaning regime that could not be removed quickly or completely enough to suit American estimates of the requirements of the situation.

Thus, the real origin of the primarily American effort to fill the collective security gap on a regional basis was the Cuban Missile Crisis. If my analysis of the international law regime concerning recourse to armed force is correct, there was no possible hope that the Security Council, in which the Soviet Union held a veto, would find the Soviet's Cuban missile adventure a threat to the peace or an act warranting acts of self-defense. But the manner in which the missiles were eased into Cuba, the blatant deceit of Mr. Gromyko's discussions with President Kennedy at a time when both parties knew, although the Russians did not know that the Americans knew, the background of recurring serious crises over Berlin, would I think, give the United States, on its own and on the merits of the case, a reasonable basis for acts of self-defense justifiable under Article 51.

But, for whatever reasons, the United States did not rest its case for the Cuban "quarantine" and for direct threats of nuclear retaliation on the right of self-defense. Instead the U.S. took the position that the quarantine was not a measure of individual or collective self-defense. The U.S. contended that since the quarantine was endorsed by the OAS and participated in by eleven nations, it was in effect an "enforcement" of a "recommendation" by the OAS under Articles 6 and 8 of the Rio Treaty of 1947 which provided for collective determination that aggression had occurred in the Western Hemisphere, and for measures, including "armed force," to meet such aggression.

In an effort to produce UN endorsement to this interpretation of peacekeeping, the United States placed heavy emphasis on Article

53 (1) of the UN Charter. Before quoting or commenting on that Article, I would point out that it is *not* included in Chapter VII, "Action with Respect to Threats to the Peace, and Acts of Aggression." It is the second Article of Chapter VIII, "Regional Arrangements," which in part supplements Chapter VII but is certainly not central to it. Article 52 of the Charter disclaims any collision between the UN and regional organizations. Article 53 as a result of the Cuban Missile Crisis and the U.S. intervention in the Dominican Revolution in 1965, has become a real sore spot for those concerned with shifting collective security from an impossible to a plausible global level. If the reader is in the least concerned over the problems of collective security, let him read, slowly and reflectively, Article 53 (1) of the United Nations Charter. It provides:

> The Security Council shall, where appropriate, utilize such regional arrangements or agencies for enforcement action under its authority. But no enforcement action shall be taken under the regional arrangements or by regional agencies without the authorization of the Security Council, with the exception of measures against an enemy state, as defined in paragraph 2 of this Article provided for pursuant to Article 107 or in regional arrangements directed against renewal of aggressive policy on the part of any such state, until such time as the Organization may, on request of the Governments concerned, be charged with the responsibility for preventing further aggression by such a state.

It seems evident that the "enforcement action" referred to in Article 53 (1) means action ordered by the *Security Council* (which is "utilizing" the regional organization and, therefore, an action based on Chapter VII of the Charter).

It is of the utmost importance to scrutinize the American argument on this point. The United States, in the debates on Cuba, distinguished three alternatives to straight-out Security Council response to a threat of peace, breach of the peace, or aggression:

1. A recommendation under the Uniting for Peace Resolution from the General Assembly for action by UN members;

2. A UN peace-keeping action basically originating from the Secretary-General, as in the 1960 Congo crisis, with supportive Security Council and/or General Assembly resolutions;

3. In the words of Abram Chayes, Legal Adviser to the States Department during the Cuban Missile Crisis:

A regional organization like the OAS is another obvious candidate for the peacekeeping role within its regional terms of reference.[11]

This approach is uncommonly convenient for the United States. It can choose to play "world policeman," a role which its real power always makes possible. It can choose to manipulate the Organization of American States so as to give both the respectability of common and regional organizational action to its acts. This may satisfy some who purport to be concerned about international law. But according to the position of Mr. Chayes, it can serve to provide the whole act with a United Nations endorsement by claiming that it is acting, under Article 53, *for* the Security Council. Thus, the United States took the position that since it claimed, together with the OAS, to be acting *for* the Security Council—athough the Security Council had never in fact ordered, recommended, or asked for the OAS so to act—the Quarantine that resolved the Cuban Missile Crisis was an "enforcement" action carried out under Article 53 on behalf of the UN.

To make things even more convenient, the United States took the position in 1962 that, the OAS was "the only regional organization in the sense of Chapter VII of the Charter of the United Nations."[12] Since the Security Council never acknowedged, much less thanked the U.S. and OAS for carrying out "enforcement" actions under Article 53 against a permanent member of the Security Council, and

[11] Covey Oliver, "The Working Paper," ed. Lyman M. Tondel, *The Inter-American Security System and the Cuban Crisis* (Dobbs Ferry, N.Y.: Oceana, 1964), p. 27.
[12] Abram Chayes, "Remarks," *Proceedings, 57th Annual Meeting, American Society of International Law,* pp. 10–12.

since the United States took the position that Security Council silence on the subject was equivalent to Security Council acceptance of the volunteer services in the spirit, certainly never the letter, of Article 53, the United States was pleased to adopt the position that, not only had it acted in its vital interests, it had acted for the vital interests of the OAS as an organization and as a collection of seriously threatened states. Thus, the U.S. seems to contend that all this had been done for the Security Council, which apparently had slept through these events and which did not have the wit, will, or U.S. backing, for a resolution thanking the United States and the OAS ever so much for having effected its unexpressed desire to employ Article 53 to preserve the peace. It would have been so simple, honest, and credible if the United States had based its stand in the Cuban Missile Crisis on Article 51 and the right of individual and collective self-defense.

Regional "enforcement" action spuriously based on Article 53 is bad enough. The 1965 Dominican debacle pushed the idea of collective security back considerably farther. At least in Vietnam one has a foreign candidate for aggressor. In Cuba in 1962 the Soviet Union was caught in *flagrante delicto*. But in the case of the 1965 Dominican Revolution there was no conceivable third-party intervention of a nature to bring into play the right of individual and collective self-defense. The existence and influence of less than a hundred assorted Communists and leftists within the rebel forces may actually have constituted a "threat to the peace" in the sense that U.S. leadership of the OAS had been defining the goals and actions of international Communism as a threat to the peace for many years. But no one could contend that there was an antecedent recourse to armed force by a *state,* or, indeed, by forces staging from a state, amounting to an act of aggression triggering rights of individual and collective self-defense. The United States did what it thought it had to do, retroactively sought and received OAS approval and support—of modest character from some of the less representative proponents of Latin American democracy and constitutionality—and, again, tried to cover its record with indications of official approval and support from the OAS.

To the normal observer of international law, it is a familiar admonition to "take it to the Court," meaning the International Court of Justice. Given the lack of sanctioned international norms, it is surprising that internationalists persist in this demand. The quality and frequency of international arbitrations are sufficiently modest. But when international idealists call for international adjudication as a central feature of a change in the international system, they call for a quantum jump as concerns international relations.

The International Court of Justice has existed since 1945. The "machinery for peace" is there. Where are the litigants? As far as I can determine, since the ICJ's first decision, in the Corfu Channel Case, (Preliminary Objection Rejected; March 25, 1948; Merits decided April 9, 1949; Amount of compensation determined, December 15, 1949) it has in twenty years considered forty-nine cases. Of these, a dozen were Advisory Opinions given for the guidance of the UN General Assembly. These include some of the most important precedents and discussions of modern international law, e.g., the decisions on Reparations for Injuries Suffered in Service of the United Nations, Reservations to the Convention on the Prevention and Punishment of the Crime of Genocide, and Certain Expenses of the UN (Article 17, Paragraph 2 of the United Nations Charter), the latter being the critical cases concerning Soviet, French, and other refusals to contribute to the financing of the Congo peace-keeping operation.

Of the forty-nine cases decided by the ICJ in the twenty-odd years hardly any involve matters of real consequence. Among the most important were the Corfu Channel Case, which is a useful precedent on international waterways and the modern law of recourse to armed force but which was ignored by Albania insofar as its provisions for compensation were concerned; the Anglo-Norwegian Fisheries Case, which has important implications for the development of an international legal order more concerned with economic, social, and geo-

graphic considerations than with legal technicalities; and the Notte-
bohm case, which provides a useful discussion of nationality although
its practical implications, namely, the rights of an unfortunate German businessman who thought he had covered himself by acquir-
ing a "quickie" naturalization in Lichtenstein but was nevertheless
treated as an enemy alien during World War II, are hardly central
to the politics in our time. There is no reason to rub it in. A simple
examination of the titles of the cases heard on the merits by the ICJ
is instant evidence of the trivial character of most of these cases.
Whenever something with real political bite turns up in the records
of the Court, the case is not settled on its merits but is choked off
on procedural grounds. Thus the ICJ never got past Iran's Preliminary Objection, granted on July 22, 1952 in the Anglo-Iranian
oil dipute. Treatment in Hungary of Aircraft and Crew of U.S.A.
(U.S.A. v. Hungary) was discontinued through nonacceptance by
Hungary of the jurisdiction of the Court, July 12, 1954. This was only
the first of nine cases involving the U.S., U.K., or Israel as plaintiffs
protesting aerial incidents, and Hungary, Czechoslovakia, U.S.S.R.,
and Bulgaria as defendants which were discontinued on the same
ground.

More recently, the International Court of Justice has frustrated
the hopes of idealists, especially in the Third World, by its decision
of July 18, 1966, in the South West Africa Cases (Ethiopia v. South
Africa; Liberia v. South Africa), Second Phase. All that Ethiopia
and Liberia were asking, as states which had been members of the
League of Nations, was that the Court rule that South Africa by its
apartheid policies and in a number of other ways was violating international obligations as mandatory power for the territory of South
West Africa. The Court, having agreed in the judgment of December
21, 1962, that it had jurisdiction over the case, now held in 1966
that Ethiopia and Liberia were not proper parties to bring the action
since the mandate relationship was with the League of Nations as a
separate legal entity and "the Applicants cannot be considered to
have established any legal right or interest appertaining to them in

the subject matter of the present claims . . ."[13] True, it was a split decision decided by the vote of the President of the Court, Sir Percy Spender. Nonetheless, for the World Court to take almost three years to decide that the plaintiffs for whom it agreed to initiate a litigation had no standing to do so was obviously not conducive to the development of international adjudication as an alternative to war.

To be sure, this must be put in perspective. Things are not quite as bad as the record of the ICJ or of international arbitrations suggest. International law and organization operate every day in thousands of ways, many of which we will quite properly never know, to prevent, mitigate, or terminate international disputes and recourse to the threat or use of armed force. But the "machinery for peace" concept has simply failed. At present there is quite adequate machinery for peaceful settlement if parties to disputes are interested. If they are not, no amount of international law and organization provides adequate alternatives to war when vital interests are at stake.

As concerns peace-research seeking alternatives to war, the same nineteenth century which produced the vision of "World Peace Through World Law," informed by the wisdom and healing qualities of legal concepts and institutions and serviced by "machinery for peace," also inaugurated the continuing epoch of social science, usually associated with the person of Auguste Comte, and the concept of inevitable "progress" which should be achieved by application or scientific (or, as its critics call it, scientistic) positivism to the practical problems which the witch doctors and savants of theology and philosophy had been unable to solve. Well over a hundred years after the death of Comte in 1857, positivists, scientists, social scientists, with or without religious or other discernible normative identifications, are still trying to clean up the mess left by the clumsy

13 Quoted from the version of the decision edited by John R. Stevenson in the *American Journal of International Law,* Vol. 61 (No. 1, January, 1967), pp. 116, 150.

practitioners of *Realpolitik* and the fuzzy-minded devotees of international law and organization.

In approaching the subject of peace research, the most recent outgrowth of the drive for social progress through the positive, scientific methods of the natural and social science, I see an interesting constancy in the extent of commitment to values in the "value-free sciences" that would lead men out of the traps laid by hypocritical moralists and legalists. As I contemplated the work of Kenneth E. Boulding, probably the most talented, erudite, and committed of the peace researchers, I thought of Comte and looked around for critiques of Comte's approach. One was that of Jacques Maritain, which, needless to say, was somewhat lacking in enthusiasm. But I think Maritain was fair, and it is relevant to the whole "scientific" approach to social problems, which is in great measure traceable to Comte, to refer to "Auguste Comte and Messianic Positivism."[14]

Now Kenneth E. Boulding is a Quaker and, as a person, far from "value-free." But his work in the field of peace research seeks to be. In my view, the most authoritative and perceptive appraisal of Boulding's work is that of Thomas C. Schelling, who is one of the most outstanding social scientists and experts on arms control and disarmament of our time and who certainly has little in common with Jacques Maritain other than ability and concern for human values. Consider the following description of Boulding by Schelling in a review of the former's principal contribution to the literature on peacekeeping.[15]

Trained an economist, by persuasion a Quaker, hooked early by cybernetics, information theory, and the mathematical biology of his colleague Anatol Rapoport, concerned about war and the evolution of civilization, Boulding has been trying to put together a new science. Six years ago, in *The Image,* he offered a name—*eiconics.* He found

[14] Jacques Maritain, *Moral Philosophy* (New York: Charles Scribner's Sons, 1964), p. 266.
[15] Kenneth E. Boulding, *Conflict and Defense, A General Theory* (New York, Evanston and London: Harper and Row, Harper Torchbooks, The University Library, 1962).

it hard to define the field, but placed its roots in the sociology of knowledge. Some idea of its scope is suggested by the three works he then
believed had contributed most toward the new science: Chester Bernard, *The Functions of the Executive;* Norbert Wiener, *Cybernetics;*
and Claude Shannon and Warren Weaver, *Mathematical Theory of
Communication.*

Since then he has fallen for Lewis F. Richardson's astonishingly
original and long-neglected work on arms races, has coupled it with
economics and games theory (particularly with the work of Martin
Shubik on "games of survival" in economics) [Martin Shubik, *Strategy
and Market Structure* (New York: 1959)] and has broadened his new
science to include virtually all social interaction processes—from war
to courtship, from competitive advertising to the lynx and the rabbit—
that lend themselves to a common style of systematic analysis.[16]

Is the reader still with me? Does he understand or have knowledge
of the better part of Schelling's comments and references? We have
come a long way from Comte, and no five-foot shelf would house
the literature necessary to stay with the avant-garde of peace research. Nor is it any less properly characterized as messianic positivism. For, as Schelling's review article progresses, he compares
Boulding's work with Rapoport's [e.g., Anatol Rapoport, *Fights,
Games, and Debates* (Ann Arbor, Michigan, 1960)]. Schelling observes:

The efforts of Boulding and Rapoport to stake out a new field of in-
quiry are, though, different, nearer to each other than to any other
work that I know of. Both men are fascinated by analytical models;
both try to transcend any specific application—economics, race, de-
linquency, war, divorce, arbitration, politics. Both offer a set of concepts, analytical schemes, and terminology with which to build up an
organized discipline.

Finally, both have a quality that is likely to confound people who

[16] Thomas C. Schelling, "War Without Pain, and Other Models," *World Politics,* Vol. 15, No. 3, April 1963, p. 466.

want to organize movements. These are men about the location of whose heart there can be no question . . . At the same time, both are intrigued by theoretical ideas—"addicted" is not too strong a term . . .[17]

Of all the diverse and arcane sources to which Schelling refers in his article review of Boulding's work, economic theory remains the core of his approach to the arms race and war. He seeks to develop, in the realm of action and reaction in the fields of arms and disarmament, parallels to the strategies analyzed by economists such as Shubik in maneuverings between rival business firms. He attempts, then, to develop a science of conflict resolution at the level of war and preparations therefore comparable to the social science of economics, informed by other social and natural sciences. In so doing he wants to show the way to systemic change in international relations.

Boulding develops the concept of LSG, "loss of strength gradient," and contends that "what we face in the modern world is a fundamental breakdown in the concept of defense as a social system, largely, as I have tried to show, as result of the constant decline in the LSG affecting almost all institutions as a result both of physical and social invention."[18] In the missile age, no state is "unconditionally viable." "We must," says Boulding, "therefore, as persons learn to live with conditional viability. This is why unilateral defense for persons has always proved to be unstable, even though new weapons and social situations may revive it from time to time, as in the cowboy era of the wild West."[19]

Boulding continues:

Now, however, we face the same problem of the breakdown of unconditional viability in the relations of national states. Unilateral national defense has created an enormous amount of human misery through history, but, up to the present century, it has been a workable system, in the sense that it has provided occasional protected heart-

---

[17] Schelling, *loc. cit.,* p. 468.
[18] Boulding, *op. cit.,* p. 331.
[19] *Ibid.,* p. 332.

lands of peace in which civilization and the arts could flourish even though surrounded by a periphery of war. Now it is no longer workable; the decline of LSG, coupled with the increasing range of the missile to more than half of the earth's circumference makes all heartlands hopelessly vulnerable.[20]

Boulding does not find the answers to the dilemma coming from peace movements or religious groups. In a statement which commands the respect of any sincere student of the dilemmas of war he says:

> Just as war is too important to leave to the generals, so peace is too important to leave to the pacifists. It is not enough to condemn violence, to abstain from it, or to withdraw from it. There must be organization against it; in other words, institutions of conflict control, or, still other words, government. The case for world government to police total disarmament seems to me absolutely unshakeable, [citing Grenville Clark and Louis B. Sohn, *World Peace Through World Law*, 2d ed., Cambridge, Harvard University Press, 1960] in spite of the fact that the march of technology has made some of their specific proposals obsolete. In general, we know the main lines of the kind of world organization that can eliminate the present dangers and give us permanent peace. What we do not know is how to get to it. The problem is how do we bargain with each other, and especially how do the nations of the world bargain with each other, to create a social contract and a machinery that will give the social contract stability. The world dilemma is illustrated admirably by the game matrix of Fig. 3.5, p. 50. We reproduce it below (Fig. 16.1) in terms of the social contract. If both parties keep the contract at *N,* all are better off; with the kind of pay off matrix shown, however, there is a pay off to either party in breaking the contract if the other party does not. If one party breaks it, however, the other must follow suit, and we end up in the Hobbesian state of unilateral defense and natural misery at *S.* The state we now seem to be in, however, is illustrated by Fig. 16.2. Here, the situation at S is worse that it is in Fig. 16.1 and if it becomes bad enough, it alters the whole character of the game, as we see from the arrows.

[20] *Ibid.*

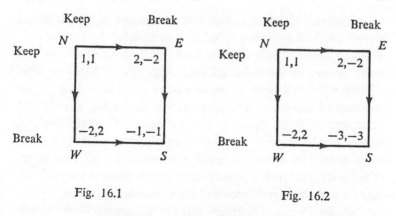

Fig. 16.1   Fig. 16.2

Now, even if one party breaks the contract, it still does not pay the other to do so; the game as it stands will end up at *E* or at *W*, depending on which party moves first. Figure 16.1 is the traditional position of unilateral defense; this has been the state of the world for many thousands of years. Now, the question arises, "Have we moved internationally into the condition of Fig. 16.2?" This might be called the pattern of unilateral virtue. It is a common pattern in human life than might be imagined . . .[21]

Thus Boulding's general concept. But *how* to get from one "figure" to another in his matrix remains a difficult problem. Boulding himself sees virtue in the arms control approach to be discussed presently and, indeed, in strengthening the bonds between the armed forces of the world at the expense of their infallible loyalty to national states. He wonders whether it might not be more conclusive to peace to exchange generals than professors and any participant in a gathering of veterans of opposing sides in a war could support this idea. In any event, the challenge is there: change the international system and change it through imaginative and scientific use of modern empirical disciplines, particularly the social sciences. Perhaps somebody's "Figure 16.1" will accomplish what *Pacem in Terris* and

[21] Boulding, *op cit.,* pp. 334–35.

the International Court of Justice and the concept of "World Peace Through World Law" have failed to accomplish.

Kenneth Boulding is a Quaker, a pacifist, and an economist and general pioneer in the social sciences. Although, as Schelling says, we know where his heart is, we are more inclined to look at the disposition of his mind. The case of another leading advocate of international systemic change is rather different. Gordon Zahn is a Roman Catholic, a pacifist conscientious objector and strong advocate of nonviolent action for moral purposes as he perceives them, and a sociologist. To the general public he is better known for his works on nonviolent resistence and the controversial role of the Roman Catholic Church in Germany prior to and during World War II than as sociologist. Deservedly or not, Zahn comes across to me as one whose heart is committed and whose brain and professional competence support that commitment rather than as a Boulding where the mixture of moral commitment and intellectual "addiction," as Schelling put it, is difficult if not impossible to sort out. Significantly, whereas Boulding discounts pacifism, individual and group war resistance and the peace movement as serious factors in changing the international system, Zahn emphasizes these factors. Moreover, whereas Boulding's work is a highly specialized series of technical exercises, Zahn seems content to sketch out general lines of social science approaches to changing the domestic and international system. He then returns to his passionate personal witness for peace and nonviolence. He also seeks to maximize by way of "demonstration effect" by using such examples as his personal hero Franz Jagerstatter, the Austrian peasant who became a martyr in the cause of resistance to a tyrannical regime and a series of unjust wars. Professor Zahn tells about the need for systemic change in international affairs, on the basis of a pamphlet he wrote for the Council on Religion and International Affairs. In *An Alternative to War* Zahn states:

This total failure of total violence to provide the security we crave presents us with what is at once a pressing need and a great opportunity to develop some alternative means to achieve the security we desire and to preserve the values we hold dear . . . our means of defense must be so organized and our policies so developed that they find their effectiveness in the identification and exploration of the essentially human qualities and capacities in ourselves and the potential enemy and not in the continued effort to destroy the greatest possible number of "them" at the least possible cost to "us."[22]

Zahn calls for a radically new international order based on the concept of nonviolence. In what conventional thinking must consider an extremely paradoxical statement he contends:

Thus, through non-violence our real and absolute defenselessness in the face of the new instruments of total destruction can be converted into power, a kind of power which could prove far more effective in the final reckoning than any break-through in megaton potential or in the accuracy and range of the instruments of delivery.[23]

Zahn, following the tradition of Gandhi, Christian pacifists, and some Black movements, would replace military force with "soul force," the "power of love," "charity." He realizes that one does not simply flip from the war system to one based on "soul force" easily or overnight. But, as a sociologist and a committed Christian he believes that nations can be *conditioned systematically* to nonviolent attitudes just as they can to the bellicose dispositions necessary to make ordinarily peaceful men go out and face hostile fire with the intent of killing as many of the enemy as possible. He would simply reverse the massive commitment of social institutions, pressures, and resources which support war preparations and wars to support nonviolent dispositions on a massive scale. He is optimistic about the possibilities of this since, he notes, revolutionary results have been achieved in the civil rights movement with nonviolent methods despite a decided lack of systematic training and allocation of resources. Unlike Boulding, who thinks the logic of his position will

[22] New York: Council on Religion and International Affairs, 1963, p. 9.
[23] *Ibid.*, p. 10.

ultimately convince everybody, Zahn supports his position, not with "figures" but with a final section on "The Role of the Churches." But the techniques involved in both Boulding's and Zahn's approaches are similar, social engineering, although Zahn relies much more on religious or humanistic imperatives than Boulding. Their common goal is to change both the domestic and international system and the outlook of the individuals who operate within both.

Professor J. Galtung, also a sociologist, Director of Research at the Peace Research Institute in Oslo, Norway, has worked out in considerably great detail Professor Zahn's basic concepts, without, however, revealing his motivation, although I rather expect that there is some Comtian "messianic positivism" at work here. In a paper read at a Conference of and to be published by the University of Nijmegen, Galtung discussed at some length the idea of nonviolence not only as a defense but as a deterrent. Interestingly, he deprecated extrapolations from the experiences of Gandhi or Martin Luther King as not paralleling "elements in the international situations [he intended] to explore.[24]

Indeed, Galtung took the position that there were *no* precedents for the kind of nonviolent national defense and deterrence to which he addressed his remarks. This makes the subject both interesting and frustrating, for, since everything is hypothetical or borrowed from some realm other than that of political science and international politics, it is difficult to prove or disprove the futuristic projections of the peace researchers. Thus, while Galtung was hesitant to apply the lessons of nonviolence in India or in the U.S. civil rights movement he moved briskly toward an analogous extrapolation from the decline of dueling as a means of settling individual disputes among Europeans to a possible decline in international war.

In any event, the thrust of Galtung's position was that fights between groups of any kind can be divided into two categories, territorial and social. Few states today have the capacity or the propor-

[24] "Mechanisms of Conflict Resolution: The Meaning of Nonviolence," address to the International Conference on Peace and Justice, Peace Research Center, Institute of Political Science, Nijmegen, Holland, April 13, 1967, p. 2 of the taped transcript of the address.

tionate need to risk defense of their territory but, in Galtung's view, any state can, with proper indoctrination and preparations, render its society so invulnerable to meaningful conquest as to deter attempts at conquest and undo them if they occur. He stated:

> Military defence is based on the assumption that I can make so much damage to you that it will outdo what you can gain from me. Nonmilitary defence is based on the idea, that I can make so much damage to myself before you get here, or I can reduce the value you can get from me that it won't be worth your effort. Here again are two subpoints.
>
> Subpoint number one is the idea of sabotage and subpoint number two is the idea of refusing to cooperate, noncooperation in the sense of disobedience as it is very often called in MD [military defence] parlance.

Galtung then continued:

> Let me then immediately add . . . Nonmilitary defence like military defence will have to be based on the idea of deterrence. That is it will have to be based on the idea that, if an organization is built up around the ideas of incapacitation and nonprofitability then this, when it is known to the attacker, will make an attack look so much less, let us say, luring, tempting to him, that he will refrain from doing it.[25]

Boulding, Zahn, and Galtung call seriously for international systemic change, the first two rather soon, Galtung gradually—although "gradualism" is a very relative term when linked with the extreme social changes envisaged by Galtung and his colleagues.

Meanwhile, there are many other advocates of international systemic change who are gradualist but rather impatient. Amitai Etzioni, the Columbia University sociologist, argues for genuine change from warlike to peaceful competitive co-existence. Etzioni says:

> The most satisfactory way to complete the shift to peaceful competition is by what has become known as the gradualist approach. This combines a set of principles for the transformation from one mode of

[25] *Ibid.*, p. 10.

operation to a quite different one, and applies to such divergent developments as the formulation of the European Common Market and the gradual growth of African political unity, as well as to the change in interbloc relations.

The essence of the gradualist approach is to break the transition into numerous limited steps. This has many advantages: psychologically, both political leaders and voters are reluctant (unless a major crisis occurs) to support drastic changes. Breaking the transition into many steps permits, at each point, only a minimal departure from the safety of the known.[26]

Professor J. David Singer, a major moving force in peace research, coeditor of the *Journal of Conflict Resolution*, is likewise impressive in the urgency and hope he places in the quest of the social sciences for alternatives to war resulting from international systemic change, but the realism with which he views the prospects for such change. He acknowledges that, "most radical but legitimate change at any level of social organization seems to be a response to forces emanating either from a parallel organization of equal or greater power, or, more likely, from a superordinate one whose capability normally exceeds that of the component parts.[27]

With no such superordinate agency in the international system, Singer asks if "good will," or utilitarian, or normative incentives, would be sufficient to bring about beneficial systemic change. He thinks not, but stresses that greater co-operation could result among nation-states if national leaders could predict with fair accuracy the reactions of other states to actions which they, the national leaders, have initiated. Nations need to know whether conciliatory gestures on their part will be exploited or reciprocated by other nations. Singer says:

[The] application of social science methods, concepts, and data to the study of international politics might well furnish the decision mak-

[26] *Winning Without War* (Garden City, New York: Anchor Books, Doubleday, 1964), p. 209.
[27] J. David Singer, ed., *Human Behavior and International Politics* (Chicago: Rand McNally, 1965), p. 455.

ers with that additional increment of accuracy and confidence in their predictions which would permit slightly less conventional policies, especially on the part of the major powers. The increment might not be large, and it is unlikely to be gained in the immediate future, but with so much at stake, we should find the challenge an important and attractive one.[28]

It is appropriate to end this brief vignette of peace research with references to two other approaches. Karl Deutsch and his followers have been following the concept of "security communities," i.e., communities free from expectation of intra-community conflict originally suggested by R. W. Van Wagenen.[29] Deutsch and his collaborators applied the concept of "security communities" with special emphasis on the Atlantic Community, including NATO and the U.K.-Canadian-U.S. relationship. It would appear that their approach to extension of the concept of "security communities" rests on stress on pluralism, preservation of national sovereignty, and emphasis on domestic issues within each nation concerned supportive of the foregoing goals. This, then, is entirely different from the fundamental systemic change enjoined by thinkers such as Boulding and Zahn.

Finally, I call attention to the conclusions of Ernst B. Haas[30] who was interested in testing the validity of a "refined version" of the *functionalist* doctrine of international relations which he viewed as an "analytical tool for criticizing the deplorable present and an ideological prescription for ushering in a better future."[31]

Haas defines functionalists in international relations theory as those who:

are interested in identifying those aspects of human needs and desires that exist and clamor for attention outside the realm of the political.

[28] *Ibid.*, pp. 456–57.
[29] R. W. Van Wagenen, *Research in the International Field: Some Notes on the Possible Focus* (Princeton, New Jersey: Center for Research on World Political Institutions, 1952), p. 10.
[30] Ernst B. Haas, *Beyond the Nation-State: Functionalism and International Organization* (Stanford University Press, 1964).
[31] *Ibid.*, p. 6.

They believe in the possibility of specifying technical and "non-controversial" aspects of governmental conduct, and of weaving an everspreading web of international institutional relationships on the basis of meeting such needs. They would concentrate on commonly experienced needs initially, expecting the circle of the non-controversial to expand at the expense of the political, as practical cooperation became coterminous with the totality of interstate relations. At that point a true world community will have arisen.[32]

Haas is willing to take the functional thesis, but he strips it of any altruistic assumptions. He rejects the assumption that nations act with the ultimate aim of furthering the common good of all nations. Co-operation among nations, he says, is the "result of convergence of separate perceptions of interest . . . There is no common good other than that perceived through the interest tinted lenses worn by the international actors."[33] In fact, what Haas is testing is the validity of the proposition that international peace and security can slowly but surely be attained as nations learn more and more of the tangible benefits of practical co-operation. After studying the workings of international organizations, most specifically one of the oldest and most effective, the International Labor Organization, Haas concludes:

> The lesson is clear. Neither functionalism nor functional analysis can bring international order out of the chaos of national confrontation. Neither a commitment to welfare nor a desire to use the analytical properties of national egotism can build the *civitas dei* or the *civitas maxima*. But functional analysis can tell us in which direction the faint ripples of common concern are likely to spread. Even chaos becomes bearable when its constituents and their movements are understood.[34]

In summary, the problem with the legal-organizational approach to war-peace questions is that it seeks to change the international

[32] *Ibid.*, p. 6.
[33] *Ibid.*, p. 497.
[34] *Ibid.*, p. 497.

system before the system as a whole, the actors in it, and the political dynamics that characterize it give sufficient indications that the system is ready for change or that the actors in it really want it to change. Since this approach is increasingly concrete, its failures are there for all to see. The problem with the peace-research approach to international systemic change is that it is highly theoretical, largely based on very new disciplines whose "scientific" character is at least open to question, prone to extrapolation from fields dealing with individuals and small groups to the nations and other actors in the international system, and frequently presented in theoretical analyses and prescriptions unsupported by historic precedent, which are virtually impossible to prove or disprove. Moreover, these analyses and prescriptions have seldom reached a form or gained a measure of acceptance by responsible decision makers for us to have the kind of concrete evidence whereby we may judge the state of their reliability, as we can in the case of efforts on behalf of international law and organization.

God bless and sustain those who labor and sacrifice for the causes of international law and organization and for peace research. May they succeed. May the day come when this book is as obsolete as a manual on dueling. That day is not in sight. So we must turn to the moral problems of war as they are, now, in the present international system. We will begin with what appears to be the worst form, nuclear war.

V Nuclear War and Deterrence: The Moral Issues

The moral issues of nuclear war and deterrence are unique and unknown prior to the nuclear age. Any sensible student of war, who does not exclude war or some form of armed coercion as morally or rationally, acceptable instrument of politics, agrees with Clausewitz that war is a continuation of politics by other means. But a major nuclear war would not fit into this concept of armed force as an instrument of politics, except a politics of ultimate despair, bitter retribution, indefensible revenge. We do not need popes, Vatican councils, and annual meetings of the World Council of Churches to explain that general nuclear war is unthinkable as a rational instrument of policy. All leaders in the United States since 1945 and all leaders in the Soviet Union since the death of Stalin have openly said this. Secretary of State Rusk has said that the nuclear decision, that is to say, the decision to engage in a major nuclear exchange, would be the last decision by an organized government in the Northern Hemisphere. Having lived through the command-post discussions of the Cuban Missile Crisis and a number of other agonizing decisions, Mr. Rusk should know. And yet preparations for nuclear war continue and, indeed, expand. Moreover, seemingly rational experts urge even greater nuclear preparation. Why?

The facts are simple and terrible. Once nuclear warfare is available to a state as a possible means of attack or defense, all of its potential enemies or victims have to confront the possibility that this supposedly "unthinkable" means might be used. No statesman or intellectual or moralist has been able to produce an acceptable argument for unilateral disarmament or renunciation of development of a nuclear capability by a state that is or might be threatened by a nuclear power. One must be blunt about this, pious hope on such matters are simply immoral. When Pope John XXIII talks about disarmament based on "mutual trust and sincerity," and Pope Paul VI talks about "loyalty" to international commitments to peace and disarmament, they are perhaps talking the language of saints, or of Professor Zahn's martyrs, but they are not addressing themselves to the real world of responsible statesmen of *any* political persuasion. As these pages are written, newspapers carry emotional accounts of the observance of the anniversary of the bombing of Hiroshima. The same newspapers report that Japan continues to study very suspiciously the Nuclear Nonproliferation Treaty of July 1, 1968. Those who govern Japan were not elected to commit that nation's security and vital interests to rest on expectations of "mutual trust and sincerity" or "loyalty" to international obligations.

At the same time, it is clear that no responsible statesman *wants* to inflict nuclear war on an adversary. Indeed, the evidence is that the closer decision makers get to the nuclear trigger the more resolved they become to keep it double-locked and to try to find ways to ensure that it will never be pulled. But, the phenomenon of nuclear wars exists; the threat exists and grows. Not all statesmen are responsible. In 1964 a United States Senator, an Air Force Reserve General, and a presidential candidate thought that nuclear weapons were just another addition to the assortment of armaments available to nations and that they could be used with impunity, even at the risk of involvement of other nuclear states, in the Vietnam conflict. That man was rather soundly defeated but he received many millions of votes and the electoral votes of many states. Senator Goldwater assuredly has his counterparts in every country that could acquire nuclear arms. Therefore, all responsible statesmen who have any occasion to fear nuclear blackmail and/or attack concern themselves with finding a nuclear power who appears reliable and willing to protect them with its deterrent capability. Failing this, or faced with growing doubt about the credibility of a nuclear ally's deterrent capabilities and intentions to fulfill its commitments, the responsible decision maker must attempt desperately to construct some minimal nuclear deterrent for his nation. This increases the number of international actors capable of launching a nuclear war on their own. It also increases the number of international actors capable of involving a nuclear ally whose reliability is in question into a war which it does not want to enter. And, since the later-arrival nuclear power is inevitably a primitive one, it assures everyone that if such a power takes a nuclear initiative it will be of the most blatantly immoral nature, namely, the threat of or the actual destruction of large population centers, the most obvious target for a weak nuclear power with modest arms and delivery systems.

Thus we are brought back to the point of the uniqueness of nuclear dilemmas, material and moral. Nuclear armaments and supportive delivery systems exist so that they will *not* be used. If they have to be used, they have failed. But there must be the capability and will to use them, otherwise they will probably not serve the deterrent function which is their only rational and morally defensible *raison d'être*. (For the moment I will not deal with limited nuclear war. I am speaking of the total nuclear capability and its ultimate uses as a deterrent threat and as a means of war.) In these circumstances, the *responsible* nuclear powers (I am aware that I am making a value judgment in so characterizing them) believe that they are behaving morally and rationally by following two basic principles:

1. Restrict the number of actors in the nuclear arena to those who are already in it and who have built up some expectations about mutual restraints on the threat or use of nuclear weapons; hence nuclear nonproliferation;

2. Avoid any destabilizing behavior that will upset the delicate balance of terror, for example, changes in the disposition of opposing decision makers, technological breakthroughs, intelligence failures resulting in under- or overestimating the intentions and capa-

bilities of the nuclear powers and those who are in some measure likely to involve allies in confrontations with nuclear adversaries.

As concerns both basic principles, the problem of "accidental war" seems to be *the* problem, both material and moral, of the nuclear age. Presumably the responsible decision makers in Washington and Moscow agree with Mr. Rusk that the decision to engage in general nuclear war would be the last decision to be made by an organized government in the Northern Hemisphere and are not candidates for the job of making *that decision*. This is a point that needs underscoring. Virtually all moral and legal analyses of nuclear war and deterrence concentrate, understandably, on the occurrence of a major nuclear war. But it is vital to bear in mind that, awesome and morally questionable as such an eventuality would be, no nuclear war has occurred. Our world has been rent wth constant, widespread, deep-rooted conflict during every day and every year since the second A-bomb was dropped on Nagasaki and World War II ended.

If nuclear war were, like the six-gun, the "great equalizer" that could be whipped out whenever tempers flared and vital interests were threatened, there probably would be no "developed nations." The "developing" nations would be making their way with difficulty. There would be no "neocolonialists" to blame for the world's problems. There have been many opportunities and temptations to use nuclear arms. *They have never been used, and it is the duty of all men of good will to see that they are never used.* And, if they are, the "just cause" must be very just indeed.

I, for one, can write about the morality of nuclear war and deterrence, because I doubt that there will ever be a nuclear war, certainly not a major one. As I said at the outset, we are all optimists about something. Were I to believe that nuclear war was remotely comparable to revolutionary warfare as a problem in terms of probability of occurrence, I would not bother to write on nuclear war, deterrence, and morality. I would either engage the services of Professors Zahn and Galtung to give me a "cram course" on how nonviolent resistance meets the problems of living in a totalitarian police state, or I would find a confessor who might assist me in facing the Last Judgment.

But I am both perverse and optimistic enough to do neither. I will undertake to discuss the moral issues of nuclear war and deterrence, not on the basis that, "it can't happen here," or "stop the world, I want to get off," but, rather, with the viewpoint of a son of the Great Depression who remembers poignantly the comment, "Yeah, things are bad all over."

Thus far, in the faltering and insufficient debate over morality and nuclear war and deterrence, two starting points, which tend to dictate the conclusions, have been established.

1. Morality first
2. Self-preservation first

Let us review these two approaches.

MORALITY FIRST

Jean Kerr's classic work, *The Snake Has All the Lines,* recounts the plight of one of her many sons who resigned from a school drama on Adam and Eve because he was not the snake and "the snake had all the lines." The only way to take the lines away from the proponent of "morality first" is to paint a torturous Gothic picture of *Darkness at Noon* or *1984* and ask, *"Would* you rather be Red than Dead?" That gambit is no longer fair or right or necessary. "Morality first" on nuclear dilemmas deserves a fair hearing. By many lights it may not get it here but I am not insensitive to the strength of the approach, which, however, I have already quite clearly rejected.

Morality first contends that:

1. Nuclear weapons are immoral *in se* and should be banned;
2. Nuclear deterrence, based on willingness to use nuclear arms, is immoral and should be condemned and discontinued;
3. Nuclear weapons systems should be dismantled and destroyed;
4. The risks of premature politically disadvantageous and non-

symmetrical disarmament must be accepted by the morally responsible decision makers and citizens of a nuclear power.

5. Such initiatives will be reciprocated by other nuclear powers
and that there can be world authority, peace, and disarmament
based on sincerity, mutual trust, and loyalty to international obligations.

Self-preservation, which should not be underestimated in terms
of the Jean Kerr reference, since it, too, has its "lines," which
include home, mother, apple pie, and the matter of survival both
for the Free World and Christianity, argues that nuclear weapons
and credible willingness to use them are indispensable for self-
preservation of a great power and for the lesser powers it protects.
Accordingly, credible willingness and capability to carry out deterrent threats cannot be impaired by or tampered with until symmetrical and reliable changes in the present state of affairs are made
by *all* nuclear powers. Therefore, no nuclear power can change its
willingness and capability to use nuclear weapons, or begin to
dismantle its nuclear weapons systems, or discontinue research
and development to any significant degree, unilaterally or without
very reliable provisions for international inspection of the actions of
other nuclear powers and adequate sanctions against violators of an
arms-control understanding.

It follows that moral judgments condemning nuclear war and
deterrence and demanding actions which are militarily, political,
and morally irresponsible are irrelevant if not outrageous, except
for pacifists and nonviolent resisters, who are invited to test their
own theories on themselves on their own time.

But, on reflection, I see that my interest and moral commitment
has led me to pose the moral dilemmas of nuclear war and deterrence
as though there were only approaches which *addressed* those dilemmas. For very few persons at any level of society and in any
country address themselves to the dilemmas of nuclear war and
deterrence. They leave them to others, or they cite them as vindica-
tions for "copping out." The housewife in suburbia is not so terribly

different from her poor little runaway daughter from Berkeley who lives in caves in the Greek Islands, occasionally checking in at the American Express office to pick up funds sent by her parents. The mother and daughter are not really so much divided by the generation gaps on issues of morality, nuclear war, and revolution (although, obviously, more so on the latter). The suburbanite mother wants "the government" to dispose of these unfathomable dilemmas. The daughter cites the same, as well as other, dilemmas as evidence that "our society" is "sick" and that it is, therefore, perfectly all right for her to live in a Greek cave with a comparatively unknown boy to whom she is not married, *because,* among other things, a society which tolerates nuclear deterrence and the threat of war is too much for this little standard bearer of *real* morality and "relevance" to countenance.

Where we are is in the "survival approach" to the moral dilemmas of nuclear war, deterrence, and morality. As Aristotle taught us before the birth of Jesus Christ, it is a good idea to try to collect the relevant facts before we begin to make policy and normative analyses. Let us consider the world from the point of view of national defense doctrine and practical capability, insofar as nuclear war and deterrence are concerned.

I have long believed it to be the case that Secretary of Defense Robert S. McNamara has done more to resolve the material and moral dilemmas of nuclear war, and of all other kinds of war, and to advance the cause of arms control and disarman t, than any other responsible decision maker of our time. It is in this light that I present U.S. doctrine and capabilities with respect to nuclear war and deterrence in McNamara's own words, in his final statement before the Senate Armed Services Committee on the Fiscal Years 1969–73 Defense Program and 1969 Defense Budget. I select those statements of Mr. McNamara's which are, in my view, most apposite to the problem of preventing and limiting war, nuclear or other. In his statement on "Strategic Forces," McNamara observed:

It seemed to us in 1961 that one of the first things we had to do was to *separate* the problem of strategic nuclear war from that of all other kinds of war. Although the matter had long been debated, the fact that strategic nuclear forces, no matter how versatile and powerful they may be, do not by themselves constitute a credible deterrent to all kinds of aggression had still to be squarely faced.[1]

A variety of terms have been produced by the literature on nuclear deterrence and some have pounced on the jargon of the "armers," "arms controllers," and "Cold Warriors," to reduce the real material and moral issues of nuclear war and deterrence to criticism of rhetoric, jargon, and attempts to avoid the real issues by reference to the unanswerable expertise of government-paid rationalists for the "merchants of death." I hold no brief for any particular theory or jargon in the sense that I support it as "the position." But I do think that it is appropriate to use the language of the Secretary of Defense of the United States of America from 1961 to 1968 to describe the doctrine and capabilities of this nation in defense matters. So I will employ two basic concepts emphasized by McNamara in his last years as Secretary of Defense without any feeling of hiding behind arguments from authority or expertise. These statements are all reported in the press. McNamara emphasized two concepts:

1. "Assured destruction"
2. "Damage limitation"

Despite heavy pressures, McNamara insisted:

1. The United States has and will have a sufficient "assured destruction," "second strike" capability to deter any rational nuclear attack.

2. While measures for "damage limitation" are to be taken where feasible and investigated seriously when they appear promising, the key to U.S. security and the security of those nations dependent on U.S. nuclear deterrence is on its "assured destruction" capacity.

[1] Statement of Secretary of Defense Robert S. McNamara Before the Senate Armed Services Committee on the Fiscal Years 1969–73 Defense Program and 1969 Defense Budget, p. 41.

Thus, McNamara comments, "a nuclear-armed offensive weapon which has a 50/50 chance of destroying its target would be highly effective. But a defensive weapon with the same probability of destroying incoming nuclear warheads would be of little value."[2]

I will now quote the better part of four paragraphs of Mc-Namara's last Defense Statement. I, like many readers, am inclined to skip lightly over extensive quotations. This one should be read carefully by anyone who cares about the morality of nuclear war and deterrence. Mr. McNamara stated:

> I believe we can all agree that the cornerstone of our strategic policy must continue to be the deterrence of a deliberate nuclear attack against either the United States or its allies. But this immediately raises the question, what kind and level of forces do we need to ensure that we have such a deterrent, now and in the foreseeable future?
>
> Having wrestled with this problem for the last seven years, I am convinced that our forces must be sufficiently large to possess an "Assured Destruction" capability. By this I mean an ability to inflict at all times and under all foreseeable conditions an unacceptable degree of damage upon any single aggressor, or combination of aggressors— even after absorbing a surprise attack. One can add many refinements to this basic concept, *but the fundamental principle involved is simply this: it is the clear and present ability to destroy the attacker as a viable 20th Century nation and an unwavering will to use those forces in retaliation to a nuclear attack upon ourselves or our allies that provides the deterrent and not the ability partially to limit damage ourselves.*[3]

There is the moral issue of nuclear war and deterrence.
McNamara then continued:

> This is not to say that defense measures designed to significantly limit damage to ourselves (which is the other major objective of our strategic forces) might not also contribute to the deterrent. Obviously, they might—if an increase in our "Damage Limiting" capability could actu-

[2] *Ibid.,* p. 42.
[3] *Ibid.,* p. 47.

ally undermine our opponents' confidence in his offensive capability. But for a "Damage Limiting" posture to contribute significantly to the deterrent in this way, it would have to be extremely effective, i.e., capable of reducing damage to truly nominal levels—and as I will explain later, we now have no way of accomplishing this.

As long as deterrence of a deliberate Soviet (or Red Chinese) nuclear attack upon the United States or its allies is the vital first objective of our strategic forces, the capability for "Assured Destruction" must receive the first call on all of our resources and must be provided regardless of the costs and the difficulties involved. . . .[4]

While emphasizing that effectiveness, not numbers, is the key to the strategic balance of power, McNamara cited the following figures as to the comparative nuclear capabilities of the United States and the Soviet Union as of October 1, 1967:

	U.S.	USSR
ICBM LAUNCHERS	1054	720
SLEM LAUNCHERS	656	30
Total Intercont'l Msl. Launchers	1710	750
INTERCONTINENTAL BOMBERS	697	155
Total Force Loadings—Approx. No. of Warheads	4500	1000[5]

[4] *Ibid.*, pp. 47–48.
[5] Mr. McNamara's successor, Secretary Clark Clifford, reiterated on October 25, 1968, the claims of Mr. McNamara as he released the following statistics to rebut the claims of a contender in the 1968 presidential campaign that the US had fallen into a "security gap."

	US	USSR
ICBM LAUNCHERS	1054	900
SLEM LAUNCHERS (SLEM-Sub. Launched Missiles)	656	75–80
Long range bombers	646	150–155
Total deliverable warheads	4206	1200

It is clear that the Soviets are "closing the gaps," but the McNamara "assured destruction"–deterrence rationale appears to be fundamentally unaffected. The basic point is second strike capability which the US clearly has and will continue to have.

McNamara was clearly of the opinion when his last budget proposals and policy statement was released that U.S. offensive capabilities, even after sustenance of an aggressive nuclear first strike, gave the U.S. an "assured destruction" capability more than adequate to its own and its allies' deterrent requirements.

Soviet doctrine and capabilities with respect to nuclear war and deterrence are difficult to evaluate. The Soviets started from a point wherein they perceived Cold War conflicts and the relevance thereto of Western nuclear capabilities in an entirely different light than the—if I may be permitted to say so—naïve Americans and others who championed the Baruch Plan in 1946. They deprecated the practical value of nuclear weapons when they still had none, while whipping up international support for the Stockholm and other declarations which appealed so strongly to men of all viewpoints who quite naturally did not want to see the civilized world blasted to pieces by nuclear weapons. Once the Soviets achieved an atomic, and then a thermonuclear capability, they were not only unresponsive to banning nuclear weapons, they were particularly opposed to clever and hypocritical Western concepts of "limited nuclear war" and to "rules of the game." Thus, when the Western powers began to discuss the option of limited nuclear defense, the Soviets promptly flattened the very concept. For example in 1956, a year of energetic and, I think, fruitful examination of limited nuclear war and graduated deterrence in the West, Marshal Georgi K. Zhukov told the Twentieth Communist Party Congress in Moscow that while the Communists were in a more favorable position to wage purely "conventional" war, there should be no doubt of their capability and willingness to employ any form of nuclear attack that appeared advantageous to them. Marshal Georgi K. Zhukov, of blessed memory, then stated:

A future war, should it be unleashed, will be characterized by the massive use of air forces, various rocket weapons, and various means of mass destruction such as atomic, thermonuclear, chemical, and bacteriological weapons. However, we proceed from the principle that the very latest weapons, including the means of mass destruction, do not lessen the decisive importance of land armies, the fleet and the air force.[6]

General Zhukov has been substantially downgraded in authority, if not in historical military accomplishments, since 1956. But the Soviet theme of all-out reaction, in the event of war, remains. Marshal of the Soviet Union V. Sokolovsky and Major General M. Cherednichenko wrote, in 1964, "Military Art in a New Stage: The Revolution in Military Matters, Its Significance, and Consequences," in *Krasnaya Zvezda* (*Red Star*), August 25, 1964:

> Classical military art was based on the fact that the main object of the conflict came down to mutual destruction of the armed forces in the theaters of operations. . . . Now the concept is radically changed. For the missile with a nuclear warhead, a front line saturated with troops is not an obstacle. The state administrative agency, the economy, the strategic nuclear weapon, the armed forces—all these are open to the new means of conflict. The availability of thermonuclear warheads and their carriers makes possible the instantaneous destruction of whole nations. . . .
>
> There is a good deal being said [by the imperialists] about "controlled" nuclear war, about using nuclear weapons only on military objectives, on the armed forces. The concept of controlled nuclear war is just the demagogism and hypocrisy of the military circles of imperialism . . . since military objectives are close to populated points.[7]

We have already seen the relative capabilities of the United States and the Soviet Union. Currently, some Western strategic thinkers are worrying about the fact that, in their opinion, the Soviets have essentially narrowed the gap between themselves and

[6] Quoted in Charles H. Donnelly, Senior Specialist in Defense, The Library of Congress, Legislative Reference Service, *United States Defense Policies*, in his *Current Strategic Thinking as to Future Wars* (Washington: Government Printing Office, May 1957), pp. 47–48.

[7] K. W. Whiting, *Soviet Reactions to Changes in American Military Strategy* (Maxwell Air Force Base: Aerospace Studies Institute, 1965), p. 75.

the U.S. Thus the issue of the "missile gap" of the late fifties and early sixties has been replaced by that of the "megaton gap." But the whole point of the McNamara analysis of the situation in his last policy statement is that numbers of missiles or totals of megatonage, at the levels of the figures cited, become relative if not irrelevant so long as there is a second-strike "assured destruction" capability which deters any rational adversary. McNamara told the Senate Armed Services Committee:

> As I stated earlier, numbers of weapons will be much more important in the future than gross megatonage. Our calculations show that, even if the Soviet deploy a substantial number of ABMs by 1972, our offensive forces (after absorbing a surprise attack) would still be able to inflict about the same percent fatalities on the Soviet population in a second strike in 1972 as they could have in 1966.[8]

British nuclear doctrine must be summarized as following the same "assured destruction," second strike logic of U.S. doctrine. The British have long recognized that their island could not survive a nuclear war and that the only hope for security lay in credible, effective deterrence, based primarily on the U.S. nuclear second-strike capability. However, it is believed in Britain that continued participation by the U.K. in a joint U.S.-U.K. deterrent force is justified. The only alternative appears to be British participation in a European independent deterrent force. But, in order to have a European nuclear force there must first be a Europe. Since the French have steadfastly blocked progress toward incorporation of the U.K. into an economic, much less a political and military Europe, the British remain frozen in their "special relationship" with the United States.[9]

France's nuclear doctrine is even more clearly one of deterrence or total destruction than Britain's. Since the British link their deter-

[8] McNamara Statement, *op. cit.,* p. 58.
[9] See Alastair Buchan's *NATO in the 1960's* (rev. ed.; New York/Washington: Praeger, 1963), pp. 80–84.

rent force with that of the U.S. they can at least contemplate the possibility of "flexible response," "graduated deterrence," or "limited nuclear war." The French *force de frappe,* on the other hand, despite pretensions that it would be available as the basis for a European deterrent for a Europe that is made impossible by French policy, is based solely on the threat of countercity attacks on enemy population centers, or, as President de Gaulle put it in his epic January 1963 press conference, on a capability to "kill in several instants millions of people."

The Institute for Strategic Studies in London, in its annual appraisal of the armed forces of the world stated in *The Military Balance, 1966–67,* that the French Strategic Air Command consisted of:

> . . . Three mixed Bomber wings, each of three squadrons with four *Mirage IVA* each, and one squadron with four C-135 tankers. A total of 50 *Mirage IVA* and 12 C-135 are operational. The force is adapted to low-level penetration with atomic bombs with a yield of 80–90 kilotons. A brigade of 25 surface-to-surface missiles, based in Haute-Provence, will enter service in 1969–70. Construction of missile silos and an under-ground operations centre began in 1966.[10]

It should be noted that although these figures and appraisals will be outdated when this book appears, they reflect a consistent pattern in the development of the French Strategic Air Command as reported by the authoritative London Institute.

Since the atomic bombs that wiped out Hiroshima and Nagasaki were "only" twenty kilotons in power, the French force would appear to have adequate means to "kill in several instants millions of people." But, obviously, the French only want to have the option of threatening such a terrible act. They must be perfectly aware that they are little less vulnerable than the British in an age when, vis-à-vis a major nuclear power, even superpowers such as the United States and the Soviet Union are vulnerable as societies, if not as possessors

[10] London: The Institute for Strategic Studies, 1967.

of assured destruction and invulnerable second-strike nuclear forces. *Why,* then, do the French insist on developing their own nuclear deterrent?

The reasons vary in rationality and are in part internally inconsistent.

First, France wants *grandeur.* It wants to be a Great Power and it is persuaded that to be a Great Power a state must have a nuclear military capability. In the words of French Defense Minister Pierre Messmer: "One is nuclear or one is negligible."[11]

Second, the French claim to doubt the credibility of the U.S. deterrent umbrella over NATO. They argue that, with the development of intercontinental missiles, the U.S. for the first time has become vulnerable to a devastating attack and that it is illogical to assume that the United States would risk such devastation to its homeland in order to live up to its alliance commitments. Working the other side of the street, however, the French give the impression that there *is no threat,* that the U.S. deterrent threat and conventional commitment to NATO are useless since the nice Communists are not going to attack anybody and the wave of the future is an independent Europe extending from the Atlantic to the Urals and finally free of the presence of and dependence on the Americans.

Third, France is concerned that its security not be closely linked with a great nuclear power such as the U.S., which, as in the Cuban Missile Crisis, may endanger its allies without their even being consulted.

Fourth, simultaneously, the French argue that *if* there is ever a need for engaging the U.S. nuclear deterrent force in defense of France and there is the expected reluctance of the U.S. to come through, an independent French nuclear force can set off a situation in which the United States has no alternative to living up to its obligations.

11 Quoted in translation by B. W. Augenstein, in "The Chinese and French Programs for the Development of National Nuclear Forces," *Orbis,* Vol. XI (Fall 1967, No. 3), pp. 846, 854 from *Journal Officiel,* January 24, 1963.

Last and most important, in the new, better Europe, cleansed of American power and influence, France intends to be the leader. Her most logical competitor is Germany, and German possession of nuclear weapons is almost impossible to imagine unless one wants to write a scenario for the beginning of World War III. If Europe ever unites, a nuclear France will have leverage which a non-nuclear Germany would find nigh impossible to overcome.

And so France continues to develop her airborne *force de frappe* and to seek to develop a rocket delivery system capability, for all of the reasons, good and bad, consistent and inconsistent, that have been recited. Note that only one of those reasons, using an independent nuclear capability to trigger a reaction by a reluctant ally, has anything to do with *using* nuclear weapons.

As will be noted in the chapter on the prospects for arms control and disarmament which follows, Red Chinese nuclear doctrine runs along lines very similar to that of the French. The main difference, which will be elaborated on in the next chapter, that the Red Chinese claim to take the idea of nuclear disarmament serious and, they argue, the more states possess nuclear arms the more serious all states will become about nuclear disarmament.

The People's Republic of China clearly shares the French view that a nation must have nuclear military power if it is to be a Great Power. Alice Langley Hsieh's authoritative and perceptive work on this subject says: How may China be prepared to exploit varying degrees of nuclear capability? There is little doubt that such achievement will considerably broaden China's options for gaining her objectives in Asia and the world. Even the experimental detonation of a nuclear device will enormously enhance China's prestige. [This was written about two years before first Chinese nuclear test in Sinkiang on October 16, 1964.] In Asia, it will be taken as another token of China's economic and scientific advance, providing Peking with additional arguments for the superiority of the Chinese Communist way to industrialization. It will also be taken as further evidence of China's emerging military power. Fear of such power may reinforce trends toward neutralism and accommodation to the

Communist bloc; it may also stimulate greater efforts toward achieving their own nuclear capabilities. In any event, China's emergence as a nuclear power is certain to aggravate political conflicts within other Asian countries as to the proper response to the Chinese achievement.

The possession of even a limited nuclear capability would underline China's claim to great power status and permit her, within limits, to practice nuclear blackmail toward her neighbors.[12]

The Red Chinese also have a problem, an increasingly obvious one, over the credibility of Soviet deterrent protection. And they have more reason than the French to raise this issue. For one thing, the Soviets once helped the Red Chinese to develop a nuclear capability, something the U.S. has never done for any of its allies. Then, in 1954 the Soviet assistance was discontinued and, indeed, the Soviets tried with what decreasing leverage remained in their possession to dissuade the Chinese from developing a military nuclear weapons capability. Red China also continues to grumble about insufficient backing from the Soviets in their 1958 confrontation with the United States over Quemoy and Matsu.

More will be said on Red Chinese policies and doctrines regarding nuclear war and deterrence in the next chapter because, unlike the French, they are inextricably bound up with their approach to disarmament. As to Red Chinese nuclear capabilities, the 1966–67 London Institute for Strategic Studies analysis was as follows:

The third Chinese nuclear test, in May 1966, contained thermonuclear material for the first time and had a yield of at least 200 kilotons (the lower end of the intermediate range). Production of weapons-grade uranium from the gaseous diffusion plant has presumably been proceeding for at least two years, and amount adequate to a small stockpile of weapons must now be available. All evidence suggests that the

---

[12] *Communist China's Strategy in the Nuclear Era* (Englewood Cliffs, New Jersey: Prentice-Hall, 1962; copyright by the RAND Corporation, 1962), pp. 170–71.

main effort for the development of nuclear delivery systems is going into ballistic missiles. The expected activity on the rocket range in Sinkiang has not, however, been observed. At present the only obvious means of delivery is the small number [estimated at about 12 at that time] of Tu-4 piston-engined bombers [described as "a copy of the B-29"].[13]

In contrasting the "assured destruction" and "damage limitation" problems of the United States as concerns the Soviet Union with those involving Red China, Secretary McNamara in his last policy statement to the Congress said:

Red China represents a somewhat different problem. Today Red China is still far from being an industrial nation. What industry it has is heavily concentrated in a comparatively few cities. We estimate, for example, that a relatively small number of warheads detonated over 50 Chinese cities would destroy half of the urban population (more than 50 million people) and more than one-half of the industrial capacity. And, as I noted last year, such an attack would also destroy most of the key governmental, technical, and managerial personnel, as well as a large proportion of the skilled workers. Since Red China's capacity to attack the U.S. with nuclear weapons will be very limited at least through the 1970s, the ability of even so small a portion of our strategic forces to inflict such heavy damage upon them should serve as a major deterrent to a deliberate attack on us by that country.[14]

These then are the doctrines and capabilities of the nuclear powers. I will discuss potential nuclear powers in the next chapter. It can be seen that the reasons set forth by the nuclear powers for their deployment and development of nuclear weapons systems and of means of damage limitation such as ABM systems and Civil Defense programs are:

1. Defense against and deterrence of attacks on their homelands or against those nations they are committed to defend;

[13] *Military Balance, 1966–67, op. cit.,* pp. 9–10.
[14] Statement Before the Armed Services Committee, *op. cit.,* p. 50, n.a.

2. Political power and prestige;

3. A capacity to affect nuclear alliance policies;

4. A capacity to affect arms control and disarmament policies.

No present nuclear power holds out the prospect of offensive first use of nuclear weapons. By this, of course, I mean that no incumbent government in a nuclear nation gives signs of serious consideration of first use of nuclear weapons. To be sure, it is certain that there are politicians and military leaders, and many who would support them, in all of the nuclear nations who would indeed contemplate first use of nuclear weapons. But leaders and people of that persuasion have not had the opportunity to do so. So we return to the fact that the primary, overriding moral problem of nuclear war and deterrence is possession and deployment of them with the intent of using them in response to a nuclear first strike by another nation. As we confront this moral dilemma it should be reiterated that we are discussing complex weapons systems set into operation under certain contingencies. These contingencies are predetermined in large measure by the nature of the weapons systems and systems of damage limitation, by the political-military command structure in the states and alliances involved, and by the degree of effectiveness achieved in efforts to prevent false information or interpretations of facts to unleash these systems unnecessarily.

In Chapter III, I stated that I hold a realist-natural law of nations view of international relations. I hold that nations have natural rights, the most fundamental of which is self-defense. In our age, very few nations have the capability of defending themselves, and they cannot turn to collective security based on a world authority for there is none. Accordingly, insecure nations must seek the protection of strong nations. Strong nations have a right, and possibly an obligation, to extend such protection as they can.

In the nuclear age, since nuclear attack is an option, nuclear deterrence and, if need be, retaliation in kind, is an essential element of the right of self-defense. Were this not the case, the right would cease to be sufficient or meaningful. While the right of self-defense does not guarantee successful defense or justify any and all measures taken in self-defense, it does justify all proportionate measures which are not clearly contrary to international law and the natural law. One perceives what is permitted or prohibited by the law of nations by examining the expectations of nations as to what can and cannot be done with a sense of legal permissibility. One judges the permissibility of an act under the natural law in the context of specific, concrete situations.

Looking at U.S. doctrine and policy on nuclear deterrence and war, it is morally permissible. Its purpose is defense and its doctrine and policies seek to maximize alternatives to nuclear war and to control and mitigate it if such a terrible war should occur. Some expressions of Soviet policy sound immoral to me, but I think I would concede that the extremity of these threats is designed to deter and defend. Soviet practice has been responsible. Between them, the two nuclear superpowers *have* maintained the delicate balance of terror and *have* a degree of stability in the international system which is incredible in view of the frequency and intensity of international conflict.

But there are prices for continued acceptance of U.S. and Soviet deterrence systems as morally permissible defense measures. As I see it the prices are summed up in these rules of nuclear war and deterrence:

1. The rule prohibiting first use of nuclear weapons and deterrence;

2. The rule of graduate deterrence;

3. The rule prohibiting countercity warfare except as a last-resort deterrence against countercity warfare by an enemy;

4. The rule requiring constant, serious, and sincere efforts to achieve arms control and disarmament, accompanied by equal efforts to improve international law and organization.

As one who once thought that limited nuclear war was practically necessary and morally permissible, I have come to believe that the critics of limited nuclear war were right when they contended that nuclear war represents a *threshold* that ought not to be crossed. Precisely because we are dealing with complicated weapons and de-

fense systems in many nations, some of which have ideological
and other reasons to mistrust and do injury to each other, and
precisely because nuclear war can very rapidly do enormous damage,
the results of which may be permanent, *no* nuclear arms should be
used, no matter how proportionate their use may appear.

I realize that this raises enormously difficult questions relating to
the tactical nuclear weapons deployed in defense of NATO. However, I would limit any use of such weapons to the guidelines suggested below regarding graduated deterrence. I would not approve
of use of tactical nuclear weapons against a massive *conventional*
aggressive attack on NATO states. If such an attack is likely contingency and the NATO states are not prepared to meet it with conventional means, as they are perfectly capable of doing if they make
the necessary plans, preparations, and sacrifices, then the first post-
1945 nuclear war is, in my view, too high a price for the defense of
an area which has been criminally remiss in not making adequate
conventional defensive plans and preparations.

The only two uses of nuclear weapons in war, against Hiroshima
and Nagasaki were wrong because they introduced this new and terrible weapon. Indeed, these sad examples make my point. The
arguments of Truman and Stimson of proportionality were not so
terribly wrong. It was true that these two terrible acts ended a war
that threatened to go on indefinitely and the inhabitants of Hiroshima and Nagasaki gave their lives in place of countless thousands
of other human beings, on both sides, who would have died had the
war gone on. Given the history of the fighting for remote islands,
imagine what it would be like to fight one's way through the
Japanese home islands. But, leaving the issue of destruction of a large
population center for rule 3, the first use of the atomic bombs was
wrong.

Since 1945 nuclear weapons have not been used. But their use
was considered. Apparently one factor in finally settling the Korean
War was a U.S. threat that nuclear weapons might be used. Such a use
would have been tragically wrong. The possibility of using nuclear
weapons to salvage the hopeless French defense of Dienbienphu in

1954 was fleetingly considered. Such a recourse to nuclear weapons would have been ludicrous as well as wrong. During the 1956 Middle East Crisis Khrushchev engaged in nuclear saber-rattling, seeming to threaten missile attacks on British and French cities if they did not desist from their invasion of Egypt. The threat does not strike one as especially plausible, but, if it was serious, it was wrong. The U. S. Naval Commander in the Far East during the 1958 Quemoy-Matsu Crisis implied that nuclear weapons might be used against Red China in an interview in which he went out of his way to emphasize the nuclear capabilities of his forces. Again, such a recourse to nuclear weapons would have been wrong, as well as dangerous, given the growing Soviet nuclear capability.

This brings us to the most crucial showdown on nuclear war and deterrence. There Kennedy threatened retaliaton in kind against the Soviet Union if missiles installed by the Soviets in Cuba were launched against the United States. *This* I defend as morally permissible because it was not a threat of first use but of retaliation in kind. This brings me to my second rule, graduated deterrence.

Graduated deterrence has been frequently discussed by experts as a theory or a policy. It should be a firm rule, one of the four prices for maintaining a nuclear deterrence posture until a better means of security and order can be found. Just as first use of nuclear weapons is unjustified, first crossing of any of the thresholds that can be discerned in a nuclear war is unjustified. By thresholds I mean, first of all, that covered by my third rule, no first attack on cities. Nuclear retaliation which may lamentably become necessary should be as much of a counterforce character as possible. If it is possible to exempt certain areas from attack, as has been done at various times in the Vietnam conflict, such sanctuaries should be respected, even—as in the case in Vietnam—at the expense of military necessities. Signs of de-escalation on the other side should be recognized with reciprocal action. What I am saying, in short, is the opposite of the official Soviet line that there can be no "rules of the game" in a general war. Everything possible should be done to avoid a general war, but, if one occurs, the purpose of fighting it should be to end it on tolerable terms, not to secure "victory."

"No cities first" is the expression of the experts in arms control and it reflects my third rule. Large population centers should not be attacked first, no matter how many important military targets and communications centers are located in them. The sole justification for attacking cities at all is to protect one's own cities, or those of an ally or non-nuclear power whose cities have been guaranteed protection from nuclear blackmail and/or aggressive first-strike attack, for example, under the 1968 Non-Proliferation Treaty or a similar arrangement. If this cannot be accomplished by countercity retaliation you have lost the war and will have to surrender. The *On the Beach* scenario of devastated nations continuing to bombard each other as long as any capability to do so remains is utterly immoral. The purpose of deterrence and defense is deterrence and defense. I state this truism because acts justified as deterrence or defense acts, especially involving attacks on large population centers, which conspicuously *fail* to deter and defend cease to be reasonable and morally permissible.

Finally, the present deterrence and defense policies of the United States and the Soviet Union will remain morally permissible to the extent that they, together with other nations, engage in constant, serious and sincere efforts to achieve arms control and disarmament. It is to this subject that I will now turn. Before doing so I have a word to say about the French and Chinese policies in terms of my four proposed rules. As an American I have enough to answer for and to worry about, so I will not venture to deliver long lectures to the French. But what they are threatening to do with their *force de frappe* violates the first three rules and, as will be seen, their record on arms control and disarmament has been downright obstructionist. Wild as their words are, the Red Chinese have thus far not clearly ruled themselves out of the category of morally responsible nuclear powers. One can only hope that this remains the case as they gain real stature as a nuclear power.

VI   The Prospects for Arms Control and Disarmament

As we enter the twenty-fourth year of the nuclear age it seems ludicrous to write, in a book that purports to be written from a moral perspective, and which has had the temerity to justify nuclear deterrence, a chapter entitled, "The Prospects for Arms Control and Disarmament," instead of, "The Accomplishments of Arms Control and Disarmament." One has the feeling of writing on the subject, "Should a man who apparently has had cancer for years be referred to a doctor?" Or, "Should surplus food be sent to starving people in India: State of the Question." But this sense of frustration and moral outrage, however warranted, does not help inform us on the actual status and prospects of arms control and disarmament.

The purpose of this chapter is to assess the progress that has been achieved in arms control and disarmament but, probably more important, to evaluate the prospects in this field. Just as it was essential to calculate the feasibility of alternative to war, so it is now necessary to judge efforts to limit and diminish preparations for war and the continuance of national security systems which could all too easily produce the catastrophic war that no sane man wants.

The point was made in Chapter II on recent Catholic teaching on war and deterrence, and it has been made by many other authoritative statements, that the material and moral problem of modern war and deterrence is not so much of justification or condemnation as one of responding to a moral and practical imperative to do something to ameliorate a morally and humanly inadmissible state of affairs. In this spirit, I will undertake to evaluate the thinking and the doing that has been going on since the first atomic bomb was detonated over Hiroshima. In so doing, I suppose that the orthodox approach would be to begin with definitions of the terms "arms control" and "disarmament." But I chose to begin differently, with a survey of the evolution of our contemporary historical predicament, our "treacherous trap," and try to see how the interlocking concepts of arms control and disarmament developed.

The predicament of our world is characterized by endless armed conflict which does not bring security, endless efforts for peace which do not bring peace. This predicament can be traced to many sources, but let us recall its immediate sources in the 1945 circumstances under which the Second World War was concluded. World War II ended in a very confused situation. The victorious Western Allies wanted to go back to the White Cliffs of Dover and the patios of Los Angeles—or to the grim tasks of restoring "liberated" nations, liberation being what it is in modern war. Those who liked that sort of thing stayed on to occupy the defeated Axis powers. One of the "United Nations," the Soviet Union, faced a very mixed situation. Its homeland was devastated, and over 20 million of its citizens dead. Yet it stood triumphant in the heart of Europe and it controlled national Communist parties in the Western nations which, tough and prestigious after their partisan success, gave promise of bringing the Urals to the Atlantic, to anticipate in reverse General De Gaulle's vision of Europe. On the other hand, the Soviets were understandably nervous about the wartime ally that had demonstrated at the cost of two great cities the most devastating weapon in history, the "A-bomb," which it monopolized. The vision of a "happy ever after" life for the Western powers was upset by the discovery of the "Iron Curtain" and the "Cold War." It was a most unsettling time altogether.

War with a capital "W" was over, but conflict and the threat of it was widespread. One thought gloomily of Trotsky's formulation: "No war, no peace." Certainly nobody had security.

One is reminded of sophisticated modern fiction about divorce. "Everyone behaved in a thoroughly adult fashion." The West, beginning to be uneasy about the real intentions and potential of its Communist wartime allies, thought that it was being very responsible in advancing the Baruch Plan, calling for *international* ownership and control over all nuclear energy at a time when only the West had access to nuclear energy. The Communist states, for their part, did not acknowledge an ounce of self-abnegation or altruism in the Baruch initiative. They responded with the classic demand of disarmament, simply disarm. They insisted on a total and immediate renunciation and destruction of the possession and use of atomic weapons which, of course, they did not possess at the time.

Meanwhile, the Soviets worked night and day to produce the atomic weapons they wanted to ban and destroy. This they succeeded in doing by 1949, to the dismay of the Western experts. The Cold War got nastier, and the West hardened its line accordingly. It is fruitless to argue at this late date over the comparative culpability of either side. There was—and still is—a Cold War, and it coincides with the atomic, or nuclear age, and with attempts to achieve arms control and disarmament. This is the context of our subject.

But there is, as it were, a second, overriding predicament. There is the nightmarish vision of what a major nuclear war would be like. Responsible decision-makers in the states most conversant with the facts found this vision, in Kahn's term, increasing "unthinkable."[1] Paradoxically, ironically, tragically a state of affairs developed in which decision-makers thought and planned every day for what they increasingly conceived as "unthinkable."

I believe that it is not surprising that no nuclear war has occurred since 1945. World War II was a terrible, extended, global conflict which inflicted still uncounted death and misery more or less indiscriminately. But it pales in comparison with the vision of World

---

[1] E.g., Herman Kahn, *On Thermonuclear War* (2d ed., Princeton, New Jersey: Princeton University Press, 1961); and *Thinking About the Unthinkable* (New York: Avon Books, 1962).

War III. It is hardly surprising that a generation of statesmen hardened to the realities of war and the threat of war and, moreover, not very hopeful about the prospects for real peace, would consistently act so as to avoid World War III. May they continue.

General war, in an age of conflict where the occasion or, in traditional diplomatic terms, the *casus belli,* was likely to occur any day became:

1. "Unthinkable" as anything more than a last, desperate option;
2. *Very* "thinkable," for nuclear states, as a deterrent to an unthinkable war.

All this seems clear enough in the 1960s. But why did it take so long for the nuclear great powers to begin even preliminary reconnaissances of the fields of arms control and disarmament? More systematic analyses will undoubtedly identify additional reasons, but the following appear to be most relevant:

1. Both sides began with "disarmament," i.e., the reduction to a very minimal level of arms and arms development, as their goals. It gradually became apparent that this goal, even if coupled with several others, was not sufficiently responsive to the problems of limiting arms stocks and their use.

2. Both sides began with a number of political-ideological-psychological blocks:

a. disillusionment about the implications of the falling out that succeeded wartime collaboration;

b. reaction from the wartime pragmatism which tended to discount doctrinal differences to a Cold War literalism, or fundamentalism, which took seriously every theoretical analysis, propaganda jab, and every implicit or explicit threat originating from the other side.

3. Hardening of Cold War oneupmanship, a zero-sum game mentality, whereby every gain for the other side was a loss for one's own side; every compromise in the name of common sense a compromise of virtually theological proportions.

4. Understandable fear and conservatism with respect to critical weapons systems in the process of development, possession of which

were vital in order to maintain the balance of power or to advance one's position.

5. Mutual distrust, not merely based on fundamental ideological-political grounds, but on incidents and accidents of early disarmament negotiations, wherein hopes and trusts were frequently dashed. It is worthwhile to give two concrete illustrations of this problem which is not as generally known as the other points I have been summarizing.

I am indebted to Bernard C. Bechhoefer for this account of an incident wherein Soviet insincerity, stalling, discipline or some combination of all three was evidenced at a time when the Soviets seemed to be willing to discuss the Baruch Plan seriously. This account is that of Frederick H. Osborn, Baruch's successor in the UN Atomic Energy Commission, quoted by Bechhoefer. Osborn tells us:

By the end of May most of the sub groups had brought their papers in for informal discussion by the New Work group, after which the respective chairmen were to give them a final redrafting prior to their going to Lake Success for presentation and formal discussion by the Committee. At an informal meeting held in New York a number of these papers were presented in fairly complete form and for the first time it was evident that the Commission was going to be in a position to put out a Second Report which would contain sound and carefully written specific proposals. Dr. Skobeltzyn was sitting in, in position as observer, flanked by the two younger members of the Soviet Staff who usually accompanied him wherever he went. As the discussion developed, one of these young men handed Dr. Skobeltzyn a paper. When he opened and read it he became highly excited and interrupted with the demand that he be given the floor at once . . . Dr. Skobeltzyn [having interrupted another speaker who withdrew] then spoke quite excitedly. He demanded, first, that a verbatim record be made of what he was about to say. When this was arranged (fortunately a stenographer-interpreter was present, although no record was being made of any other talks) Dr. Skobeltzyn launched into an extraordinarily bitter attack on the meetings and the people taking part in them . . . [etc.,

etc.,] None of the other delegates who were present at this outburst made any reply. The procedures we were following had been approved in great detail in the formal meetings of the committee at Lake Success. Dr. Skobeltzyn had been urged in the strongest possible terms to take part in the work of the sub groups and had been present in all the meetings of the group as a whole. *It was the feeling of the other delegates that this outburst was due to Skobeltzyn's sudden realization that the work had advanced further than anything reported to Moscow, and his fear that he would be criticized for having permitted so much of a constructive nature to be done.*

Dr. Skobeltzyn's outburst was the beginning, and in a sense, the end of Soviet participation in the constructive work of the Commission.[2]

A more serious, and apparently more honest, misunderstanding seriously jeopardized disarmament negotiations in the late fifties. It arose out of the comparatively uncontrollable factor of changing scientific estimates of problems and their effect on political negotiations. In 1958 a U.S. panel of scientists headed by Dr. Hans Bethe had investigated the possibility of cessations of nuclear tests. Although they began with a skeptical attitude their conclusions tended to a position that continued testing would be of comparatively marginal advantage to the United States. Since there was so much concern about the world-wide fallout problem of testing, the Eisenhower administration agreed to consider a voluntary test ban and to meet with the Soviets to discuss the scientific problems of instituting a formal test ban by all the nuclear powers. Meanwhile the Soviets, having completed extensive tests, announced a unilateral moratorium on nuclear tests, March 31, 1958.

In these circumstances, the United States approached the Soviets with proposals resulting in a Conference of Experts, July 1–August 21, 1958. Khrushchev waxed hot and cold on the utility of these talks and the implication of the Soviet attitude was that it was a Western idea which had to be vindicated by the West.

[2] Frederick Osborn, "Negotiating on Atomic Energy," Chap. in Raymond Dennet and Joseph E. Johnson, eds., *Negotiating with the Russians* (1951), pp. 209, 225–26; quoted in Bernard C. Bechhoefer, *Postwar Negotiations for Arms Control* (Washington, D.C.: Brookings, 1961), pp. 52–54.

The fundamental questions concerned the possibility of cheating on a general test ban and the feasibility of detecting forbidden tests, mainly underground tests. Obviously this was a highly touchy question, since the standard Soviet attitude from 1945 had been that inspection of disarmament measures was unnecessary and the Western position had been that effective inspection was essential. Nevertheless, the Conference of Experts proved to be one of the more fruitful East-West disarmament discussions.

But one underlying difficulty lay in the sparseness of data about key topics. The U.S. experts started out the discussions on the basis of data from only *one* underground test, the "Ranier" 1.7 kiloton detonation in Nevada, September 10, 1957. By extrapolation from this one shot it was concluded that science was on the threshold of a capability for detecting underground detonations. The state of the art was primitive, and little thought had been given to possible ways of hiding or camouflaging nuclear detonations. It was to be several years before arms control discussions really dug into the question to be posed by RAND's Aaron Katz: In a disarmament situation where cheating was suspected, would you rather be a "hider" or a "seeker"? This primitive state of knowledge on the subject resulted in greatly varying estimates as to the number of inspection posts on the ground (i.e. in a foreign country's territory) would be necessary in order to satisfy parties to a test ban agreement.

I will not continue with the details. But the general situation, then, was that the West had the Soviets talking seriously about detecting nuclear tests in violation of a formal international test ban and that this was progress. However, in October 1958, further tests in Nevada produced new data which indicated that it would be more difficult to identify underground nuclear explosions than the Western experts had believed to be the case during the meetings of the previous summer.

Accordingly, when the Geneva Conference resumed, January 5, 1959, James I. Wadsworth, chief of the American delegation, was obliged to hold a brief informal meeting with Semyon K. Tsarapkin, head of the Soviet delegation. In this meeting, Wadsworth informed

Tsarapkin that the new data revised U.S. estimates as the magnitude of the problems and, obviously, the requirements for adequate inspection. Specifically, the United States now believed that the difficulty of distinguishing earthquakes from nuclear explosions was greater than had been thought and that the number of earthquakes equivalent to a given yield of a nuclear explosion was about double that previously estimated.

Tsarapkin apparently felt that the Soviets had been double-crossed. He insisted that the discussions proceed on the bases of the estimate reached in the Summer 1958 Conference of Experts. This the United States could not do, not only because it honestly believed the new data invalidated the old estimates, but because it was faced with formidable domestic opposition to a test ban which was reinforced by the new data. Wadworth later wrote that the introduction by the U.S. of the new data, spread a pall over the negotiations from which they never completely recovered.[3]

To return to the list of reasons explaining the lateness and paucity of arms control and disarmament efforts and results:

6. Inadequate research and thinking on the subject, grossly inadequate governmental staffing and co-ordination, including coordination between disarmament planners, diplomats, scientists, and the military, and lack of political muscle behind initiatives in this area. The United States in particular had a wretched record on these counts until the early sixties, and the situation still leaves much to be desired. The Soviets, on the other hand, have closely coordinated their disarmament policies with major political and propaganda lines and have, above all, staffed their negotiation teams with professionals whose names reappear constantly in the history of the subject, whereas the Americans have entrusted the subject to a fantastic variety of undoubtedly well-intentioned men who, particularly in the fifties, were quite often unprepared for their

[3] James J. Wadsworth, *The Price of Peace* (New York: Praeger, 1962), p. 124, quoted in Harold Karan Jacobson and Erie Stein, *Diplomats, Scientists, and Politicians* (Ann Arbor: University of Michigan Press, 1966), p. 137. This invaluable work, together with Bechhoefer's, briefly cited, is my principal source on this subject.

jobs. To be sure, the field of arms control and disarmament as a sub-discipline has been developed in the United States and Britain much more than in the Soviet Union. But most of this initiative came from the scientific and academic communities, and even today the U. S. Arms Control and Disarmament Agency leads a precarious existence.

7. Finally, one must cite general lack of experience. The modern world has had little experience with disarmament except in the form of the kind of irresponsible abandonment of military forces needed for defense and, perhaps, collective security, that characterized the American unilateral rush to disarmament in the twenties. It still remains to be seen whether genuine arms control and disarmament can be made to work.

There are, however, substantial incentives for arms control and disarmament. At least nine developments are discernible. First, there is the increasing knowledge of the horrible consequences of modern, especially nuclear, war. For example, the whole world has access to estimates such as those given by Secretary McNamara to the House Sub-Committee on Department of Defense Appropriations in 1965. He said at that time that if no additional investment were made in a damage-limiting program based on a 1970 U.S. population of 210,000,000 an early urban attack would cause 149 million fatalities, a delayed urban attack, 122 million fatalities. Whereas with an investment of $25,000,000,000, the number could be reduced to 78 and 41 million fatalities respectively.[4] The effects of a nuclear attack on Red China have already been noted.

Second, post-World War II, Cold War disillusionment and distrust have at least intermittently been pierced by a certain grudging admiration for and partial understanding of adversaries who have, in the end, frequently acted responsibly.

Third, with the breakup and liberalization of the Communist world, came realization that the Cold War zero-sum game model is not an accurate, and certainly not a helpful, basis for thought

[4] U. S. House of Representatives, Sub-Committee on Department of Defense Appropriations, *Hearings*, pt. 3, 89th Cong., 1st Sess. (Washington, D.C.: Government Printing Office, 1965), p. 41.

and action. (For our purposes, a zero-sum game model is one which assumes that in any competition, either economic or political or military, each side's gain is the other's loss. The nuclear era has taught us that a development may be either both sides' gain or loss.)

Fourth, there have been internal problems within alliances in all camps accompanied by a seeming tendency of the nuclear superpowers to identify more with each other on many issues than with their ungrateful and troublesome allies. Indeed, I wonder about these alliances. Several years ago it was suggested in Washington that the U.S. and NATO trade France to the Soviet Union and the Warsaw Pact for Romania. The Czechoslovak debacle of 1968 notwithstanding, the implications of this political joke are still relevant to the contemporary European situation and may become relevant in other parts of the world.

Fifth, the Cuban Missile Crisis seems to have had a sobering and salutary effect on everybody except the American hard-liners who use it as a model to be improved and built up to a Pax Americana and their Soviet counterparts who are playing catch-up and would like to pull ahead and have another showdown where the Americans back down. More on this presently.

Sixth, there has evolved greater progress in research, thought, diplomatic initiatives and responses, and mutual education in this field. This evolution is based largely on the growing realization that we all have to work at educating each other as well as ourselves if meaningful progress is to be made in arms control and disarmament.

Seventh, there is the perhaps decisive factor of the economic consequences of the arms race. As Arms Control and Disarmament Director William C. Foster put it, in arguing for the Nuclear Non-Proliferation Treaty: "It is plainly in the national interest of the United States and the Soviet Union to constrain spiraling risks and costs of the strategic arms race."[5]

[5] Address of October 19, 1968, to 150 of the nation's top corporation executives at Hot Springs, Virginia.

Eighth, there has been the development of the idea of "arms control" more as a comprehensive and useful concept than "disarmament."

Finally, we find an ever-increasing expression by religious authorities and men of good will that arms control and disarmament are moral imperatives.

"Disarmament" is historically related to the idea that wars occur because nations have the arms to wage war. Get rid of arms and you will be rid of war. Disarmament assumes basic change in the international system. As the reader has been made aware from the outset, I do not see any early prospect for such a change and I do not believe that the classical notion of disarmament would, if applied, necessarily bring about a beneficial change in the international system.

The framers of the League of Nations Convenant were optimistic about change in the international system. They placed high hopes on the alternatives to international war discussed in Chapter IV, pacific settlement of disputes and collective security. They failed. They also made disarmament an essential and integral feature of the League system, providing in Article 8 of the Convenant that:

> The members of the League recognise that the maintenance of peace requires the reduction of national armaments to the lowest point consistent with national safety and the enforcement by common action of international obligations.

Note the emphasis on *reduction* to the *lowest* point consistent with obligations of collective security. Ironically, the same generation which had unimaginatively and tragically slaughtered millions of soldiers because of its *quantitative* approach to armaments was now to approach disarmament in much the same way. To be sure, some qualitative issues were to be raised in inter-war disarmament negotiations, but generally on a blatantly selfish basis, i.e., the British wanted "offensive" submarines banned or unrealistically restricted while the French and Italians defended submarines as necessary "defensive" weapons. By 1934, when Germany was rearming, no viable theory of the case as to how disarmament should be accomplished had received broad assent. Disarmament was dead.

And it was just as well, for it was almost too late for those nations, particularly Britain, which had taken disarmament seriously, to rearm to meet the challenges to the peace that were fast developing. Pluck, pluck, the United States, and the Soviet Union finally bailed out the world that the League had misled and mismanaged. The process, of course, was long and ghastly. The lesson was not lost upon those who drafted the United Nations Charter. It contains nothing like Article 8 of the Covenant. The Charter enjoins disarmament as a goal, and the first action of the First General Assembly was to pass a disarmament resolution. But the problem of war was not handled in terms of disarmament. It was handled in two ways:

1. By a solemn reiteration of the obligation not to use force or the threat of force as an instrument of foreign policy;

2. By potentially elaborate collective security measures ordered and conducted by the significantly named "Security Council."

In other words, management of force rather than physical elimination of it by destroying weapons was the principal *motive* of the UN system. Since that system has not worked out either, such world order as exists is maintained by deterrence and by arms control. The concept of arms control in the sense that employ the term is that of Thomas C. Schelling and Morton H. Halperin. They say:

We use the term "arms control" rather than "disarmament." Our intention is simply to broaden the term. We mean to include all of the forms of military cooperation between potential enemies in the interest of reducing the likelihood of war, its scope and violence, if it occurs, and the political and economic costs of being prepared for it. The essential feature of arms control is the recognition of the common interest, of the possibility of reciprocation and cooperation even between potential enemies with respect to their military establishments. *Whether* the most promising areas of arms control involve *reductions* in certain kinds of military force, *increases* in certain kinds of military force, *qualitative changes* in weaponry, differing modes of deployment, or arrangements superimposed on existing military systems, we prefer to treat as an open question.[6]

Schelling and Halperin go on to state that their notion of arms control is not in opposition to disarmament. "It is intended rather to include such disarmament in a broader concept." They continue, "We do not, however, share the notion, implicit in many pleas for disarmament, that reduction in the level of military forces is necessarily desirable, if only it is 'inspectable' and that it necessarily makes war likely."[7] Nor do I. I agree with Schelling and Halperin that reducing *incentives* to go to war or to wage it without limitations are as much if not more important than reducing capabilities.

The extent to which this approach has affected U.S. policy is reflected in the name of the agency designated to take primary responsibility in this field, the U. S. Arms Control and Disarmament Agency. Increasingly, those concerned with this subject use the term "arms control" to mean "arms control and disarmament." On the other hand, the usage "disarmament" remains in effect in UN and other international organizational and diplomatic contexts, e.g., the Eighteen Nation Disarmament Committee (ENDC) which meets at Geneva. Moreover, since the United States follows the Schelling-Halperin concept of "arms control" in its defense and foreign policies but also follows the classical "disarm and verify" approach of "disarmament," I will use the term "arms control and disarmament."

I have no intention in this chapter of attempting to provide a catalogue of arms control and disarmament issues, although the more important will be analyzed. I think it more important to summarize attitudes and approaches with respect to arms control and disarmament, for it is here, I believe, that we are most likely to find the basis for an evaluation of the prospects for arms control and disarmament.

[6] *Strategy and Arms Control* (New York: Twentieth Century Fund, 1961), p. 2. [Emphasis added]
[7] *Ibid.*, pp. 2–3.

I will start with American approaches to arms control and disarmament and then assess prevailing approaches in other nuclear
nations as well as in some of the non-nuclear nations. This will
necessarily involve a more elaborate treatment of American approaches, first, since Americans have done more thinking about the
subject than anyone else, and, second, because the American open
society permits more debate. Many of the American approaches may
be supported in some other nations, but those nations speak with a
single voice, one moreover, that can often change its tune without
warning.

There are, basically, three American approaches to arms control
and disarmament: the arms-control approach, the legal-disarmament
approach, and the Pax Americana approach.

The *arms-control approach,* associated with Thomas C. Schelling,
Morton H. Halperin, Henry A. Kissinger, Herman Kahn, and
like-minded (though frequently disagreeing) thinkers, in addition to
making the assumptions already quoted, assumes the following:

1. International stability is based on deterrence and on rational
understandings, even among enemies or competitors. Anything that
destabilizes a global or regional balance is dangerous and to be
avoided. It works two ways, essentially. First, a precipitate or major
unilateral disarmament measure which critically improves the position of potential adversaries may be dangerous because it tempts
those adversaries to take advantage of the new relationship. Second,
a major increase in power may be dangerous for the beneficiary,
because the adversary who is now in a weaker position may become nervous and do something rash which is in no one's interest.
Thus if Dr. Teller were to announce triumphantly that he had just
invented a new super-bomb or delivery system that left the Soviets
far behind in the arms race, the effect might well be to increase
the likelihood of a desperate Soviet preventive or pre-emptive war.

This applies to so-called passive-defense or damage-limitation
measures as well as to armaments and delivery systems. On the face
of it, Civil Defense seems like a good thing. Who should complain
if ABM (anti-ballistic-missile) systems are developed to protect

cities? But if one side really goes all out on Civil Defense preparations and deployment of ABMs, a potential adversary may rightly become worried and reason, "They must be preparing to attack, otherwise why should they be so anxious to protect themselves?" For, of course, the other party's intentions are always suspect. Nations tend naïvely to believe that if *they* know their own intentions, and the intentions are pure, this will be evident to other nations.

Arms control as an approach, then, begins with the system as it is. It works in any way that seems to make sense to improve it, but always by stabilizing, qualitatively and quantitatively, any change in the system, always keeping it, as it were, fair to all sides, symmetrical.

2. Accordingly, continued nuclear deterrence is a necessity; limited war is a necessity; a capacity to "signal" and communicate with potential and actual enemies is a necessity. All of these things, as previously pointed out, are based on material and moral assumptions which can rightly be questioned, but this is true of all approaches.

3. As mentioned in the quotes from Schelling and Halperin, the arms-control approach is extremely skeptical about the prospects of fundamental change in the international system and for treaty provisions that are not sanctioned either by strong motivation based on mutually perceived interests or on a capacity to enforce them by some kind of effective coercion.

The *legal-disarmament approach* is best characterized by Grenville Clark and Louis B. Sohn's, *World Peace Through World Law* (3rd ed.; Cambridge, Mass.: Harvard University Press, 1966), and the Draft Treaties on General and Complete Disarmament Under Strict International Control, submitted by the Soviet Union and the United States, which have been under consideration since 1962. These will be discussed later in this chapter. This approach relies upon elaborate, detailed blueprints, embodied in draft treaties, sanctioned by intricate inspection and administrative arrangements, ultimately to be carried out under an International Defense Organization (IDO). These proposals assume the possibility of international systemic change, producing a disarmed world governed by a world authority. As against faith in enlightened power politics carried out by hard-headed politicians and military leaders, the legal-disarmament approach places great faith in the ability of lawyers to draft language which will deal with virtually all foreseeable contingencies and which will facilitate administrative or judicial peaceful settlement of disputes over the operation of the new system. To this is added a tendency to trust in the universality and objectivity of science and the integrity and ingenuity of relevant science in solving technical problems which have political-legal-military ramifications. This, as we have seen, is the approach favored by the Catholic Church and other influential religious and humanitarian institutions. This is true, however, with one important qualification. The churches want men to build world peace, law, and order on the basis of moral imperatives. The principal proponents of the legal-disarmament approach prefer to build such a condition on "strict control," on virtually foolproof arrangements that will dispel distrust. However, as in the churches' approach, it is believed that a multiplier effect will operate to increase the degree of mutual trust as the blueprint unfolds and proves efficacious.

The *Pax Americana approach,* the so-called "hard line" of thinkers such as Edward Teller, Stefan Possony, William Kitner, General Curtis LeMay, Senator Barry Goldwater, and Robert Strausz-Hupè, takes an almost completely negative approach to arms control and disarmament. The hard line holds:

1. We are engaged in "protracted conflict" with the Communists that must end either in victory for one or the other or in abandonment of fundamental values by one or the other. We should never abandon our values and our opposition to theirs. They will never abandon their values unless forced to by our power. Meanwhile, the protracted conflict can be kept manageable by maintaining a constant, unrelenting program of scientific-military development to ensure constant Western superiority over the Communists.

2. There are, contrary to the conventional wisdom of the scientific

and governmental establishment, substantial possibilities for militarily decisive breakthroughs. We should pursue those possibilities. The Communists certainly will. They have already closed the gap of superiority which we have held since the Cuban Missile Crisis of 1962. They may soon surpass us. When they do, the political and military consequences will be disastrous.

3. The Communists can be expected to cheat on any international agreement, especially on disarmament. Arms control and disarmament agreements should only be contemplated if there are iron-clad methods of inspection, and prospects for such agreements are not sanguine.

The *official U.S. approach to arms control and disarmament policy* has been based on an eclectic mix of the arms control, legalist-disarmament approaches with, I think, strong influences from the Pax Americana approach, especially as regards U.S. policy toward Red China. For it is extremely important to distinguish U.S. Soviet policy from U.S. policy on Red China. Policy toward the Soviets works hard for *détente* and for arms control and disarmament. Policy toward Red China is hotly debated within the U.S. government, and there are important forces that would leap at any sign that that nation was willing to be more conciliatory. But it seems evident to me that the whole strategic policy in Asia is, to use a favorite phrase of the hard-liners, based on "forward position" toward Red China in a situation of "protracted conflict." So my following remarks have to do with arms control and disarmament exclusive of Red China.

First, the U.S. follows an arms-control policy in that it consciously interrelates political-military policies with arms control and disarmament policies. Graduated deterrence and limited war are arms-control policies.

The United States also follows an arms control policy in its decisions on developing weapons systems and damage-limitation systems. It consistently resists hard-line pressure within and outside of the government to heat up the arms race. Idealists and pacifists who concentrate their moral outrage on the "crackpot realists" need to be reminded from time to time that things could have been worse and might become worse. We could still be contaminating the atmosphere with dirty hydrogen bomb tests, and we could have become involved in a number of Christian Crusades Against Godless Communism. Even the war in Southeast Asia could have been worse and one can be sure that there are powerful persons in the executive and legislative branches of the U.S. government, as well as in the conservative establishment, who would, for example, like nothing better than a Red Chinese intervention into the Vietnamese war, providing the opportunity for "taking out" the Red Chinese nuclear and rocket installations. Thank God this has not been U.S. policy, and responsible citizens must work to see that it does not become U.S. policy.

A second element in U.S. policy has taken the form of the legal-disarmament approach. This is represented by the submission at the Eighteen Nation Disarmament Committee, April 18, 1962, of an "Outline of Basic Provisions of a Treaty on General and Complete Disarmament in a Peaceful World." This draft GCD treaty has since been amended in 1962 and in 1963. The Draft Treaty seems to indicate a commitment to trying seriously the legal-disarmament approach. How seriously the United States really takes its own proposals, and whether they would be acceptable to the Congress and the people if presented to them, remains to be seen.

The third element in U.S. policy is, in my view, a combination of the arms control and the legal-disarmament approaches. It is exemplified by individual measures, not necessarily forming part of a clear, broader "package," tending toward arms control and disarmament progress. The two best examples of this mixed approach are the Partial Nuclear Test Ban Treaty of 1963 and the Nuclear Non-Proliferation Treaty signed July 1, 1968. Both take the form of an international agreement but both reflect attitudes and patterns of behavior which had been developing as a matter of unilateral practice for some time. Let us now turn to Soviet approaches to this subject.

Since the Soviets reject the term "arms control," I will not saddle them with it. But they practice it. This gets us off to a good start in discussing a subject that requires high tolerance, arguments, and positions which might be called dialectical, inconsistent, opportunistic, honest changes of position, or whatever, depending on one's analyses and disposition. This is undoubtedly true. The shifts in the power elite in the Soviet Union and in their ideological, political, and military thinking, not to forget their economic reckonings, are important factors in a state which is still desperately trying to find resources for all of the necessities of a progressive modern society.

Since the Soviet Union usually presents one position at any given time, which it presents to the world, it seems best to enumerate some of the recurring characteristics of Soviet approaches to disarmament without trying to break down schools of thought as we did with respect to the Americans. The following generalizations may be made:

1. The Soviets, like the United States, follow no single approach. They are eclectic and sometimes inconsistent, indeed, contradictory in their approaches.

2. The existence of Marxist-Leninist doctrine does not result in consistent, "scientific" positions on disarmament. This parallels the early decision of the Soviets in the twenties not to follow the logic of inevitable conflict with the imperialist and to reject imperialist international law. Instead, they took the pragmatic view that in pursuing their ideological-political-strategic interests they should use Western international law as an instrument of policy to be used against the hostile capitalist states and in defense of the Soviet Union.

Their method in accomplishing this was to place heavy emphasis on an extreme version of the classical notion of absolute sovereignty and on these corollaries:

a. A state cannot be bound without its consent. In defending their interests the Soviets virtually limit their admitted international law obligations to *treaty* obligations. Customary international law and general principles *as interpreted by others* are rejected. However, when the Soviets are attacking the conduct of others, they invoke the full spectrum of sources of international law including opinions of text writers and precedents, especially if they are embarrassing to the foreign nation.

b. Absolute sovereignty means absolute non-intervention in the affairs of a state. The Soviets are especially insistent on this and understandably, since, from their standpoint, they have suffered more from foreign intervention than most nations. This, together with their native as well as political propensity toward maintaining a society that is comparatively closed to the world, tends to make any suggestion on international inspection by foreigners in the Soviet Union the object of instant and, from the Soviet standpoint, principled denunciation. Obviously, the Soviets, and Communists generally, constantly intervene in the internal affairs of other states. But this is simply denied or explained by the contention that the incumbent governments in those states are repressive and undemocratic and that individual Soviets or other Communists have a right and duty to help the people combat such governments.

3. The Soviets reject arms control in both senses in which the concept is accepted in the U.S. First, the Soviets have, in public statements and official publications rejected as absurd the ideas of "limited war," "counterforce," "no first use," "graduated deterrence," in short, the "rules of the game" for modern general war. Second, arms control in the sense of "arms control and disarmament" is rejected. For the Soviets, "disarmament is disarmament, period." Nevertheless, they do in fact follow the arms-control approach. Their "disarmament" policy is simply a part of an integrated foreign and defense policy, very much—if not more so—than in the United States.

4. Much like their Western adversaries, the Soviets are greatly influenced by the implications of political, strategic, and technological developments for disarmament. Both sides became more seriously interested in disarmament after Sputnik in 1957, after the Cuban

Missile Crisis of 1962, and after the Moscow-Peking break of July 1963.

5. The Soviets are evidently influenced by their economic situation and prospects, as they look to their security requirements and the possibility of lessening through (whether they will use the term or not) arms control and disarmament measures. Indeed, there existed in the past and may still exist an American point of view that we should push the arms race to the limit and thereby drive the Soviets to economic ruin. In the face of rising demands for economic, social, and racial justice in the United States and the reaction to the Vietnam War, this eminently "capitalist" option is now clearly out of the question. But it raises a serious point with respect to Soviet attitudes on this subject.

6. In keeping with the classical concept of disarmament, the Soviets like to stick to simple concepts. They like to talk in quantitative terms, for example, number of divisions demobilized or of weapons whose destruction is *announced*. The complications and sophisticated concepts and machinery of Western legal-disarmament approaches, strongly influenced as they are by ingenious scientific-technical concepts, are rejected, ridiculed, or finessed. At least this has been the tendency. Soviet-Western arms-control and disarmament talks in the last few years have apparently indicated a growing willingness on the part of the Soviets to take such proposals seriously. It is my hope that this characteristic of Soviet attitudes and behavior is changing so that this point (6) may be put in a more qualified manner and with emphasis on the past rather than the present and future.

7. Finally, and it must be said that this is a characteristic that has been discernible in U.S. behavior but which I have saved until now to emphasize the common nature of the problem of the nuclear powers and the frequently common tendency they show to follow a zigzagging course. This is the "double-take" syndrome. A proposal is made by one side. The immediate reaction of the other, especially the Soviets is: No, Ridiculous! Hypocritical! Unnecessary invasion

of privacy! Then, somehow, the proposal is seriously considered and sometimes adopted. There was a time when the Soviets would not countenance any arms-control and disarmament treaty before *first* obtaining a treaty banning the possession and use of nuclear weapons. Then they obtained their own nuclear weapons and, while still advocating a ban, were willing to talk about other things. Both sides have at times insisted that any arms-control and disarmament measure must be part of a comprehensive package of agreements. No such package has been achieved, but we have the Test Ban Treaty of 1963 and the Non-Proliferation Treaty of 1968. Indeed, both sides have at times been adamantly against limitations on nuclear testing. Having apparently satisfied themselves, but not Dr. Teller and his Soviet counterparts, that they had tested enough, what had been out of the question became the first order of business. So, while there is life there is hope. How much more time remains for the complicated operation of this "double-take" syndrome to get us out of the "treacherous trap" is the hard question.

Considerable problems are raised by the French approach to arms control and disarmament. Once the French approach to this subject was very positive. Until the French decided to develop their own nuclear capability, French diplomacy, led by an outstanding statesman, Jules Moch, worked with the British to be the "go-betweens" with the Americans and the Soviets. Since France began to go her own way to nuclear grandeur, her position has been highly skeptical on arms control. It may be summarized as follows:

1. The odds are entirely against any arms-control and disarmament measure that contravenes a state's national interest. France, at least, will take no risks on this score.

2. The nuclear super-powers are all too anxious to limit and disarm others. Let them disarm themselves first, and then one will see. If they are serious about it, let them go about the process systematically and comprehensively.

These attitudes have been advanced consistently since the late 1950s. They are not solely those of General De Gaulle. Specialists trace the Test Ban Treaty of 1963 to the Conference of Experts, July 1–August 21, 1958. But on August 21, 1958, French Foreign Minister Maurice Couve de Murville reiterated his government's position in a talk with President Eisenhower:

France was determined to push ahead with its plan for the development of an independent nuclear capability, and, as a consequence, continued to oppose a test ban as an *isolated* measure of arms control.[8]

In the subsequent Thirteenth General Assembly discussions wherein India proposed an immediate suspension of the testing of nuclear weapons, Jules Moch, the most able and imaginative French arms-control negotiator, answered that this country would not discontinue its nuclear weapons program unless, "the 'atomic powers' should immediately cease to increase and begin to reduce their stockpiles under international control."[9] General De Gaulle has reaffirmed this position a number of times, for example on April 7, 1960, before a Joint Session of the U. S. Congress, six days after the second detonation of a French nuclear device.[10]

This viewpoint was reinforced with an interesting variant when France refused (as it continues) to participate in the Eighteen Nation Disarmament Committee sessions at Geneva. Not only did France cite the failure of the other nuclear powers to destroy their nuclear capabilities, it—now a nuclear power, though of modest proportions —added a new objection. The subject of nuclear arms control and disarmament *should be limited to nuclear powers*.

The Red Chinese approach to arms control and disarmament is even more negative than the French. Its principal components seem to be:

1. Whereas the French are skeptical about disarmament concessions as risky to the national interest, Red China had a much more grandiose reason for skepticism on this subject. It perceives itself as

[8] Jacobson and Stein, *op. cit.*, p. 89.
[9] *Ibid.*, p. 104.
[10] *Ibid.*, pp. 250–51.

the true, pure, leader of the Communist world. For it to limit itself
in this matter without prior disarmament of all nations would be to
do what the scorned Soviets have done, let cowardly fear of
nuclear war (as well as bourgeois tendencies and fuzzy thinking that
has strayed far from the true Marxist-Leninist-*Maoist* line) drive
them into treacherous collaboration with the capitalist imperialists.

2.   Collaboration with arms-control and disarmament negotiations
is presently out of the question because it takes place primarily in
the ENDC, a United Nations organization and in the UN itself.
Excluded from the UN, formerly attacked by so-called "United
Nations" forces in Korea, Red China wants no part of present
arms-control and disarmament efforts.

3.   Whereas French concern for her security seems rather far-
fetched, Red China is very aware of her vulnerability, the unrelia-
bility of the Soviets, once their protector, and, therefore the need
to develop her own nuclear capability, as we have seen earlier. In
a note of August 15, 1963 (just after the signing of the Test Ban
Treaty), the government of the People's Republic of China said:

> In fighting imperialist aggression and defending its security, every
> socialist country has to rely in the first place on its own defense ca-
> pability—and only then—on assistance from fraternal countries and
> the people of the world. For the Soviet statement to describe all the
> socialist countries as depending on the nuclear weapons of the Soviet
> Union for their survival is to strike an out-and-out great power chau-
> vinistic note and to fly in the face of the facts.[11]

The official Peking release concerning the first Chinese nuclear
test said:

> This is a major accomplishment of the Chinese people in their struggle
> to increase their national defense capability and oppose the United
> States imperialist policy of nuclear blackmail and nuclear threats . . .

[11] Augenstein, "The Chinese and French Programs for the Development of
Nuclear Forces," *op. cit.,* p. 846.

China cannot remain idle and do nothing in the face of the ever-increasing nuclear threat posed by the United States. China is forced to conduct nuclear tests and develop nuclear weapons.[12]

4. The Red Chinese would, given their doctrinaire belligerence, appear even more unlikely to accept the American arms control concept. But it should be noted that they already have experienced fighting under tacit "rules of the game" in Korea and observed the operation of such rules, especially as concerns bombing in North Vietnam close to their borders, in the Vietnamese conflict.

5. Finally, and saddest of all, except for the painful negotiations at Panmunjom, and the unhappy Geneva Accords of 1954 to which the U.S. was not a direct party, the Red Chinese have had little occasion to develop techniques of negotiation on questions of arms control and disarmament. Except for some of the coldest years of the Cold War, the Soviets and the West have been haggling over arms control and disarmament, and gradually there has been less haggling and more communication, education, and progress. We do not even have the beginnings of such a process with Red China, a sad and dangerous fact.

Finally, let us turn to some approaches of other nations to arms control and disarmament. I have not gone into British approaches to arms control and disarmament, not for lack of appreciation of their importance, both on their merits and because Britain is a nuclear power, but because they pretty much tend to fit either into the American "arms control" or the "legal-disarmament" approach. Suffice it to say that the intermediary role played in earlier days by Britain and France has, since the French experiment in remaining a great power by having a nuclear capability, been continued by Britain alone. The British has been an unending source of optimism and patience throughout the ups and downs of the arms-control and disarmament negotiations, from 1945 to the present.

As to the non-nuclear powers, three themes recur:

---

[12] Hshinhua press agency, October 16, 1964.

First, the nuclear powers have been irresponsibly endangering the world by their nuclear tests, preparations, and threats, and the non-nuclear powers have a right to demand that they get on with progress in arms control and disarmament. India was originally the leading proponent of this point of view.

Second, in a softer sell, the nuclear powers have locked themselves into ways of viewing their problems and are understandably unable to escape from the impasses which they have created. Therefore, it would be helpful to have some non-nuclear powers actively influencing arms-control and disarmament negotiations, to get some fresh perspectives from non-nuclear powers, some of which, technically quite advanced, such as Sweden, might be able to come up with acceptable new ideas on the subject.

Third, pulling in another direction, non-nuclear states ask, "Who protects us from nuclear blackmail and/or aggression if the major nuclear power or powers on whom we rely begin to play around with arms-control and disarmament schemes threatening the credibility of their nuclear deterrents?" I will save further comment on this very real problem for my discussion of the nonproliferation treaty.

The opening wedge in the move to meet points (1) and (2) had been the creation of a Ten-Nation Disarmament Committee established outside of the framework of the UN on the basis of parity of East and West. For, in the summer of 1959, the Foreign Ministers of France, the U.S.S.R., the U.K., and the United States agreed in Geneva that such a committee be established. This was important in that it provided the ultimate basis for the ENDC. The Ten-Nation Disarmament Committee met in Geneva in March 1960. It consisted of Canada, France, Italy, the United Kingdom, and the United States from the West, and Bulgaria, Czechoslovakia, Poland, Romania, and the U.S.S.R. from the East. The Ten-Nation Disarmament Committee at least gave some answer to charges that the great nuclear powers were not sufficiently meeting their responsibilities with respect to nuclear testing, preparations, and threats, to the non-nuclear nations. But, I think, more importantly, the Ten-Nation

Committee established a model for a medium-sized arms-control and disarmament working group, something between the 1955 Subcommittee of five (U.S., U.K., France, Canada, and the U.S.S.R.) and a free-for-all to no purpose in the General Assembly.

Thus, the desire of the non-nuclear and neutralist powers to enter into the mainstream of arms-control and disarmament negotiations was met by the negotiations on a nuclear test ban resumed on March 11, 1962, at Geneva, in the Eighteen-Nation Disarmament Committee (ENDC) Jacobson and Stein observe:

> This committee had been created as a result of bilateral talks between the United States and the Soviet Union in the summer and fall of 1961, and its composition had been endorsed in General Assembly Resolution 1722 (XVI). In the same resolution, the Assembly requested that the Eighteen-Nation Committee should report to it, and directed the Secretary General to facilitate the Committee's work by supplying the necessary services. The Eighteen-Nation Committee thereupon met, as the Conference on the Discontinuance of Nuclear Weapons Tests had previously, in the *Palais des nations,* in Geneva. By virtue of the Assembly Resolution 1722 (XVI), however, the Eighteen-Nation Committee had a somewhat more definite link with the United Nations than the previous conference, and this was underscored during the subsequent negotiations.[13]

To the Ten-Nation Committee were added: Brazil, Burma, Ethiopia, India, Mexico, Nigeria, Sweden, and the United Arab Republic.

Did it make any difference?

Yes, I think so, although without the basic commitment of the nuclear great powers to progress in arms control and disarmament, only propaganda and wounded pride might have resulted from this move.

It is arbitrary and unfair to select out the approaches and contributions resulting from the broadening of the ENDC. As to the

[13] Jacobson and Stein, *op. cit.,* p. 356.

first of them of the non-nuclear powers, there is little doubt that the presence of eight non-nuclear powers of very diverse orientations placed them on their mettle. On the other hand, one has the impression that it was salutary for the formerly excluded non-nuclear powers to grapple themselves, and see others, both nuclear and non-nuclear, grapple with the dilemmas of arms control and disarmament.

As to the second theme, positive assistance, it is not surprising that Sweden has been outstanding in the ENDC in its contributions to solution of practical dilemmas. Sweden, along with India, is a nation that could produce nuclear weapons before 1970. Sweden has been particularly helpful in bridging the once uncrossable gap between U.S. insistence that all arms control and disarmament measures must be inspected by checked-out international or national inspectors of the soil of the possible violator to an agreement, and the Soviet position that (1) such an invasion of sovereignty and privacy is inadmissible and; (2) it is unnecessary because existing national and international networks reporting scientific phenomena are in themselves sufficient to detect cheating on disarmament agreements, leaving the requirement for international inspection nonexistent or greatly below Western estimates. Sweden has taken the lead in checking out this Soviet contention with respect to monitoring underground nuclear tests in violation of a total test ban and, for example, presented to the ENDC in the summer of 1962 a detailed survey of the world's meteorological and seismological facilities relevant to this problem.

As concerns the third problem, that of responsible nuclear protectors of non-nuclear states, India, of the members of ENDC, has increasingly shifted from the position of the utterly unaligned opponent of all nuclear preparations and commitments to a state which, in the light of the development of the Red Chinese capability, must increasingly concern itself with the question. "Must we build our own nuclear deterrent, a course we have so often deplored when followed by others, or must we rely on 'nuclear guarantees' from both sides?" This raises the further question, that the Federal

Republic of Germany was not formally represented either at the ENDC discussion or in the United Nations of which it is not a member. It was to play its role, particularly since it is not a long drive from Bonn to Geneva, in the negotiations on the Nuclear Non-Proliferation Treaty, albeit informally. States such as Israel and Japan had similar serious problems and made them known, notwithstanding the fact that they were not members of the ENDC.

What all this brings home to me is that the "scorpion in the bottle" analogy of Oppenheimer has long since ceased to be a useful basis for discussion of nuclear arms control and disarmament, if it ever was. So many states, with so many approaches and *nuances* of approaches and problems, are caught up in the dilemmas of nuclear arms control and disarmament, that, as in any wild political campaign, you pick a leader or a theory of the case and go with it. If you miscalculate, you lose, and perhaps the world loses.

In the light of these differing approaches, I propose to survey some, certainly not all, of the issues outstanding in the field of arms control and disarmament in the light of the approaches and problems mentioned. The issues concern:

1. Participants, procedures, and pace in arms-control and disarmament negotiations;

2. Nuclear testing;

3. Nuclear non-proliferation and its enforcement;

4. The relationship of "progress" in arms control and disarmament by the nuclear powers to the behavior of non-nuclear powers;

6. The ABM (anti-ballistic-missiles-systems) issue, Civil Defense and "Vertical Proliferation";

7. Communication and avoidance of accidental war;

8. Nuclear free zones;

9. Prospects for blueprints for GCD (general and complete disarmament). Following this I will undertake to analyze the prospects for arms control and disarmament in an overly dangerous world where all morally responsible men call for progress in this field.

First, there is the UN General Assembly where, annually, up to 122 members have the right to express their views and to engage in off-the-floor lobbying, politicking, and negotiation. Then there is the currently central forum in the Eighteen-Nation Disarmament Committee, meeting at Geneva. Thirdly, there is the Non-nuclear Conference (NNC) which began meeting in August 1968, and which has recently forwarded a series of resolutions on arms control measures to the United Nations.[14]

It seems clear that serious business is only going to progress, in most foreseeable cases, in the ENDC and in small, private negotiations involving the principal nuclear powers. To the extent that progress does occur in these arenas, it is certainly useful for educative purposes to air the issues in the General Assembly, tedious as this may sometimes become. There appears to be one major difficulty with the present fairly happy mix of the three models. This is the fact that important and highly interested parties are not members of the United Nations. The Federal Republic of Germany is one of those most interested in and affected by negotiations on this subject. It has shown extraordinary restraint and co-operativeness and the United States has sought to assure the Germans that their interests would be respected and protected. Nevertheless, future arms-control initiatives must find better means of providing the Federal Republic of Germany with a voice in negotiations. The Communist states will not like this, but, particularly in the wake of the Non-Proliferation Treaty to which it is hoped Germany will adhere, they will have to treat the Germans reasonably. Indeed, the Federal Republic would not be acting unreasonably if it required some implicit or explicit assurances on this point before signing the Non-Proliferation Treaty.

Then there is the extraordinarily difficult problem of Red China. I can foresee no specific solution to this problem. But I would expect that if it is ever solved it will be part of an extremely comprehensive package deal involving relations with Taiwan, the United Nations,

[14] The Non-nuclear Nations Conference met in Geneva, August 29–September 28, 1968. The ninety participating states agreed to present resolutions to the Assembly concerning security assurances for adherents to the nonproliferation agreement and peaceful use of atomic energy, looking to further conferences and *ad hoc* committees on these subjects. No firm draft of an Assembly resolution concerning these vital issues emerged.

the security of Asia, the military posture of Japan, the role of the United States in the Pacific, and similarly staggering issues, which some incredibly talented and patient collection of diplomats will produce, perhaps on some mountain top in the Himalayas. When we are told to "study the question," the admonition seems difficult to respond to, but feasible, with respect to the issues of arms control and disarmament. But studying the Red Chinese part of the question puts most dedicated and optimistic arms controllers in deep depression.

As to the other states not represented in the United Nations and not usually consulted on arms control and disarmament, such as East Germany, North and South Korea, and North and South Vietnam, one can only say that until the central issues as to the future of Germany and of China are worked out, they will only be as involved as their allies care to involve them.

As to procedures, a subject already implicitly dealt with in part, it appears that, ultimately, there is only one procedure for progress in arms control and disarmament. That is tireless, patient negotiation, line by line, on a challenge-and-response basis. On these subjects above all, nations are not and ought not to be content with generalities. To be sure, they will sometimes agree to the broad lines or principles of an approach and fill in the details through subsequent negotiation. But certainly the experience of negotiating the Test Ban Treaty and the Nuclear Non-Proliferation Treaty, no matter at what point one considers to be the true origin of the negotiations, indicate a time span of roughly three to five years, because of the procedures that must be followed.

This, then, brings us to the question of the pace of negotiations. Can they be speeded up? Can more issues be treated simultaneously so that three or four major agreements are being worked out during a particular three- to five-year period? If one doubled the amount of political and scientific talent and influence contributed, the budgets of the agencies or offices working on the subject, the attention accorded arms control and disarmament by influential heads of state, could we get more and better arms control faster? No one really

knows the answer to that question because, to the best of knowledge, no major participant in arms-control and disarmament negotiations has ever tried an all-out, crash effort. It is obviously about
time that somebody tried such an effort. But no nation will until
its elites and general public opinion insist that they do so, a question
which I will return to in the last chapter.

Bearing these points in mind, what is the status of efforts to limit
nuclear testing? As earlier remarked, the first stages of progress
toward cessation of nuclear testing were unilateral and, in the
American sense, arms-control measures. The Soviets announced a
unilateral moratorium on nuclear testing in the atmosphere in March
1958 and ended it in November of that year. In the same month,
the United States initiated its own unilateral moratorium on testing,
whereupon the Soviets, apparently having tested as much as they
thought they needed to, announced that they would not be the first
to resume testing. They did so, however, on September 1, 1961. The
Soviets at that time denigrated the importance of a test ban as a
disarmament measure. Moreover, they called attention to the French
nuclear tests. The weapons detonated were reportedly of fantastic
magnitude, ranging from an estimated 20 to 100 megatons. It will
be recalled that this was a period of tense East-West confrontation
over Berlin. Since it was estimated that Soviet preparations for the
tests must have required six months to a year there is also an obvious possible link between them and the collapse of the Spring
1960 Paris Summit Conference, following the U-2 affair.

In response, on September 3, 1961, President Kennedy and Prime
Minister Macmillan proposed an international agreement not to
conduct nuclear tests "which take place in the atmosphere and produce radioactive fallout." The agreement was to have no control
measures. They proposed to meet in Geneva by September 9, 1961
to sign such an agreement. The proposal was, admittedly, designed
to embarrass the Soviet Union. But it was also a serious proposal.
Meanwhile, the United States did not resume testing in the atmosphere until April 5, 1962.

Despite their differences and despite continuation of Soviet nuclear tests in the atmosphere through October 1961, the United States and the Soviet Union were able during the meetings at the General Assembly of that year to agree to the expansion of the Ten-Nation Disarmament Committee to the Eighteen-Nation Disarmament Committee which went into operation March 11, 1962. In the year that followed, the 1963 Test Ban was worked out. I will not go into detailed calculations that once again altered U.S. estimates of the possibility of detecting underground tests. For a key point was raised in the ENDC by Brazil, July 25, 1962. Since virtually all disagreements obstructing a test ban concerned underground tests, why not concentrate on atmospheric and outer space tests, which "are the most dangerous, actually and potentially, and the ones which have a most disturbing effect on mind, body, and nerves."[15] And, indeed, this was in effect what the U.S. and U.K. had proposed to the Soviet Union on September 3, 1961.

It took exactly a year (a good example of the problem of "pace" just discussed) to sort out the international and domestic problems involved, but on July 15, 1963, one year after the Brazilian proposal, the Test Ban Treaty was initialed by the U.S., U.K., and Soviet negotiators. It was formally signed in Moscow, August 5, 1963. In that year a lot had happened, to put it mildly. The Cuban Missile Crisis and the open break with Red China had obviously sobered the Soviets considerably. The Soviets seem also to have been genuinely impressed with the fact that the Kennedy administration expressed a desire for peace, notably in Kennedy's American University Commencement Address of June 10, 1963. Interestingly, the treaty was initialed the day after the major Soviet document on its rift with Red China was issued. Were the parties "sincere"? Is the agreement based on "mutual trust"? I am not at all sure. But it does appear that they felt it to be in their mutual interest, and that is all that the realist arms control approach requires.[16]

---

[15] Jacobson and Stein, *op. cit.,* p. 394.

[16] Article 1 obliges the parties "to prohibit, to prevent, and not to carry out any nuclear weapon test explosion, or any other explosion, at any place under its jurisdiction or control" in the atmosphere, underwater, and outer space. It

There remains the question of underground testing. A ban on such tests will not be easy to obtain but it appears much more conceivable today than it did five years ago and enormously more plausible than it did ten years ago. I say this because of recent developments in Soviet and U.S. arms control attitudes and policies.

The Soviet line, for whatever reasons it was taken, and some of them were self-serving, that science and technology would increasingly render unnecessary international inspection of suspected nuclear detonations in violations of nuclear test bans seems, to a non-expert reading the histories of arms-control developments, to have been borne out. A similar line is taken by Sweden, which certainly can be trusted insofar as motives are concerned. It will take scientists to determine what if any risks of cheating remain on a ban against underground nuclear testing. But it will be interesting to see the U.S. reaction to point 7 of Kosygin's memorandum to all governments on the occasion of the Moscow signing of the Non-Proliferation of Nuclear Weapons Treaty, July 1, 1968. Mr. Kosygin proposed: "A ban on underground nuclear tests on the basis of present national detection methods."

In 1965 the United States intensified its initiatives for a nuclear nonproliferation treaty. These efforts reaching an important point on August 17, 1965, when the U.S. tabled a draft treaty on this subject at the ENDC in Geneva. The Soviets followed with their own draft a month later. The issues that most troubled the negotiators were:

---

also bans underground testing "if such explosion causes radioactive debris to be present outside the territorial limits of the state under whose jurisdiction or control such explosion is conducted." Finally, the parties agree not to assist any other states in carrying out the prohibited nuclear explosion.

It is clear that the U.S. does not interpret the treaty as affecting in any way the option of using nuclear weapons in time of war. For the text of the treaty and numerous authoritative documents and statements about it, see United States Arms Control and Disarmament Agency, *Documents on Disarmament, 1963* (Washington: Government Printing Office, 1964; United States Arms Control and Disarmament Agency Publication 24, Released October 1964).

1. Soviet opposition to any nuclear-sharing arguments by the U.S. and its allies;

2. The concern of the non-nuclear powers that the nuclear powers would deprive them of the possibility of developing nuclear capabilities while failing to make significant progress toward arms control and disarmament;

3. Fear of nuclear blackmail, particularly from Red China;

4. Concern over the effect of the treaty on Germany, on NATO, and on EURATOM, since the draft treaties looked to supervision of the agreement by the International Atomic Energy Agency, IAEA, and over the competence and objectivity of IAEA.

Indeed, the whole problem of safeguards was and remains extremely troublesome.

Before proceeding to a discussion of these issues, it is necessary to say a word about the pre-1965 background of this subject, for it does cast light on the German and NATO problems. In 1963 the United States proposed the MLF (Multi-Lateral Force) wherein NATO forces would be integrated on ships from which nuclear weapons could be launched. This was supposed to give the non-nuclear NATO powers, especially Germany, more importance and control in NATO's nuclear defenses. It was also designed to head off France's unilateral, nationalistic initiatives, which others might be tempted to follow. As long as some form of MLF was under consideration, a nonproliferation treaty was blocked by Russian insistence that MLF created a new nuclear entity and therefore constituted proliferation. Late in 1964 President Johnson decided that MLF was not working out as a viable or necessary concept and, in effect, told its advocates in the U.S. government, who were mostly in the Department of State, to forget about it. This opened the way in 1965 for initiatives for a nonproliferation treaty.

In an impressive display of great-power co-operation, the U.S. and U.S.S.R. proceeded in 1967 to replace their competing draft treaties with a single draft treaty, which each submitted independently but with identical texts. The Seventh Annual Report of the U. S. Arms Control and Disarmament Agency states:

At 4:25 A.M. on the morning of January 18, 1968, Adrian S. Fisher, the United States delegate at Geneva, informed the White House that the Co-chairmen (delegates of the U.S. and U.S.S.R.) had reached final agreement, and that a complete draft treaty was to be submitted to the Disarmament Committee later that day.[17]

The Draft Treaty on the Non-Proliferation of Nuclear Weapons was submitted to the ENDC on March 11, 1968. After changes were made in the ENDC to meet remaining objections of the members, the final nonproliferation treaty was placed before the United Nations General Assembly which endorsed the treaty on June 12, 1968. Ninety-four nations voted for the resolution endorsing the treaty. Only four voted against it. Some of the twenty-one abstaining nations subsequently signed the treaty.

As will be shown, every effort was made in the treaty to meet the objections that had existed throughout discussion of this subject. But the one thing that could not be persuasively accomplished through words in a treaty was the fundamental assurance that the two nuclear super-powers were prepared to make real and immediate progress in arms control and disarmament. The Soviets knew this, and they apparently wanted the treaty very badly. Accordingly, on June 27, Soviet Foreign Minister Gromyko announced to the Supreme Soviet that the U.S.S.R., "is ready to enter an exchange of opinions" on "the mutual limitation and later reduction of strategic weapons, both offensive and defensive, including antimissile missiles." Thus an offer by President Johnson in 1964 and again in February 1967, to discuss limitation and reduction of offensive missiles and to halt deployment or plans for deployment of ABMs was accepted. The Treaty on the Non-Proliferation of Nuclear Weapons was signed in Washington and Moscow on July 1, 1968, three days after Gromyko's statement.

There is reason to believe that the prospects of great-power nuclear arms-control talks enhanced prospects for wide adhesion to

[17] 90th Cong. 2d Sess., House of Representatives, Doc. No. 256, *Seventh Annual Report of the U. S. Arms Control and Disarmament Agency*, p. 3.

the long-pending treaty. The non-nuclear nations appeared to feel that the super-powers really meant business.

The purposes of the Non-Proliferation Treaty are:

1. To prevent any further spread of nuclear weapons;

2. To permit the development of nuclear energy for peaceful purposes under international controls that will ensure that nuclear facilities are only used for such purposes and to allay fears that clandestine military nuclear preparations are being carried out;

3. In Mr. Arthur Goldberg's words "to establish a new and solemn treaty obligation, especially upon the nuclear-weapon powers, to press forward the search for nuclear disarmament."[18]

4. To guarantee non-nuclear adherents against nuclear black-mail by commitments made by the United States, the Soviet Union and the United Kingdom through a Security Council Resolution.

In pursuance of these purposes the treaty made the following provisions. In quoting parts of them I will italicize language which was added to the original U.S.-Soviet version. It will be evident that they relate to the concerns mentioned at the outset of this section.

As to the first purpose, prevention of proliferation of nuclear weapons, Article I requires the nuclear-weapons powers to "undertake not to transfer to any recipient whatsoever nuclear weapons or other nuclear explosive devices or control over such weapons or explosive devices directly, or indirectly; and not in any way to assist, encourage, or induce any non-nuclear weapon state to manufacture or otherwise acquire nuclear weapons or other nuclear explosive devices, or control over such weapons or explosive devices."

Article II lays down a complementary obligation for "Each non-nuclear weapon-State Party to This Treaty," not to receive any forms of nuclear-weapons-capabilities transfer of which is prohibited to the nuclear-weapons powers in Article I.

---

[18] Statement by Ambassador Arthur J. Goldberg, United States Representative to the United Nations, in Committee I, on the Draft Treaty on Non-Proliferation of Nuclear Weapons, May 31, 1968 (United States Mission to the United Nations, Press Release USUN-84 (68), May 31, 1968), p. 9.

The second purpose, development of nuclear energy for peaceful purposes under proper internatonal inspection is provided for by:

1.   Article IV stating, "the inalienable right of all the Parties to the Treaty to develop research, production and use of nuclear energy for peaceful purposes without discrimination and in conformity with Articles I and II of this Treaty."

2.   Article V, whereby all parties undertake *"to take appropriate measures to ensure that, in accordance with this Treaty, under appropriate international observation and through appropriate international procedure* potential benefits from any peaceful applications of nuclear explosions will be made available to non-nuclear-weapon States Party to this Treaty on a non-discriminatory basis and that the charge to such Parties for the explosive devices used will be low as possible and exclude any charge for research and development . . ." The italicized portions represent additions and changes made as a result of exchanges between the great nuclear powers and the non-nuclear members of the ENDC.

3.   Article III, by which the non-nuclear states undertake "to accept safeguards, as set forth in an agreement to be negotiated and concluded with the International Atomic Energy Agency . . ." It should be noted, however that the IAEA need not be the international organization responsible for the implementation of the provisions of Article V. While the U.S. would prefer to see IAEA monitorship, there are strong pressures from several nations to establish a new international organization to undertake the implementation of provisions of Articles IV and V. On the other hand, the safeguarding of the provisions of Articles I and II as stated in Article III must be conducted by the IAEA.

The third purpose, progress toward arms control and disarmament, is expressed in Article VI, under which, "Each of the Parties to this Treaty undertakes to pursue negotiations in good faith on effective measures relating to cessation of the nuclear arms race at an early date and to nuclear disarmament under strict and effective international control."

The fourth purpose, a guarantee against nuclear blackmail for the non-nuclear states, is explicitly implied, according to Ambassador Goldberg, by the insertion as a final paragraph in the Preamble to the Treaty that recalls, "that, in accordance with the Charter of the United Nations, States must refrain in their international relations from the threat or use of force against the territorial integrity or political independence of any State, or in any other manner inconsistent with the purposes of the United Nations, and that the establishment and maintenance of international peace and security are to be promoted with the least diversion for armaments of the world's human and economic resources."[19]

Thus at the time this chapter was written, the U.S., U.S.S.R., U.K., and eighty-two others have signed the treaty. Of course it must be ratified in accordance with the constitutional processes of each nation. The main stumbling block appears to concern the fourth issue, nuclear blackmail. The implication of the insertion of the paragraph in the Preamble just quoted is that the U.S., U.S.S.R., and U.K., operating in the context of the Security Council, would enforce the Charter. Since they have not been doing much enforcing, except by unilateral actions, this is quite a questionable kind of "guarantee." We need some gifted improvisor of "scenarios," such as Mr. Herman Kahn, to draft some scenarios of the U.S., U.K., and U.S.S.R. coming in with a threat of nuclear retaliation in the event of aggression by Red China. Obviously if one of the three of them is the alleged aggressor things are complicated. If it is envisaged that the Charter finally operate as it was supposed to because of U.S.-Soviet agreement there is now the technical complication of France's independent and somewhat eccentric behavior, and France has the veto too.

Thus among those who have not signed the Non-Proliferation Treaty are three nations with legitimate concerns about its implications for their security: The Federal Republic of Germany, India, and Japan.

The Federal Republic of Germany, which could quickly become

[19] Goldberg's May 31, 1968 Statement, *op. cit.*, p. 6.

a nuclear power, is reluctant to sign the treaty without strong assurances from the United States that it would guarantee West Germany's security with its nuclear deterrent. But in hearings before the Senate Foreign Relations Committee on July 10 and 11, 1968, Secretary of State Dean Rusk and Deputy Secretary of Defense Paul Nitze flatly denied any U.S. commitment to defend Germany other than under NATO. West Germany is concerned over the possibility that NATO will wither away, leaving her without a U.S. commitment to collective defense. Whether the brutal Soviet intervention into Czechoslovakia will reverse the trend toward a declining NATO remains to be seen. In his July 11, 1968, testimony before the Committee, Nitze argued, however, that a "new federated European state" could "succeed" to the nuclear-weapons-power status of one of the nuclear powers existing on July 1, 1968, e.g., either the United Kingdom or France. Since French policy renders unlikely either a reliable presumption that NATO will continue very long or that a new federated European state, including the United Kingdom, will emerge, the Federal Republic is confronted with the possibility of standing all alone, facing the problems of East Germany and Berlin with only the vague assurances of the Treaty's Preamble about the principles of the Charter which have never been enforced in the way they were intended to be, and, with no nuclear capability. It is not surprising that the Federal Republic has not rushed to sign the treaty. Additionally, elements in German political life fear that the most honest and sincere U.S. security guarantees are inadequate over the long range. Finally, some West Germans have expressed concern over the prospects of industrial sabotage occasioned by foreign inspectors inquiring into West Germany's peaceful nuclear program.

India has equally frustrating dilemmas. While West Germany could easily afford a significant nuclear capability, India could not. India may well require more of an independent nuclear capability than West Germany, since a threat or attack on India is not, in American or most Western eyes, the equivalent of a threat or attack against West Germany. (I realize that I am speaking in terms of comparative catastrophes.) Apparently the majority in every sense of Indian governmental and public opinion is against becoming a nuclear power because of the exorbitant cost in a country desperate for positive allocation of resources, India's stake in promoting the stability of the international political system, a widely shared moral aversion to nuclear weapons, and the pressures of foreign friends on both sides of the Iron Curtain, especially the Soviet Union and the United States. A minority view, apparently of some strength, is that India's security, her status as a world and Asian power, and her interest in decreasing Red China's position as a world and Asian power, all argue for development of an Indian nuclear capability.[20]

As another state that could become a nuclear power before 1970, India faces enormous material and moral problems, as do those who would advise and/or defend her.

If I may be clinical about a profoundly difficult and morally significant subject for a moment, Japan is in an interesting position in this matter. Japan is protected by the U.S. nuclear umbrella against Red Chinese attack, or against any attack. Japan is the third most advanced nation in the world, many claim, in space technology, and has already produced a 9½-ton rocket with a range of 1300 miles. It has a modern delivery system easily within its capacity. Moreover, Japanese restiveness over reliance on undependable supplies of oil from the Middle East has apparently induced a major development of nuclear energy for peaceful purposes. This could be easily applied to military purposes. Japan can go one of two ways, basically. It can continue to rely on the United States for its security, which would have fundamental material, legal, and moral implications for the United States, or it can apparently become a much more plausible version of the model that France sets for itself.

The problems of Japan, as a potential nuclear power, are difficult and complex. Its decisions, on the nonproliferation treaty, on taking on the burdens of self- and regional defense, on the relation of both to pressing the U.S. to leave the Ryukyus and to move back

[20] See Sisir Gupta, "The Indian Dilemma," in Alistair Buchan, ed., *A World of Nuclear Powers?* (Prentice-Hall, 1966), pp. 55–67.

on its strategic posture in the Pacific, may well be critical to a number of issues, most pressing of which is, obviously, Red China as a nuclear power in the 1970s. Ultimately, however, the critical point for Japan, unresolved at the time of writing, appears to be whether and when the U.S. will ratify the treaty.

To sum up, the price for the adhesion of the Federal Republic of Germany, India, and Japan to the Nuclear Non-Proliferation Treaty involves at least a serious effort by the nuclear powers to provide some reassurance concerning nuclear blackmail. This must be squarely faced. No ban on nuclear weapons, no rule of no first use or no cities first *in terms of a "guarantor"* nuclear power, is possible if such nations are to be assured relative security in exchange for attainment of nuclear power which is well within their range. Would it be a terrible crime to "take out" a city in Red China if that nation had already destroyed an Indian city? Thus the highly moral goal of nuclear non-proliferation collides with the inescapable fact that in the present international system, with its present actors and expectations, nuclear war in defense of a threatened or attacked non-nuclear nation is perhaps more of a moral problem than retaliation-in-kind by a nuclear state subjected to a nuclear aggressive attack.

As to the first of the purposes of the Non-Proliferation Treaty, the prevention of the spread of nuclear weapons, the prospects seem fairly good, provisionally, contingent on the possible repercussions of the point four, just discussed. There appears to be little likelihood of deliberate transference of nuclear capabilities or military decisive research facilities, equipment, or information from the principal nuclear powers, i.e., the U.S., U.S.S.R., and U.K. The nagging question, already discussed, is whether nations close to the nuclear-weapons threshold will hold the line. The answer to that question will depend on confidence in the "guarantees" of the nuclear powers, the behavior of Red China, and the the result of U.S.-Soviet arms-control and disarmament negotiations and actions. Here I must recall the realist arms-control caveat that not everything that looks like "progress" in this area will necessarily maintain international

stability. The case of India alone makes this point. India wants
real progress in arms control and disarmament, but it also wants
security, particularly from nuclear blackmail by Red China. Issues
may well arise in which these considerations clash.

Any way one looks at the future, serious material and moral
issues are raised. If the material or moral concerns of the nuclear
great powers place in question their deterrent guarantees, possible
targets of nuclear blackmail or attack will in proportionate measure
face their own material and moral dilemmas. If a new nuclear
power, having gone against the grain of the overwhelming world-
community desire for the prevention of the spread of nuclear weapons,
can only rely on something like General De Gaulle's *aboutistes*
countercity threats, is it materially and morally better off than
before? Indeed, may it not be the case that the most desperate
material and moral issues in this area are those faced by the non-
nuclear or weak nuclear, rather than the strong nuclear powers
who are the point of the most discussions, condemnations, and demands for progress in arms control and disarmament?

I will not discuss the third purpose of the Non-Proliferation Treaty,
encouragement of the right to develop nuclear energy for peaceful
purposes except to the extent that it is relevant to the other purposes
of the Treaty. The key element in this part of the Treaty is the
challenge to the IAEA. Will it be able to monitor peaceful development of nuclear energy and foreclose fears that someone may be
cheating? On the other hand, will the nations possessing the facilities
for development of nuclear energy really co-operate with the IAEA?
In addition to the nations that could produce nuclear weapons before
1970, namely Canada, the Federal Republic of Germany, India,
Israel, Japan, Sweden, and Switzerland, the following nations possess
nuclear reactors: Argentina, Australia, Austria, Belgium, Brazil,
Bulgaria, Colombia, Congo (Kinshasa), Czechoslovakia, Denmark,
Egypt, Finland, East Germany, Greece, Hungary, Indonesia, Italy,
South Korea, Netherlands, Norway, Pakistan, Philippines, Poland,
Portugal, Romania, South Africa, Spain, Taiwan, Thailand, Turkey,

Venezuela, South Vietnam, Yugoslavia. This is a formidable beat
to police!

In this connection it should be noted that among the present non-
signatories to the Treaty are Israel, Sweden, Italy, Belgium, Luxem-
bourg, Spain, South Africa, and Pakistan, all of whom are expected
to sign it at some time but who are in various ways checking
out the operation of the IAEA or some other aspect not, apparently,
having to do with fear of nuclear attack or blackmail, even in the
case of Israel (since Egypt, Syria, Jordan and Iraq had signed the
Treaty). But Brazil appears to be an adamant holdout because it
believes the Treaty does not sufficiently ensure its rights to development of nuclear energy for peaceful use, and Argentina will apparently not sign until Brazil signs.

With respect to the third purpose of the Non-Proliferation Treaty,
there are some propitious signs. As previously noted, the Soviets
undertook prior to the signing of the Treaty to engage in across-
the-board discussions with the U.S. with respect both to offensive
and defensive weapons systems. Kosygin set forth a ten-point agenda
for such discussion at the time that the Treaty was signed in
Moscow, July 1, 1968.[21] It was reported on August 4, 1968 that
U.S.-Soviet talks were likely to begin in the month of August. The
Washington *Post* reported:

> The buttoning up of time and place is now going on in Moscow
> between U. S. Ambassador Llewellyn E. Thompson and Soviet officials.
>   Meanwhile, the State Department's top expert on Soviet arms, Ray-
> mond L. Garthoff, has been summoned back to Washington from his

[21] He called for an effective arms freeze in the Middle East, a convention prohibiting use of nuclear weapons, negotiations on mutual limitation and reduction of strategic missile systems, prohibitons of nuclear-armed bomber flights
outside national frontiers and of nuclear-armed submarine patrols, prohibition
of chemical and biological weapons, elimination of foreign military bases, and
prohibition of military establishments or activities on the ocean floor under
the high seas. Unfortunately, such negotiations, some of which have long been
sought by the U.S. have at time of writing been blocked by the repercussions
of the Soviet intervention in Czechoslovakia.

NATO assignment in Europe to help shape up U.S. position papers with an interdepartmental team headed by Deputy Under Secretary of State Charles E. Bohlen, former U. S. Ambassador to Moscow.[22]

Thus far, then, the nuclear super-powers seem to be taking arms control and disarmament more seriously than they ever have. Perhaps there is now a momentum for progress after all these years. Let us turn now to some of the main outstanding issues in the field, some of which have already been dealt with and some of which remain troublesome. These will be the other issues identified at the outset of this chapter.

The model for progress in arms control and disarmament of the idealist has always struck me as being based on a vision. The vision is one of a world wherein the dynamics of power politics are stopped in place and everyone leaves whatever he is doing to gather around an Athenian forum and work out all problems. My version of the vision is admittedly prejudiced, the more so since I see a Greek forum as an arena for contention as frequently as an arena for unity. Another version of the vision appeared in a U.S. documentary film shortly after the signing of the United Nations Charter. The film showed a carefully selected collection of nice-looking people of all races and nations walking up a grand flight of stair toward a noble building, most of them carrying briefcases. That is the way that arms control and disarmament, as well as pacific settlements of disputes, are supposed to look, according to the vision.

The reality is that arms control and disarmament is an exercise more akin to painting a moving train which is in danger of major or minor wrecks or mishaps at every moment. Formal negotiations and informal attempts to develop rules of the game proceed in a world of constant political activity, much of it bitter and partisan— some of it fanatic—as well as of armed conflict. But, as we have seen in this chapter, somehow progress is made. But future progress,

[22] Warren Unna, "U.S., Russia Expected to Start Missile Talks This Month," the Washington *Post,* August 4, 1968.

even on the Non-Proliferation Treaty, which is signed but not yet sealed and delivered, will depend on many political developments, international and domestic. Just to cite some of the more obvious:

1. The outcome of the Vietnamese conflict and the future position and policy of the United States in the Pacific;

2. Internal developments and the foreign policy of Red China;

3. The status of the Indian-Pakistan disputes;

4. The Middle East situation;

5. Resolution of the problem of divided Germany, of the future of Western Europe, Eastern Europe, and the relation of all these issues with the Soviet Union, especially in the light of the chilling effects of Soviet intervention in Czechoslovakia;

6. Developments in Black Africa.

I saved Africa for last deliberately. There have been threats by African nations to refuse to sign the Nuclear Non-Proliferation Treaty unless the UN or somebody intervened in South Africa against the apartheid regime there. This seems ludicrous to me, but it underscores an important fact. All nations are "for disarmament," but when it comes to signing an agreement they can usually think of many reasons for not doing so or for doing so with crippling reservations, as well as concessions which might be best sought as part of the price of agreement. Hence my skepticism about "sincerity," "mutual trust," and "loyalty."

Next we must address the paradoxical issues of vertical proliferation, principally with respect to anti-ballistic-missile systems, ABMs, and civil defense programs.

Experts term the proliferation of nuclear weapons *horizontal proliferation*. They use the term *vertical proliferation* for measures which increase the strength of an existing nuclear power. The two principal issues involved in vertical proliferation are ABMs and civil defense programs.

ABMs are missiles designed to destroy incoming enemy missiles sufficiently far away from their targets as to negate or greatly decrease their destructiveness. For many years the United States has studied

the feasibility of ABM defenses. These studies tended to find that
no ABM defense system would be very effective against a major
nuclear attack from a nation like the Soviet Union. It was also
concluded that a large-scale ABM system would be inordinately
expensive. The U.S. policy was to emphasize research and development in this field and not actually to deploy ABMs to any great
extent. The Soviets, on the other hand, were test-firing missiles for
an ABM system in late 1966. The U.S. position was to persuade
the Soviets that this was vertical proliferation, which would unnecessarily—and expensively—add a new dimension to the arms race.

Still there were heavy pressures on Defense Secretary McNamara,
who, time and again, had expressed the view just stated. Finally, on
September 19, 1967, McNamara announced that the United States
would start building a five-billion-dollar ABM system over a five-
year period. The U. S. ABM Defense System, designated "Sentinel,"
will consist of:

1. "The PAR . . . a low frequency phased-array radar used
for long-range surveillance, acquisition and tracking." . . . The
MSR . . . a phased-array radar used to control the Sprint and
Spartan interceptors . . ."[23]

2. "The SPARTAN missile (which) as presently designed, will
have three stages and utilize an advanced warhead and should
be able to intercept objects at ranges in excess of several hundred
miles and at exoatmospheric altitudes . . . (McNamara added that,
"we plan to make some further improvements in the Spartan to
enhance its capability against FOBS." The FOBS, Fractional Orbit
Bombardment System is Soviet ICBM system designed to be launched
at a very low trajectory across the northern or southern approaches
to the U.S. and thereby reducing the possibility of timely detection.
"The SPRINT missile (which) is designed to attack incoming warheads after the atmosphere has helped to separate out the ac-
companying decoys, chaff, etc. The missile is capable of climbing

[23] McNamara Statement Before the Senate Armed Services Committee, *op cit.*,
p. 74.

thousands of feet in a few seconds to make intercepts between
5,000 and 100,000 feet at ranges between 15–25 miles . . ."[24] The
system is to be tested in early 1969.

In his September 18, 1967 statement, McNamara stressed that
the "thin" ABM system was only designed as a "prudent" measure
to protect the U.S. against an "irrational" Red Chinese attack. It
would also add to the invulnerability of our second-strike capacity.
He reiterated that it would cost forty billion dollars to construct
a so-called heavy ABM shield of this kind but that the cost was not
the reason for not doing so. The reasons for not deploying a heavy
ABM shield are twofold: (1) it would not give significant protection
against a Soviet attack; only our effective deterrent can give that;
(2) it would accelerate the arms race and the United States does
not want to do that.

Many advocates of arms control and disarmament were dismayed
by what they considered a vertical proliferation implicit in even
"thin" ABM deployment. They considered that a "threshold" had
been crossed, a concept with which we have already had to deal.
Once crossed, it is argued, where does one stop? Will there not be
heavy pressure from the defense community and from worried citizens to extend the system? I, for one, tend to be impressed by the
"threshold" argument. Men much more knowledgeable than I on
this subject, whose judgment I trust, are not. In any event, there
is now reason to hope that the Soviets may accept the original
American position on the ABMs and agree to discontinue deployment of their ABM systems. This was implied by Gromyko's June
27, 1968, statement. One is further encouraged by reports on
August 1, 1968, that the Soviets have been slowing work on and
reappraising deployment of an ABM system around Moscow. It is
an ill wind that blows no good. Ironically one of the reasons for
this slowdown, in the opinion of American specialists, is the per-
formance of Soviet anti-aircraft missiles in Vietnam, which, while
shooting down many U.S. bombers, have let a number through

[24] *Ibid.,* p. 75.

to their targets that would be catastrophic if they were carrying nuclear weapons.

In a sense the larger problem of whether or not to deploy ABMs is that of civil defense. Civil defense sounds inoffensive. But, to the extent that a nuclear power becomes serious in its civil defense preparations potential, adversaries are given reason to question the reasons for this seriousness. Is it possible that the reasons relate to expectations that nuclear war, perhaps initiated by the nation emphasizing civil defense measures, is considered more likely? At present the United States has a civil-defense program which is either criminally ineffective or expressive of a high expectation that nuclear war is close to "unthinkable." Thus the paradoxes of the age of the balance of terror. We turn now to communication among potential adversaries.

Communication and avoidance of accidental war are critical issues today. The essence of the arms-control approach to war and deterrence is that you always keep talking, even when you are fighting or threatening to fight. You keep in communication, particularly, in crisis situations where a wrong interpretation or intelligence estimate of the facts could lead to tragic and unnecessary conflict. For some time the United States sought to establish a so-called "hot line" between the two nations. Typically, in an otherwise polemic speech, Tsarapkin, Acting Soviet Representative at the ENDC, indicated on April 5, 1963 that the Soviets would be willing to discuss establishing a hot line. No doubt their experience in sweating out messages during the Cuban Missile Crisis had influenced their thinking. On June 20, 1963, therefore the U.S. and U.S.S.R. released a "Memorandum of Understanding . . . Regarding the Establishment of a Direct Communications Link," consisting of "two terminal points with telegraphic-teleprinter equipment between which communications shall be directly exchanged . . . One full-time duplex wire telegraph circuit, routed Washington-London-Copenhagen-Stockholm-Moscow, which shall be used for the transmission of messages . . . One full-time duplex radio telegraph circuit, routed Washington-Tangier-Moscow, which shall be used for service communications and for coordination of operations between the two terminal points."

The hot line was used, at the Soviets' initiative, during the 1967 Middle East Crisis, with extremely helpful results.

In addition to formal exchanges, in emergencies through the hot line, normally through diplomatic and other communications, nations "talk" to each other by their behavior, a phenomenon called "signaling" by arms-control experts. Let us take one crisis in which actions were taken which really did not critically alter the political-military situation but which "signaled" intentions unmistakably. In the 1961 Berlin Crisis, President Kennedy wanted to persuade the Soviets and the East German Communists that the U.S. would not back down. Of many actions taken, three were in varying degrees symbolic and of the nature of "signals."

President Kennedy called up a large number of Reserve Units. Most of them were of little or no immediate importance. Some never accomplished anything more than reactivating unused military facilities so that they could have a tolerable place to spend their unhappy year of active duty. But the act of calling up these Reserve Units signaled U.S. seriousness, while at the same time bringing home to millions of affected American families the crisis nature of the situation. Kennedy also had troops moved to and from West Germany and Berlin, to demonstrate that we had a right to do so and that the troops were not hiding in Berlin basements, trembling in fear of Soviet threats. Thirdly, he sent Vice President Johnson to Berlin to show the flag for the United States, the Berliners, and the Communists. None of these moves really affected the political-military balance decisively, but they did signal U.S. determination. It was a good thing for the Soviet Union to receive these and probably other signals. West Berlin is still free, and we did not stumble into World War III to try to keep it free, partly because of international signaling.

One final thought comes to mind on the subject of communications and avoidance of accidental war. Honesty is not only a virtue, it is an invaluable instrument of international politics. Cynics define diplomats as people whose profession it is to lie for their country. Admittedly, diplomats have to conceal or interpret away unpleasant facts. But the closer one comes to the subject of war and deterrence, it seems to me, the closer one comes to appreciation of the truth that honesty is the best policy. Temporary advantages may be achieved through dishonesty in matters concerning war and deterrence. But the risks engendered by an opponent's lack of faith in your honesty are horrendous. For once some rudimentary mutual reliance on honesty concerning critical matters is lost, arms control and disarmament is hopeless. I am not recanting on my skepticism about agreements based on "sincerity," "mutual trust," and "loyalty." I am, rather, saying that the necessary basis for arms control based on mutual expectations of rational behavior founded on shared interests is out of the question if utter loss of confidence in the honesty of an adversary exists.

Another hardy perennial is the subject of *nuclear-free zones.* In the 1950s Poland presented several versions of the so-called Rapacki Plan, which would designate certain areas of Europe as nuclear-free zones in which nuclear weapons could not be placed or utilized. In the Cold War atmosphere of the times and during the height of the ascendancy of the limited-nuclear-war concept in NATO, little serious attention was given to this concept. But gradually areas of the world had been placed by treaty "off limits" insofar as deployment or use of nuclear weapons is concerned. The key treaties effecting these developments are:

1. The Antarctic Treaty of December 1, 1959, while ensuring freedom of scientific investigation in that area, provides that "Antarctica shall be used for peaceful purposes only," and prohibits nuclear explosions in Antarctica. I do not share the euphoria invoked among international lawyers by this treaty, since I have little reason to believe that the nuclear powers were racing to see who could turn Antarctic into a nuclear testing range or battlefield. Nevertheless, I suppose it must be cited as a beginning.

2. The Outer Space Treaty of January 27, 1967 (entered into force October 10, 1967) "prohibits the installation of military bases,

installations, and fortifications, the testing of weapons, and the conduct of maneuvers on the moon and other celestial bodies with
inspection rights to check compliance with the treaty. Of more immediate importance, it prohibits the placing in orbit around the
earth, stationing on celestial bodies, or otherwise stationing in outer
space weapons of mass destruction."[25]

3. The Treaty to Prohibit Nuclear Weapons in Latin America
of February 14, 1967, signed by fourteen nations at Tlatelolco,
Mexico. Under the treaty, the parties agree to use nuclear energy
exclusively for peaceful purposes and to prohibit testing use, manufacture, or acquisition by any means whatsoever of any nuclear
weapons, or the receipt, storage, installation, deployment of such
weapons, within their jurisdiction.

The basic question with respect to all of these nuclear free zone
agreements is, of course, their practical consequences. Have any
likely options concerning testing for, preparing for, and engaging
in nuclear war been significantly affected by them? Are they "steps
in the right direction" or are they steps on trails well removed from
the beaten tracks of possible nuclear confrontations? I, for one,
will be more impressed when nuclear-free zones are established
with respect to areas wherein the testing, threat, or use of nuclear
weapons is a serious practical option. For this reason I am most
impressed by the Latin American Treaty than the others. One has
only to recall the Cuban Missile Crisis to see that this treaty might
well place meaningful constraints on international actors with respect
to situations which are likely. I will gladly concede the field to
speculation on the achievements of the exclusion of nuclear weapons
from Antarctic and Outer Space for the internationalists who are
forever seeking some evidence of progress in arms control and
disarmament. Let us now turn to a subject which I obviously do
not relish, comprehensive blueprints for general and complete disarmament.

[25] Seventh Annual Report of the United States Arms Control and Disarmament
Agency, January 30, 1968, quoted in, United States Arms Control and Disarmament Agency, Documents on Disarmament, 1967, p. 767.

We have seen that, at various times, both the United States and the Soviet Union have deprecated "partial measures" and pushed for comprehensive arms-control and disarmament agreements. We have further seen that, in fact, what progress has been made in this field has been in the realm of partial measures which combine the pragmatic arms control with the legal-disarmament approach. Since 1962, both the United States and the Soviet Union have had outstanding draft treaties for GCD which have been amended several times.

These proposals have in common a similar format. They both envisage three stages of progress from where we now are to a situation of GCD. They both end up with a world that is disarmed except for domestic security forces and whatever forces are required to keep the world orderly after international law and order have finally been achieved. They both envisage an IDO, International Disarmament Organization, inspecting, administering, policing the disarming and disarmed world. They are both vague about the hard questions as to who deals with "revolutions" once the world is happily peaceful, orderly, and disarmed and as to how such revolutions should be dealt with. The main differences between the blueprints seem to be that the Soviets would move faster and more radically—on paper at least—and that they would introduce the IDO in Phase I rather than in Phase II.[26]

Having already expressed my opinion on peaceful alternatives to war as a means of solving international conflicts and disputes, I will concentrate my comments on the U.S. and Soviet GCD draft treaty proposals on the single issue of *enforcement*.

Article 26 of the Soviet draft treaty provides:

1. After the complete abolition of armed forces, the States parties to the Treaty, shall be entitled to have strictly limited contingents of po-

---

[26] A convenient compendium of the two draft treaties and one proposed by Clark and Sohn is to be found in *Current Disarmament Proposals,* as of March 1, 1964 (Preliminary Edition; New York: World Law Fund, 1964). For a serious analysis of these proposals, see the companion volumn, Marion N. McVitty, *A Comparison and Evaluation of Current Disarmament Proposals,* as of March 1, 1964, (New York: World Law Fund, 1964).

lice (militia), equipped with light firearms, to maintain internal order, including the safeguarding of frontiers and the personal security of citizens, and to provide for compliance with their obligations in regard to the maintenance of international peace and security under the United Nations Charter.

The 1962 U.S. draft looks, even at the completion to Stage II, to a similar situation of internal security forces and providing "agreed manpower for the United Nations Peace Force."

I return to the question with which I began this book. What will be the policies of this wonderful United Nations Peace Force? Since the possibility of surreptitious, treacherous development of a nuclear capability will presumably remain possible, will it have a nuclear deterrent? If so, how will its material and moral problems vary from those of a national state? If the United Nations Peace Force is confronted by conventional or unconventional resistance, what means does it use? Are the means it uses, *more or less restrained,* because it is acting for the world community which had finally achieved GCD? There is no indication in the proposals. GCD is at the end of the rainbow. But, as long as man is sinful, is there really a GCD end to the rainbow?

It is difficult to maintain a sense of reality as one works through the Phases of the GCD plans. It is impossible for me to see them even if ever accomplished, as the end of the rainbow. In any event, there is no imminent likelihood of these plans being adopted and executed, and the problem of management of conflict still afflicts us. I shall address them in a chapter on revolution and a chapter on the laws of war.

VII   Revolutionary War and Intervention

Most contemporary discussions of morality and war deal with nuclear war and extreme forms of "total" war of a "conventional nature." Yet, despite the persistent threat of either form of warfare, there have been few conventional wars and no nuclear war since 1945. But in the last twenty-five years there has been widespread and almost continuous, highly destructive, armed conflict. This conflict has taken the form of revolutionary war, often mixed with various forms of indirect aggression and military intervention.

Modern revolutionary war has certain characteristics which obstruct political, military, and normative analyses. Absent early support from outside regular armed forces, e.g., close to one million Chinese Communist "volunteers" in the Korean War, rebellion in a state that has even a very minimal level of governmental organization and military/paramilitary capability cannot challenge the incumbent authorities in the manner of the American patriots at Lexington and Concord, Bunker Hill, and Yorktown. They must use the various forms of guerrilla or "unconventional" warfare.

But it is not sufficient to characterize the majority of contemporary revolutionary wars as "guerrilla" wars. They are more complex. In one way or another, modern revolutionary wars are influenced by revolutionary theories, primarily of Marxist origin, which purport to propound scientifically sound doctrines concerning man, society, and revolutionary change. These doctrines, moreover, claim to be

based on solid and successful experience in violent revolution. This
addition to traditional concepts and techniques of guerrilla warfare
cannot be overemphasized, for it adds complex dimensions both to
the character of revolutionary war and to that of counterinsurgency,
as modern counterrevolutionary theory used to be termed, until it
was labeled "stability operations," or "internal defense." The latest
label for the operation and the problem will race this book to its
final submission to the printers. The labels change, but the answers and the results do not seem to change sufficiently, sad to say.

One of the most important and illusive of these dimensions is that
of perception and intent as well as estimate of capability. Each side
studies the doctrine as well as the behavior of the other and acts as
much, if not more, on the basis of its own doctrine and its reading
of the other's doctrine as it does on its estimate of its own capabilities
and policies, or those of the adversaries. Why has this doctrinaire
confrontation of revolutionary warfare and counterinsurgency dominated the warfronts since 1945? The reasons are quickly recalled:

First, the great powers' mutually recognized need to avoid direct
confrontation has led them to limit their thrusts and counterthrusts
to wars by lesser allies and/or wars of indirect aggression.

Perhaps more relevant to our contemporary predicament, it
seems increasingly evident that much of the existing threats and
engagements in armed conflict do not result from "orders" given to
"puppets" by scheming imperialist great powers. On the contrary,
the increasingly stability-conscious great powers keep getting involved in conflicts cooked up by lesser allies or unwanted friends
over whom they have inadequate control but whom they cannot desert for reasons of prestige, ideology, and global strategy.

Further, direct, conventional military attack across international
borders has proven, as in Korea, to be difficult to accomplish, as well
as impossible to defend in the forums of whatever world law and
opinion exist. Indirect aggression, assistance to essentially indigenous
revolutionary forces, on the other hand, permits the adventuresome
state to have its cake and eat it. Ideological, strategic, and other interests can be furthered by willing allies, especially revolutionaries,

at great expense to the material and moral resources of domestic and foreign counterinsurgents. Meanwhile, the malevolent *éminence grise* looks on innocently, and the world grapples hopelessly with charges of intervention and counterintervention by foreign powers variously enmeshed in the conflict.

Finally, there is the mystique of "revolutionary warfare." This term, usually associated with Mao Tse-tung and his followers, was widely publicized by the French theorists and practitioners of counterinsurgency. They had learned about revolutionary warfare the hard way in Indo-China and tried unsuccessfully to defeat it in Algeria. The saga of "revolutionary warfare" has tended to hypnotize revolutionaries and counterrevolutionaries all over the world. As previously observed, revolutionary warfare in this sense differs from old-fashioned guerrilla warfare, which, after all, is familiar to Americans in terms of the Revoluntionary War and Civil War experiences. This new "revolutionary warfare" purports to have the support of a "scientific" theory behind it. It is rooted in Marxist theory of human nature, society, and revolutionary change. Respect for doctrine breeds a tendency to be almost as much concerned with "going by the book" as with the concrete results obtained. In the unanswerable manner of all doctrinaire approaches to human problems, evidence that the doctrine has not worked is usually met with the assertion that the doctrine was inadequately or insufficiently understood or applied. But the doctrine cannot be wrong. (If it turns out to be, traumas set in.) Thus there exists a mystique of revolutionary warfare.

There are three principal components of the science, doctrine, or, as I prefer to call it, *the mystique,* of *"revolutionary warfare."* They are:

1. Marxist-Leninist-Maoist political and social thought, particularly with respect to revolution;

2. The theory and practice of Marxist-Leninist-Maoist thought as developed in China;

3. The further development of Marxist-Leninist-Maoist theory and practice regarding revolution by Ho Chi Minh, General Giap,

and their Vietnamese followers, and by various other Communists and assorted revolutionary theorists and activists. It is highly doubtful whether Fidel Castro, Che Guevara, the Algerian F.L.N. and other revolutionary leaders were particularly influenced by these doctrines and policy prescriptions. The latter seem, somewhat in the manner of the fascists of the 1920s and 1930s, to have acted first and developed theories afterward. In any event, at the present time, the real focus of attention with respect to both the theory and practice of "revolutionary warfare" is on its home grounds, China and Asia.

The most noteworthy characteristics of the theory and practice of revolutionary war may be summarized as follows:

1. Like some of the fascist theories and patterns of behavior, there is a copious, quasi-hypnotic emphasis on spelling out exactly what is to be done to whom with what results. Consequently, there tends to be an infusion of certainty and inevitability into the revolutionary process which greatly heartens the revolutionaries and alarms their targets.

2. Specifically, revolutionary warfare is divided in theory and practice into three phases:

   a. *Phase 1.* Propaganda, subversion, political "education," of the "oppressed masses," on a selective basis. Occasional acts of terrorism, coldly calculated for symbolic effect. Exploitation of existing grievances and of the shortcomings of the government and the existing political, economic, and social systems.

   b. *Phase 2.* Guerrilla warfare in earnest. Acceleration and expansion of acts of terror calculated to shake confidence in the existing order. A persistent campaign to kill, kidnap, intimidate, or discredit any individual or institution which reflects real and effective concern for the society's problems and indicates some prospect for success in meeting them. When circumstances permit, two types of individuals, the *best* and the *worst,* in the governmental hierarchy, are dragged before isolated communities and executed ceremoniously and hideously, often with their families.

As Phase 2 develops, the revolutionaries seek to drive the incumbent government (and its external allies) to countermeasures of repression and reprisal involving innocent people and thereby increasing resentment and hatred against those in power. The hardliners of the incumbent regime easily fall into this trap. They recommend drastic countermeasures, for example, the practice in South Vietnam of writing off whole areas as "VC controlled," so that indiscriminate attacks against anything that moves or remains standing in such areas are condoned or encouraged.

c. *Phase 3.* Open conventional combat is invited as the government collapses and its armed forces are defeated and demoralized. "Victory" is not usually to be anticipated in the traditional sense but the plight of the incumbent government becomes so desperate, its prospects so poor, and the will to continue of its external elements or allies fails (whether in an imperial metropolitan state such as France after the 1954 Dienbienphu defeat, or the Algerian stalemate, or in the case of a foreign ally, such as the United States, which is racked by profound disagreement over Vietnamese policy). Then "revolutionary war" wins its victory.

Since all of this is very difficult for the counterinsurgents to swallow, the doctrine of revolutionary warfare calls for a "national unity," popular-front coalition government wherein safe and manageable representatives of virtually all segments of the political spectrum are, for at least a time, represented. Those who cease to be safe, manageable, or important—from the viewpoint of the revolutionaries—will predictably be purged in good time for counterrevolutionary tendencies or treasonable contacts with "foreign agents."

The theory is plausible. It is frightening to its potential victims. Its successes and her consequences are well known. Many contemporary Communist societies are more liberal, but the victims of the processes just outlined are not around to enjoy life in those liberalized societies. The mystique takes hold. It gives doctrinaire certainty to the revolutionaries and fascinates their opponents to the point where they tend to become morbid and paralyzed. To shake off the hold of this mystique, the counterrevolutionaries understandably develop a countermystique, that of *counterinsurgency.*

Modern counterinsurgency theory and practice have been dominated by the French. Their main roots are to be found in the French
defeat in Indo-China, the "generous" policy of Ho Chi Minh which
first "educated" and then liberated French prisoners of war, who returned home with an abiding respect for the theory and practice of
"revolutionary war," Asian Communist style, and, in the determination of key French officers to learn how to wage and defeat revolutionary war.

Algeria provided the testing ground, and the French theorists and
practitioners of counterinsurgency did very well in many respects.
They were never defeated militarily, as in Indo-China. Indeed, it is
important to remember that they were not even defeated *militarily*
in Indo-China, they were defeated in one battle, Dienbienphu, which
came at the precise moment when a home front eager to quit the
war and an administration positively committed to end the conflict
within a given time span were promoting international negotiations
to that end. In any event, the French were ahead on points in
Algeria right up to the end. But the French nation tired of the effort
and, under the helpful umbrella of De Gaulle's resurrection, gave
up the struggle and left the Algerians to mismanage themselves. In
the process the counterinsurgency experts tried a little revolutionary
warfare themselves, both in Algeria and in France, but they had little
success. Those who were not jailed or discredited retired to their
studies to write frightening books on revolutionary warfare and counterinsurgency. These books usually predicted that anyone who tried
counterinsurgency against a real revolutionary war opponent was
likely to fail. After all, the French, who know more about this painful subject, and who have tried harder to master it than anyone else,
had failed in counterinsurgency.

About the same time, however, other strands of theory and experience were receiving attention by active or potential counterinsurgency successes of the British in Malaya, the Greeks, and the
loyal forces of the Philippines were noted and carefully studied.

Then the third, and most conclusive development in counterinsurgency theory, practice, and the building of a mystique occurred.

The Americans discovered the subject and took it over. The strategists and experts, whether in the Pentagon, Cambridge, or Santa Monica, who had been pondering "unthinkable" dilemmas of nuclear deterrence, limited nuclear war, nuclear testing, arms control and disarmament, and the like, became interested in counterinsurgency. It became the "in" subject in these circles. Generals and lieutenant colonels concerned with professional advancement flocked to any activity, course, or source of wisdom that dealt with counterinsurgency. To top it off, President Kennedy visited Fort Bragg, lent priority and prestige to the Green Berets, and "special warfare" became the wave of the future.

As the war in Vietnam expanded, as the Berlin and Cuban crises abated, as revolutionary situations in the Third World became more alarming, particularly in the Western Hemisphere, a great number of people realized that *the* subject of professionals in the field of national security, indeed, of international relations, was revolution and counterinsurgency.

The American approach was to cull what seemed positive and relevant from French, British, and other sources, scarcely pausing to ponder the dire predictions and caveats often contained in these sources, and to search for new, uniquely American concepts of counterinsurgency. These came to incude the following:

1. Emphasis on "special forces," possessed of great physical qualities and all sorts of technical skills, who could be deployed in the rough terrain favored by guerrillas, to advise and, if necessary, direct, the counterinsurgency efforts;

2. Emphasis on technological means of reaction to guerrilla activities, e.g., improved communications, helicopters, and overwhelming firepower;

3. Various forms of political-economic-social development ranging from the concept of "nation-building," the most ambitious, to "civic" action, the most marginal and potentially gimmicky. "Nation-building," of which the characterization "presumptuous" may be more accurate than "ambitious," involves across-the-board efforts through aid and advice to build a disorganized, backward society

into a viable political state. "Civic action" stressed encouragement
of initiatives by the incumbent government in a developing nation,
particularly the military, to "help the people help themselves" by
co-operative projects such as road-building, sanitation measures,
building bridges or digging wells, wherein the capabilities and equipment of the government are joined with the active participation of
the people to achieve something that is good in itself and which
also improves the image of the government and the military with
the people. The reason I say that this can be marginal and gimmicky
is that all too often "civic action," whether engaged in by an
indigenous government or an intervening ally of that government, is
spotty, fortuitous, and often takes the form of, in effect, a handout
in the sense that troops move in and build something *for* the people
and then leave rather than taking the form of a truly co-operative
effort.

In any event, the United States government and its advisers and
consultants proceeded to develop its own mystique of counterinsurgency. Special training, maximum exploitation of technological
and scientific know-how, "nation-building," and dedication would
accomplish what the French and others had failed to accomplish
—successful and positive counterinsurgency.

South Vietnam had the misfortune of providing the testing ground
for the mystique of revolutionary warfare, Asian Communist style,
and counterinsurgency, American style. All parties to the conflict
have acknowledged and indeed emphasized this fact. U. S. Army
Chief of Staff Harold K. Johnson summed this up well when he
said:

One of the basic considerations in the communist strategy—and this
one attributed to Lenin—says:
  ". . . and finally we will encircle the last bastion of capitalism—the
United States. We shall not have to attack it, it will fall like overripe
fruit into our hands."
  The Chinese Communist leaders are dedicated to a bellicose, Mao
adaption of the Marxist-Leninist doctrine of world revolution. This

strategy involves the mobilization of the underdeveloped areas of the world—which Chinese communists liken to "rural" areas—against the industrialized and prosperous areas—termed the "urban" areas. Envisioned in this strategy is a so-called "people's war" whose climactic act will be "wars of annihilation."[1]

I believe that it is appropriate to quote General Johnson on this subject because as Deputy Chief of Staff for Operations, U. S. Army and as Chief of Staff, he was a driving force behind the American counterinsurgency effort, based on the analysis of the nature of the threat of revolutionary war as a concept as well as a reality in Vietnam. His reference at the end is to the September 1965 policy statement of Marshal Lin Piao who is both Chairman of the Military Affairs Commission (MAC) of Red China's Central Committee (CC) and its Politburo and Minister of National Defense.[2]

All major Red Chinese newspapers published an article by Lin Piao on September 3, 1965. The key portions of the article for our purposes are summarized in the following excerpts from it:

The countryside, and the countryside alone, can provide the revolutionary bases from which revolutionaries can go forward to a final victory. Precisely for this reason, Comrade Mao Tse-tung's theory of revolutionary base areas in the rural districts and encircling the cities from the countryside is attracting more and more attention among the people in these regions.

Taking the entire globe, if North America and Western Europe can be called "the cities of the world," then Asia, Africa, and Latin America constitute "the rural areas of the world."

Since World War II, the proletarian movement has . . . been temporarily held back in the North American and Western European capi-

[1] Address delivered at the 36th Anniversary Dinner, Honorary Directors Association, Rockhurst College, Kansas City, Missouri, November 7, 1967, *Vital Speeches,* XXXIV, January 1, 1968, p. 169.
[2] General Samuel B. Griffith, "Military Posture and Doctrines," in *China, Vietnam, and the United States,* Highlights of the Hearings of the Senate Foreign Relations Committee (Washington, D.C.: Public Affairs Press, 1966), pp. 61, 63.

talist countries, while the people's revolutionary movement in Asia, Africa, and Latin America has been growing vigorously. In a sense, the contemporary world revolution also presents a picture of the encirclement of cities by the rural areas.[3]

It is equally appropriate to quote General Maxwell D. Taylor, whose role in Vietnam and as an adviser on Vietnam is well known on this point. General Taylor told the Foreign Relations Committee in 1966:

Most [Witnesses before the Committee] have referred to the most recent statement of the Chinese Communist political goals, the Lin Piao position paper of September 1965, but it is variously interpreted. The Aesopian dialogue of the Communist world is not always easy to follow and this effort was clearly designed to achieve several purposes at the same time. In my view it should be taken seriously as a general indication of the objectives and strategy of the Peking wing of the movement. It is based on the assumption that the revolution is not going to occur in the great industrial states, that the Achilles heel of the West is the Third World, that the promotion of wars of national liberation in Africa, Latin America, and Southeast Asia will distract and waste the energies of the Western powers, confuse their peoples and demoralize their leaders. . . .

The main question that leaders and peoples of Southeast Asia are asking is *who is going to win?* Under the above condition it would have seemed that the Chinese brand of Communism was in the ascendant: Lin Piao's statement would have looked like a curtain-raiser rather than noisy bragging or defensive defiance. China is obviously in no position to seek a head-on collision with the United States and is most unlikely to give us the opportunity to declare war on her, but she is quite capable of fostering wars of national liberation wherever opportunities are provided. We have chosen to assist in blocking one of these wars in South Vietnam, under the most unfavorable conditions for us that could have been selected. If we succeed it will not stop the Chinese

[3] "Excerpts from Peking Declaration Urging World 'People's War' to Destroy U.S.," New York *Times,* September 4, 1965, p. 2.

from aiding others to promote similar wars of national liberation; if we fail we do not necessarily lose the whole of Southeast Asia but it would be that much harder to defend.[4]

In like manner, President Johnson said in his San Antonio speech of September 29, 1967:

I cannot tell you tonight . . . with certainty that a Communist conquest of South Vietnam would be followed by a Communist conquest of Southeast Asia. But I do know there are North Vietnamese troops in Laos. I do know there are Communist supported guerrilla forces in Burma, and a Communist coup was barely averted in Indonesia, the fifth largest nation in the world.[5]

It is virtually impossible to say which side came closest to "winning" in this confrontation of mystiques. To begin with, the definition of "winning" such a conflict is extremely difficult, no matter what perspective one brings to the analysis.

Normally, it would seem that the definition of winning such a test case would be simple: the other side quits. But, given the doctrinal and psychological aspects of the two mystiques it is as important to establish *why* one side or the other quits or compromises as it is to cite withdrawal from the conflict. All sides in the Vietnam War introduced so many new elements into the supposed classic revolutionary war-counterinsurgency showdown that it became impossible to view the war in the terms which all parties to the conflict claimed they viewed it at critical moments of commitment and justification. There were so many wars—military, political, economic, social, ethnic, psychological, international public opinion, domestic discord in the intervening states—that it has been hard to say who has been getting the best of which war and when.

To the responsible decision-maker it is undoubtedly an academic question whether it was one side or the other that was primarily responsible for changing the showdown of the two mystiques, rev-

[4] "Containing Aggression," *Ibid.*, pp. 131–33.
[5] *Vital Speeches*, October 15, 1967, Vol. XXXIV, p. 3.

olutionary war and counterinsurgency, into a new and terrible combination of such a confrontation and a large scale conventional conflict. But, conflicting with and ultimately overcoming the pragmatic reactions of the interested parties is the residual legacy of the two mystiques, revolutionary war and counterinsurgency.

This is the kind of reality which the Church and morally concerned persons must face. It is not enough to isolate issues of peace, justice, and order in a revolutionary situation. It is essential to understand what the adversaries perceive to be the stakes in revolutionary wars. There seems to be adequate evidence that both indigenous and external forces committed to revolutionary conflicts are substantially influenced by the broad—open-ended—concept of such conflicts as testing grounds for other conflicts. Future conflicts will be shaped in large measure, according to this view, not only by the outcome but by the conduct of present conflicts and by the extent to which both the outcome and the conduct confirm revolutionary doctrine.

From the American point of view, the classic revolutionary war-counterinsurgency showdown met with bad luck. It may well be that, for very different reasons, this view is held by the other side. Reports from Hanoi and Peking indicate grave differences in both capitals over the strategies imployed by the Vietcong and the Army of North Vietnam. In any event, from the American point of view, just when the spanking new techniques of counterinsurgency were succeeding, our luck ran out. The Buddhists misbehaved to no particular purpose except to divide the country and furnish copy for correspondents and horrible pictures for photographers. Diem's friends and relations outdid themselves in perpetuating attitudes and actions designed to alienate the people, frustrate efforts at "nation-building," and provide ammunition for the press with which to arouse highly critical world opinion. Finally, the military deposed Diem and his regime. However necessary that was and however inadequate Diem's government and conduct of the war, the processes of government and the conduct of the war were obviously set back incalculably by this development and by the predictably inept efforts of the generals to learn on the job how to build a nation while at the same time fighting a highly motivated and effective guerrilla opponent supplied and directed from adjacent Communist states across borders impossible to survey much less to defend.

At the point when defeat appeared imminent, the United States changed the nature of its intervention and thereby the nature of the confrontation. The occasion for this change was the direct attack by the Vietcong on U.S. advisory forces at Pleiku. This attack was a breach of the tacit rules of the game under which all parties to the conflict, each for its own reasons, acted as though the U.S. was not a direct party to the conflict. Whatever the legal or moral pros and cons of this decision, the showdown of the two mystiques was at an end. A new test case began in which it would be determined whether Maoist theory and practice of revolutionary warfare supported by external, "fraternal," support amounting under international law, in my view, to indirect aggression could be overcome by massive military intervention of a major power on behalf of the target state and its incumbent government. Revolutionary warfare and counter-insurgency remained major problems for all sides, but the Vietnam War after 1965 became a new kind of war for which there are no precedents, not even within the "Stage 3" experience of past revolutionary wars.

There are many lessons to be learned from these experiences in Vietnam and elsewhere. Among the material lessons are the following:

1. Counterinsurgency requires security. There must be security for the people, as far as possible. There must especially be security for the leaders of "revolutionary development" teams and for the civil servants of the government, above all for the good, effective, respected civil servants. *They* are the prime targets of the guerrillas.

2. Counterinsurgency requires means of combat that are discriminatory and controllable. A platoon of skilled combat troops operating with good intelligence is worth a dozen helicopters capable of enormous—but often indiscriminate—firepower, or a bomber,

or long-range artillery. It still remains difficult to avoid killing
civilians, especially when you cannot tell who the noncombatants
are or where they are, or if the enemy deliberately hides among
them. But one of the gravest mistakes made in Vietnam—and, for
that matter, in the Dominican Republic—has been misuse of firepower.

3. Conventional wisdom has it that the key to counterinsurgency
is winning "the hearts and minds" of the people. In a revolutionary
situation, it seems to me, that this is nonsense. All that you do, once
you provide security and show by your policies and their successes
that you—meaning the incumbent government and its allies—
intend to and are probably able to last out the conflict, is to try to
improve the lot of the people and to make needed reforms where
necessary. Whether, in the process, you will "win" their "hearts
and minds" is something that the future will reveal.

There are also moral lessons to be learned from recent interventions in revolutionary wars. They cut across the stale clichés of the
"Dove-Hawk" debate. I would contend that they are the following:

1. Intervention is morally irresponsible if there is not an intention
on the part of the intervening government, and a reasonable belief
that the public shares this intention, to continue the intervention as
long as there is reasonable hope for success. This takes us back to
our discussion of the domestic political prerequisites for limited war.
They are very demanding. If the decision-maker does not have good
reason to believe—and of course this is a difficult prudential judgment—that the home front will stay the course, he should not intervene, even if he thinks that intervention is either morally required
or permissible. This is the more so because we have increasing
evidence that intervention, no matter how well-intentioned and what
form it takes, is extremely difficult and frustrating.

2. The revolutionary-war-counterinsurgency war is a dirty war.
Critics of the war in Vietnam say that it is by far the dirtiest war in
which the United States has ever engaged. Of course it is; that was
unavoidable, given the nature of such wars. The moral and legal
problems, which will be further discussed in the next chapter, is to

try to mitigate the nastiness of this, and all other, forms of armed conflict.

There is little reason to believe that "peace will break out" if the war in Vietnam is somehow ended. This is a revolutionary age. There will be more revolutions, and the moral issues raised by violent revolution require continuous study and debate. As Christians and as human beings we cannot turn and look away when societies are torn by violent revolutions. Let us consider some of these issues.

The moral and legal categories relevant to violent revolution and counterinsurgency appear to be substantially the same as those applicable to international war, namely:

1. Recourse to violent revolution and resistance to revolution: the moral decision;

2. The morality of the means employed by revolutionaries and counterinsurgents.

This chapter will emphasize the first question, the decision to revolt or to suppress revolution. It will, however, be necessary to mention in general terms the second category, since one cannot evaluate the legitimacy of a claim on either side without considering in general terms the means that will probably be used by both sides. In Chapter VIII, I will consider in greater detail the legal and moral issues raised by contemporary revolutionary war, together with the overlapping issues of the law of war generally applicable to all forms of warfare.

I do not pretend to have mastered the contemporary Protestant literature on morality and revolution which seems to be considerable and increasing and which, on the whole, seems sympathetic to revolutionaries in societies wherein governments are oppressive or unresponsive to the needs and rights of the people.[6] As remarked in Chapter II, Catholic thought is in some disarray on this subject.

[6] For example, in June 1968, the general board of the National Council of Churches issued a statement saying: "We recognize that when justice cannot be secured either through action within the existing structure or through civil disobedience, an increasing number of Christians may feel called to seek justice through resistance or revolution." At the same time, the board of the NCC called for, "a study . . . of the alternatives of resistance and revolution in the light of Christian principles and experience."

The official teaching of the Church deplores the possibility of revolution and condemns guerrilla warfare without addressing the question what oppressed peoples are to do when their government, or indeed, the entrenched institutions of the society, deny them the rights which the Church says they should have. It appears to me to be a field which is relatively independent of normative analyses.

But if official Church thought is comparatively sparse and negative on revolution, there has been a different reaction among post-Vatican II theologians and ethicists. Many influential moralists seem to place the presumptions in favor of revolutionary change. This applies not only to violent revolutions in foreign countries but to revolutions in seminaries, colleges, political parties—almost anywhere. As usual, the realists end up in the middle. I would argue, in terms close to traditional natural law, the following general principles:

1. The right of revolution is one of the most fundamental of human rights, ranking with that of self-defense. When a society manifestly fails to provide the rights and necessities for which societies are formed and, on the contrary, oppresses its people, they have a right to overthrow that society.

2. But, much as a just war must give promise of probable good results exceeding probable evil, a violent revolution should be undertaken only when good—even if only very distant and problematical—seems likely to be proportionate to the foreseeable evil resulting from a violent revolution. However, just as a war of legitimate self-defense may be morally undertaken with the odds desperately against it, revolt against attack by the government on a segment of the population, as in the case of genocide, certainly is justified, as in the tragic cases in some African states, where the physical extinction or reduction to a sub-human condition is the official government policy.

3. Not all change, violent or nonviolent, is good in itself. Evident? No, not in the present state of revolutionary euphoria all over the world. Not all change is good, and existing orders are not necessarily unbearably bad or manifestly immoral, even if they are

distressingly imperfect. Moreover, the mere destruction of that which is unjust or imperfect does not constitute a sufficient goal or justification for violent revolution. Revolutionaries like to disclaim this as their real goal, but, if pressed, often argue that you need not have a better solution if you believe something is bad. It is sufficient to believe that it is bad and must be torn down. This is surely a highly prevalent view in the black ghettos, on college campuses, in the peace movement. I cannot accept this view. It is not enough to know that the state of affairs in a society may justify violent revolution. One must know what chances the revolution has, who will control it, who will emerge to conduct public affairs if it is successful, and what life will probably be like in the new state.

With these principles in mind, consider the moral decision to embark on violent revolution. It cannot be too strongly emphasized that this decision must take cognizance of factors which come very close to terming its form and outcome. They are:

1. The geography of the country, the advantages and disadvantages it provides for revolutionaries and for counterinsurgents;

2. The respective strengths and characteristics of the revolutionary forces and those of the incumbent government;

3. The will and staying power of each side;

4. The prospects on one side for outside assistance, particularly from an adjacent state or from organizations able to operate within adjacent states, or otherwise able to send personnel and materiel.

There are many factors involved in the success or failure of a revolution, but it will be noted that the principal cases of counterinsurgent victories against formidable revolutionary forces have been:

1. In Greece, after Yugoslavia broke with Moscow and ceased to be the chief base for assistance to the Greek Communists, who then made the mistake of moving into a Phase III conventional war challenge, which the Greek government, with American aid, crushed;

2. Malaya, where there was no adjacent Communist state, and

where the core of the revolution was made up of persons of Chinese origin, therefore more distinguishable and more readily cut off from the rest of the population;

3. The Philippines, where the Huk rebels were not in a position to receive foreign aid.

Note that despite ten years of threats and organization of revolutionary activity in Havana, there has been no Communist-inspired supported revolution in an area which obviously provides many occasions for revolution and many propitious locales and situations. It is significant that Che Guevara died in a ridiculous revolutionary foray in Bolivia. How does one rig a Ho Chi Minh trail to Bolivia? In passing, I may say that I consider the U.S. charges of Communist foreign intervention in the Dominican Republic in 1965 to be patently wrong, if by intervention one means a large-scale and continuing interference in a revolution by a foreign state or organization operating from a foreign state.

It may seem odd to omit from this list of basic factors the disposition of the generality of the population. In some cases this factor might indeed be important if not determinative. But most modern revolutionary wars are won or lost by a minority of dedicated revolutionaries who manipulate, terrorize, or skillfully mobilize the general population. In the process, if they are successful, they cause the society to collapse or suffer intolerable dislocation. They do *not* necessarily or even usually "win the hearts and minds of the people." They persuade the people by every means, fair or foul, that *they,* the revolutionaries, will be the future rulers of the society and that the incumbent regime, its supporters, and its collaborators are doomed. This is not to say that the generality of the population approves of or supports the incumbent regime. It is to say that most modern revolutions are not popular in leadership. The revolutionary situation exists and is exploited by the revolutionary elite, as Lenin explained and demonstrated fifty years ago.

In brief, if the revolutionaries' estimate of the situation is accurate and encouraging to their prospects in terms of the factors listed and if the good of revolutionary change seems probably to exceed the foreseeable evil of revolutionary strife, the decision to make a violent revolution would appear to be morally tenable—if violent revolution under most modern conditions can be morally tenable, which I think is the case.

It must be emphasized, however, that, even more than in the case of a nation contemplating recourse to what it considers a just war, the moral or just violent revolution must be viewed in terms of very restrictive alternatives. Concretely, it is almost out of the question for a modern revolutionary force, even in a very primitive and badly run state, to aspire to an open, "fair" trial by combat with the incumbent regime. This is substantially the case whether the revolution occurs in Vietnam or Nigeria or Detroit. As previously discussed, the principal, tried and proven, means of violent revolution are:

1. *Terror*—destroying the structure and substance of a society by sheer terror; making life unlivable for a substantial majority of the population, the government, and all essential co-operating elements of society.

2. *Destruction of progressive elements*—destruction or obstruction of every individual, program, or institution which seems to respond to the needs of the society and, therefore, to imperil the claims of the revolutionaries that progress within the existing system is impossible and that progress will only come after the system is overthrown.

3. *Successful manipulation of "attentisme"*—coercing and persuading the uncommitted or faltering majority of the population, those who in Edgar Furniss' studies of French counterinsurgency he called *attentistes,* those who are watching and waiting to see who is going to prevail ultimately, that the rebels will outlast and succeed incumbent regime.[7]

[7] Edgar S. Furniss, Jr., *Counterinsurgency: Some Problems and Implications,* with commentary by Charles Burton Marshall and William V. O'Brien (Ethics and Foreign Policy Series; New York: Council on Religion and International Affairs, 1966). Furniss, who died shortly after publication of this analysis, was one of the best-informed and most insightful American experts on France, its modern internal and external problems, and, especially, on the trials of the contemporary French Army.

What about nonviolence? Gandhi had some success with non-violence, principally because the British were tolerably civilized in their treatment of his resistance. The civil rights movement succeeded in the United States to the extent that it has, because it sought to force subordinate entities within a system of law to obey the law and because it was backed up at every critical turn by armed force. Try nonviolent resistance to overthrow the government in the states that are ripe for revolutionary change and you will see bodies that are dragged away by the police and military in limp fashion because they have "gone limp." They probably will either be permanently limp or close to it.

At this point it is appropriate to move the focus from the means to the ends. What *is* the end of modern violent revolution? Is it not something like this: A chance for fundamental change for the better purchased at a very great price. Modern revolution exacts a great price. What are some of the costs of violent revolution, aside from the necessity of using some of the odious means characteristic of modern revolutionary wars? They seem to include:

1. Co-operation with and extension of rewards to radicals of the left, right, or nihilistic undefinables, depending on the composition of the society and the way the revolution unfolds;

2. Consequently, agreement to coalition and popular-front revolutionary governments, the hazards and short tenure of which are notorious;

3. The real possibility of a takeover by totalitarian or other elements who step into the power vacuum caused by the revolution.

If you are optimistic you will hope that courage and skill in combat will obviate the need for the dirtier means of revolutionary war, that the positive elements in your revolutionary program *will* win the hearts and minds of enough people so that your revolution will succeed with a minimum of evil-doing. Then you will hope that bad elements in the revolutionary movement can be handled and that reasonable and efficient men will take over the government. But in a real violent revolution, one involving fundamental change, not merely replacement of personnel or changes within the prevailing system, is it not the moderate, the liberal, who usually loses out, and the radical or charismatic demagogue who usually ends up on top? It need not always be so, but these are some of the problems that Christian and other well-intentioned enthusiasts for revolutionary change will have to ponder.

We must also ponder the moral responsibilities and dilemmas of counterinsurgency. They are less obvious but no less difficult than those of violent revolution. Viewed morally, and in terms of fundamental human compassion, there is at least as much agony in accepting the challenge of a violent revolution as in deciding to wage one. Only the most dense or heartless ruler could be insensitive to the stakes and costs of civil war. Just as the revolutionary must attempt to calculate the probable cost of violent change, so the defender of the existing order must calculate honestly both the prospects for necessary nonviolent change and the cost of repression of efforts at revolutionary change.

If the revolutionary begins with the assumption that the system as it exists is incapable of adequate change and must be destroyed, the morally responsible adherent of the system sees the good in it, the potential in it, the likely results of an internal conflict which will tear it apart. He sees the possibility of destruction of that which is good and worth preserving, what the chances are for change within the system. He sees and fears not only the means that will be used by the revolutionaries but also the consequences of their violent rejection of the system. He too must make his decision. If it is a decision for defense of the system, even a greatly changed version of it, his first priority is security. As remarked with respect to the lessons of Vietnam, you cannot have "nation-building" and internal development without security. Without security, counterinsurgency is doomed.

Yet, this is the dilemma, material and moral. Excessive concern over security has time and again retarded or obstructed positive measures of internal development. Specifically, security may mean rough treatment by patrols in areas where enemy activity has occurred or is suspected, deprival of fundamental civil rights, relatively indiscriminate measures against segments of the population, reprisals against whole "rebel controlled" areas, and far-reaching population-control measures, displacing people and placing them in often unpleasant camps.

Such problems can be identified, controlled to some extent, minimized. But they are endemic to counterinsurgency and, to some extent, will predictably arise. When a government accepts the challenge of violent revolutionary activity, it takes on these problems. When another government comes to the assistance of any side in a revolutionary war it also assumes that side's problems. It is to this problem area that we now turn.

Intervention in a civil war raises serious questions of international law and morality. They concern both the permissibility of the intervention if it constitutes the threat or use of armed force and the permissibility of the means used both by the party to the internal conflict aided and the interventor. Since many of these issues are both legal and moral, I will deal with them together under the rubric *legal-moral*. There are other issues which are not covered by international law but which are serious moral issues. They will be dealt with at the end of the chapter. As in other sections of the chapter I will concentrate on the *decision* to act, referring to the *means* only in a general way, since we shall discuss that subject in the next chapter.

The legal-moral issues of intervention may be divided into two categories, which are readily distinguished logically but devilishly difficult to divide in practical analyses:

1. Intervention without direct, overt recourse to armed force;
2. Direct military intervention with armed force.

A state may intervene in a revolutionary situation or war (for, we must remember, revolutionary war is a *process* in which it is difficult to say at what point preparation for revolutionary war becomes revolutionary war) by use of the political, psychological-ideological, or economic instruments of foreign policy, or, generally, some combination of all of them. The use of such instruments may originate at home or anyplace in the world. When it originates within a society vulnerable to or beset by violent revolution, such activity generally takes the form of aid, both in the form of materiel and money and personnel rendering technical assistance. The latter varies greatly with respect to the degree of interference by the foreign state in the nation receiving the aid. The problems of deciding whether such aid is legally and/or morally permissible are complex. Some of the problems confronting normative analysis are the following:

1. The problem of deciding *when* there is a revolutionary war situation and when foreign aid, which, in principle is not only morally desirable but a duty for those who can afford it, should be viewed primarily as a contribution to suppression of a possibly just revolution and when it should be judged as legitimate assistance to a developing nation through its incumbent government.

2. The problem of whether such assistance to an incumbent regime violates international law once it is reasonably clear that a revolutionary war is in progress. This is a more difficult legal question than many experts who participate in war-peace debates admit. Moreover, even if there is an international law presumption against intervention in a civil war, there is the possibility that appeal might properly be made to a higher moral right, e.g., in the case of massive injustice or genocide by one side or another.

3. The problem establishing that covert assistance, including covert armed force, violence, subversion and the like, is extended to either side in a revolutionary war. If directed against an incumbent regime, particularly when combined with other, non-military coercive policies may constitute "indirect aggression" under international law. If, on the other hand, it can be demonstrated that such activity is necessary and proper in support of a morally justifiable revolution, then we have a collision of legal and moral norms. In any case, it should be recognized that international law tends to place order and non-recourse to armed force over justice as a priority in an imperfect world public order. International law encourages acceptance of governments that exist rather than their overthrow to produce governments which, by some moral or ideological criteria, "ought to be."

Let us look at these three problems concretely. Much of the de-

mand for a "theology of revolution" concerns Latin America. In
Latin America the United States has a twofold counterinsurgency
policy:

First, it extends aid under the Alliance for Progress. This aid is
primarily not military nor does it take the form of assistance that
is really motivated by and related to political-military objectives, except in the broadest sense that improved government and political-
economic-social development in Latin America should preclude violent revolution, often Communist-related, inimical to the strategic
interests of the United States.

Second, it extends explicitly military aid through military techni-
cal-assistance, especially concerning counterinsurgency and civic action operations to incumbent regimes.

Is this legal? Is it moral? Obviously the questions are too broad,
but they are a valid starting point. Certainly one could not say that
the vast majority of U.S. programs under the Alliance for Progress
variety are either illegal or immoral. Certainly, many of the recipients of such programs are governed by regimes that are far from
democratic or efficient. Certainly the political, economic, and social
systems in many of these nations are and have been unfair and
slow to change. But, to the extent that U.S. assistance encourages
change and provides leverage with which to press for reform, it certainly does not violate either international law or morality. Indeed,
on more than one occasion, suspension or withdrawal of aid has been
used, together with non-recognition, as a practical means of putting
pressure on a regime or a new military junta to follow more enlightened policies, for example, after the military coup in Peru in
1963.

But suppose more liberal elements, naturally in association with
leftist elements that are understandably unpalatable to the U.S. government, actually appear to be mounting a revolution that will bring
fundamental change, definitely for the better, but with the risks
earlier noted about modern violent revolution. In my view, international law and morality may split here. Legally, I see no reason
for not continuing assistance, particularly of a positive, essentially

non-military character, even though, admittedly, *all* assistance to a threatened government tends to enhance its military capacity to sustain itself. Morally, though, it might well be the case that all aid, except straight-out humanitarian aid (emergency food, medicine, etc.) should be discontinued while the unhappy nation fights its revolutionary war, regardless of U.S. strategic interests.

Thus, as to the first question, non-military aid of the Alliance for Progress is certainly legal as long as a government is in power, even if threatened by a revolutionary war. Primarily military aid I would term participation in the war and, once it is determined that there is war, such aid would be assimilable into the subject next to be discussed, military intervention.

As to the second question, I dispute the position that international law prohibits intervention in a civil war. If it does, then it seems to me, all assistance, military or not, must cease. The exception would be a higher law right to prevent genocide. I would not hesitate, for example, to justify intervention by any means if, as I hope is not the case, Nigeria really followed a policy of genocide in Biafra. I would urge measures to protect tribal or other group targets of such policies. At the present time, the nations of the world have been all too prone to wring their hands over the starvation and suffering caused by Nigeria's blockade of Biafra. Nigeria is not an invulnerable state and a great number of non-military means could be used to change the state of affairs in that unhappy country.

However, this is a very extreme case. The point that I would like to leave foremost in the reader's mind is that there is an overlap between "military" intervention and aid and "non-military," that legally the cut-off point is a determination that the militarily relevant aid or intervention amounts to recourse to armed force in the sense of the UN system. Morally, the crucial question is whether or not the aid or intervention interfered with the natural right of a society to resolve fundamental differences by that most unfortunate of all means, civil war.

As far as the third problem identified, thus far, indirect aggression, if the use of primarily non-military means does in fact, initiate, direct, sustain a revolutionary war, it is the legal and moral equivalent of aggression and gives rise to the legal and moral right of coming to the defense of the target government. The U.S. engaged in indirect aggression against a left-leaning regime in Guatemala in 1954. This was illegal and its morality rests on determinations I cannot make as the actual threat of Communist domination, what that would have meant to that nation, and the alternatives, which recently have not been inspiring. Thus, to make my point again, it is perfectly legal for the U.S. to give both non-military and military assistance to the incumbent government of Guatemala but it may very well be immoral, or come to a point where it is immoral. One does not have to be a renegade missionary to see that.

As to recourse to armed force in the form of military intervention in a civil revolutionary war, the key concept is collective self-defense. If either an overt military aggression or indirect aggression as just described occurs, the right of collective self-defense goes into operation legally and morally. There is obviously a classic case, the Vietnam conflict. Here both the U.S. and the Communists claim that the other was guilty of military intervention amounting to aggression and that its intervention constituted counterintervention, justified legally and morally as collective self-defense.

This matter has been so thoroughly and acrimoniously debated that it is best to state my view of the legal and moral case in this conflict. Basically, I accept the U.S. version. I believe that it was the case that the civil war was organized, directed, supplied, and initiated by North Vietnam and was therefore aggression. The United States counterintervened, first by primarily military assistance and advisory activity that became more and more involved in participation in combat, then in open deployment of U.S. forces. Why did the U.S. do these things? As I suggested earlier, it did them because it wanted a forward posture in Asia; it believed the revolutionary war supported by indirect aggression mystique; it found the South Vietnamese more willing to fight than most of their neighbors; and so it chose to use its rights under Article 51 of the UN charter and under the natural right of individual and collective self-defense to assist the government of South Vietnam.

To those who say there is no South Vietnam I say that existence as an independent nation for fifteen years, most of them years of conflict, treatment as an independent nation by most nations of the world, including the Soviet Union, which once proposed the Republic of Vietnam, along with North Vietnam, for membership in the United Nations, and a number of other facts qualifies South Vietnam for statehood and the rights of statehood and the legal and moral right of collective defense with states whose policies lead them to exercise their legal and moral rights of collective defense.

This does not mean that the United States was not more concerned with its strategic interests as it saw them than in the rights of the South Vietnamese, or that it was terribly worried about democracy in South Vietnam (although this point does not impress me one way or the other, since democracy is not common in the world), or that it was a prudent policy, or that at some point in time the war may not have become too disproportionately destructive to the people of Vietnam to justify its continuance. I merely state that it is a matter of the most common form of modern conflict, revolutionary civil war either precipitated or heavily abetted by indirect aggression being met by, first, partial military assistance measures and general aid, then, major military intervention. Whatever one's interpretations of facts or intentions, it is vital that the reasonableness of the U.S. rationale be granted, if, for the sake of argument, one hypothesizes a South Vietnamese state with a right of individual and collective self-defense.

Mine is hardly a comfortable position, given the international and domestic trends of the times concerning Vietnam. But it is appropriate for a diehard defender of the U.S. intervention in Vietnam to go on to make the point that if there is *no* plausible basis for contending that a revolutionary war is made possible by indirect aggression, then there is no legal right to intervene with armed force as the United States did in the 1965 Dominican revolution. This was clearly illegal, since by no stretch of the imagination could the presence of fewer than a hundred odds and ends of Communist and other leftist activists in a deeply indigenous revolution be likened to the initiative and support of North Vietnam for the N.L.F. in South Vietnam. In other words, my model for that kind of military intervention justified legally and morally as collective self-defense against indirect aggression against an ally the U.S. version of the Vietnam War.

This model is useful—if one still wants to stay in the business of military intervention—for areas such as Asia. It could be applied, not to Communist indirect aggression but to indirect aggression and revolutionary warfare in the Middle East, e.g., Egypt in Yemen, and in Africa, e.g., a number of African states in the Congo when Tshombe was Prime Minister. But in the area where U.S. military and other intervention in revolutionary war is most likely, the model is inapplicable. Cuba has turned out to be a highly overrated staging area for subversion and revolution. Unless some fairly powerful Latin American country becomes Communist or adopts some home-grown revolutionary crusade policy and manages to influence events in adjacent states as North Vietnam and Red China do in Asia, the Vietnam model in inapplicable to Latin America, and the Dominican model is, in my view, illegal, possibly immoral, and very bad policy. Concentration on the agonies of Vietnam must not delay a profound consideration of the problems implicit in this state of affairs by responsible decision-makers and citizens.

There remains the tricky business of justifying support of revolutionary elites who, as is so often the case, may or may not represent a "true" revolutionary spirit in a country, but are, by *your* standards just and right in their desire to overthrow a regime, for example, the Bay of Pigs affair. Clearly the Bay of Pigs invasion, mounted, supported, timed by the United States was an illegal act of aggression, even if it had serious moral considerations supporting it. I will not linger on this theme, since I trust that the United States has learned that overt support to initiation of a revolutionary war is, whatever its moral merits, something at which the United States is not very adept and had better pass by.

There remain some moral issues that are beyond the realm of international law as I interpret it. They are:

1. The impact of revolution and intervention on the revolutionary society;
2. The effects of the experience of intervention in the home society of the intervening state;
3. The effects of intervention on regional and global peace and order.

Any intervention of the kinds discussed disrupts the values and behavior patterns of the tormented society wherein the conflict rages. Although there is no necessary, logical reason why intervention, including beneficent, self-sacrificing intervention, should do more harm than good, the record appears to indicate that intervention has profound, often negative, effects, regardless of the intentions of the intervening party. If the interventor of today, like the colonialist before him, cannot leave "somthing of value" behind him after he has departed, something proportionate to the costs of uprooted institutions, battle-scarred areas, dislocated and often perverted patterns of life, it is difficult to defend a major intervention on moral grounds.

I think that the strongest part of the U.S. defense of its intervention in Vietnam is the proposition that this intervention may prevent many more of the same. The weakest part is that it is all for the good of the South Vietnamese people. At best, their sacrifice will help others, just as the sacrifice of some victims of Nazi aggression helped others. At worst, perhaps, they should have been left to the mercies of the Communists and be done with it.

Moreover, the more ambitious the intervention, the more likely it is that it will have deep repercussions in the domestic society of the intervening state. The French experienced this; the Americans are now experiencing it. The conflict of will and commitments fundamental to intervention in revolutionary war strains all of the societies concerned. In brief, when the decision is made to intervene, or to continue or increase intervention, or to withdraw from interventionary activity, a moral calculation has to be made as to the effects of the decision on the intervening society as well as on that society in which the intervention is contemplated. These effects must be measured against the prospects for "success" in the endeavor.

Finally, intervention in revolutionary war affects the peace and order of the area wherein it occurs and, usually, that of the whole world. It might be thought that this is a legal-moral, rather than a moral, issue, as the two categories have been distinguished here. But I myself doubt that there is an international law governing either a right to intervene or refrain from intervention in a revolutionary war, not because of the rights of one nation, but because of the rights and security of whole regions and ultimately of the world public order. "World policeman" is not a term welcome in Washington these days, but if, as is the case, there are no world policemen, and, seldom, regional policemen, there is a need for volunteers for such roles.

This tends to run counter to what I have been saying about the feasibility of intervention, I know. This is a real dilemma in a subject beset with dilemmas. Whatever the practical, legal, and moral presumptions against intervention in revolutionary wars, it is the lot of great powers, and perhaps of other powers, as well as international organizations, to face the prospect of engaging in such interventions. This is the case because revolutionary war continues and it is not usually a strictly domestic problem. It threatens regional and world peace and order. But it can also contribute to both and to the achievement of a more just world. Power engenders responsibility. In a decentralized world public order, those who have power will sometimes be forced to intervene in dangerous, ambiguous, revolutionary situations, or forbear their power and responsibility. There is always isolationism or Fortress America. But in the absence of a world authority, or even much progress toward regional authorities, when great-power force is needed to sustain order and, if possible, justice, with limited means, can anything be more irresponsible or immoral than an isolationist policy based on dedication to total nonintervention?

Thus the dilemmas: intervention is abnormal but frequent, often selfish but often self-sacrificing, difficult to accomplish, inclined to disrupt more than it builds, particularly when carried out in a patient, limited manner difficult to explain to the home front and to find support for over the long haul, the source of domestic discord that can be crippling, contrary to the theoretical assumptions of international law and organization—*and* a continuing practical possibility which cannot be responsibly ignored.

VIII   The Laws of War

Whether viewed in primarily legal or moral terms there are certain basic concepts and principles governing the conduct of war. The *basic concepts* are the following:

1.   War must be fought with the realization that enemy forces and noncombatants are human beings possessing rights which must be respected even in the heat of war.

2.   The ultimate end of war is a just and lasting peace. Measures not essential to the achievement of reasonable end by permissible means and even seemingly essential military measures which threaten to defeat this ultimate end are prohibited.

3.   The purpose of the positive laws of war is to give concrete content to the foregoing concepts. Nations, their leaders, responsible commanders, and citizens of belligerent nations of groups are legally and morally obliged to develop the laws of war toward the accomplishment of this purpose. Neglect of the laws of war as long as war remains a feature of international relations means neglect of millions of victims of war as well as neglect of the goals of international peace and justice.

The basic principles of the laws of war are:

1. The principle of legitimate military necessity, which justifies all measures proportionate to legitimate military ends, provided that they conform to the laws of war and the natural law (the concept of the principle of humanity could be substituted for natural

law), when taken on the decision of a responsible commander, subject to judicial or other review.

There are two corollaries of the principle of legitimate military necessity:

a. Superfluous suffering and unnecessary destruction are prohibited.

b. There is no open-ended "right of necessity" which justifies violation of the laws of war on grounds of alleged great need, desperation, or "higher value."

2. The principle of immunity from attack of unresisting enemy nations, whether noncombatants or prisoners of war who have surrendered, although rendered difficult of application by the character of modern war, remains valid and must be applied to the greatest possible extent.

3. The principle of responsibility of belligerents to provide the necessities of life, governmental and/or administrative services, law, order and protection to enemy nationals under their control, whether in the relationship of Detaining Power to prisoners of war or of belligerent occupant of occupied territories is the most widely recognized and developed of the principles of the laws of war.

These principles govern all acts of war and are applicable under international law in the absence of more specific rules, as recognized by the preambles to the principal conventions of the laws of war, namely, the Hague Conventions of 1899 and 1907 and the Rules of Landwarfare and the four Geneva Conventions of 1949.

Before proceeding to an analysis of the laws of war it is appropriate to say a few words about the lawmaking process and the role of morality and public opinion in it.

Law and the law-making process are not divorced from morality and public opinion. This is true even in advanced legal orders within states which sanction their laws with sovereign powers. Experience refutes the contention of extreme legal positivists and of pure theories of law that such a divorce is possible or desirable. The need to understand and build on the interrelation and interaction between law, morality, and public opinion is the more clear in international relations where there is no sovereign power to enforce the law.

This is not to say that law, morality, and public opinion must not be distinguished. They are no more synonymous than they are mutually exclusive. Serious mischief may result from attributing to one of the tenets of either or both of the others. Accordingly, a controversial part of international law such as the laws of war should be analyzed from the threefold perspectives of law, morality, and public opinion, in the context of the actual behavior and expectations of contemporary belligerents.

We have already summarized that part of the laws of war concerning the decision to have recourse to armed force, traditionally known as the *jus ad bellum.* We turn now to the content and organization of the laws of war in the sense of the *jus in bello,* literally, the law that operates *in* the conduct of war. Traditionally the laws concerning the conduct of hostilities have been organized in the following manner:

1. Belligerent status;
2. Protection of prisoners of war and of the sick and wounded;
3. Limits on the means of destruction;
4. Communication between belligerents; truces and armistices, and the closely related question of perfidious behavior;
5. Protection of occupied societies.

This sequence will be followed. However, the degree of attention accorded each subject will vary greatly, depending on its relevance to modern warfare and its complexity. It should be further noted from the outset that the laws of war embodied in international conventions were primarily directed to the conduct of what we now call conventional war whereas, as we know, armed conflict increasingly takes the form of unconventional warfare and grave difficulties arise in applying the traditional rules to these new situations.

Belligerent status, and hence qualification for the rights and duties of the laws of war, is accorded automatically to "Members of the armed forces of a Party to the conflict, as well as members of militias or volunteer corps forming part of such armed forces."[1]

Further, and most relevant to most modern conflicts, belligerent status is accorded:

1. Members of other militias and members of other volunteer corps, including those of organized resistance movement, belonging to a Party to the conflict and operating in or outside their own territory, even if this territory is occupied, provided that such militias or volunteer corps, including such organized resistance movements, fulfill the following conditions:

"(a). that of being commanded by a person responsible for his subordinates;

(b). that of having a fixed distinctive sign recognizable at a distance;

(c). that of carrying arms openly;

(d). that of conducting their operations in accordance with the laws and customs of war."[2]

A common Article 3 of all of the four Geneva Conventions of 1949 provides:

"In the case of armed conflict not of an international character occurring in the territory of one of the High Contracting Parties, each Party to the conflict should be bound to apply, as a minimum, the following provisions:

(1). Persons taking no active part in the hostilities, including members of armed forces who have laid down their arms and those placed *hors de combat* by sickness, wounds, detention, or any other cause, shall in all circumstances be treated humanely, without any adverse distinction founded on race, colour, religion or faith, sex, birth or wealth, or any other similar criteria.

To this end the following acts are and shall remain prohibited

---

[1] Geneva Convention Relative to the Treatment of Prisoners of War, August 12, 1949, Art. 4 (A) (1). The Convention will henceforth be cited as GPW. This Article closely resembles Art. 1 of the Annex to Hague Convention No. IV of October 18, 1907, henceforth cited as HR.

[2] GPW, Art. 4 (A) 2. Essentially the same conditions are laid down by HR Art. 1.

at any time and in any place whatsoever with respect to the above-mentioned persons:

(a). violence to life and person, in particular murder of all kinds, mutilation, cruel treatment and torture;

(b). taking of hostages;

(c). outrages upon personal dignity; in particular, humiliating and degrading treatment;

(d). the passing of sentences and the carrying out of executions without previous judgment pronounced by a regularly constituted court affording all the judicial guarantees which are recognized as indispensable by civilized peoples.

(2). The wounded and sick shall be collected and cared for."

An impartial humanitarian body, such as the International Committee of the Red Cross, may offer its services to the Parties to the conflict.

"The Parties to the conflict shall further endeavor to bring into force by means of special agreements, all or part of the other provisions of the present Convention."[3]

The application of the preceding provisions shall not affect the legal status of the Parties to the conflict.

Influential publicists have argued that unrecognized rebel forces, such as the Vietcong before the Vietnam War became clearly an international conflict and the FLN in the Algerian civil war are *only* protected by common Article 3 of the Geneva Conventions of 1949. My view, reflecting my natural law background, is that the law of nations arises out of natural law, or the principles of humanity, or the universal conscience of mankind—the terminology is immaterial. Whenever there is widespread, more or less continuous fighting over public issues of the kind at stake in a revolutionary war, it is my belief that the principles of the law of war clearly apply to *all* participants in the conflict, that wherever relevant, the detailed

[3] N.B. Since this is a common Article in all four Geneva Conventions, this means that Parties to such conflicts are encouraged to extend the full array of humanitarian provisions for the mitigation of suffering to civil and other conflicts not clearly covered by the four Geneva Conventions.

rules of the law of war should be applied, and that the criteria for belligerent status set forth in Article 1 of the Hague Rules of 1907 and Article 4 of the 1949 Geneva Convention on Treatment of Prisoners of War should be very liberally interpreted so as to provide the maximum possible protection of the laws of war (and they are inadequate enough) to people who are fighting a public war. Admittedly, this proposition confronts some serious difficulties:

In the first place, parties to a conflict whose status as international persons (subjects of international law, entitled to all rights under it and obligated by all duties under the law) is clear, and, who stand to lose psychological or politically by recognition of a revolutionary force and/or foreign volunteers, are never going to characterize the enemy as anything but "bandits" with whom they would never make any of the agreements suggested by common Article 3 of the Geneva Conventions of 1949—unless the enemies are so successful that some kind of recognition becomes necessary.

Second, it is extremely difficult to distinguish widespread crime and disorder from revolutionary war. (I must say that, as a resident of Washington, D.C., I was made acutely aware of this problem during the April 1968 riots, when my street was patrolled at five-minute intervals by jeeps containing four armed members of an armed cavalry regiment of the United States Army.)

Perhaps the most agonizing dilemma concerns attempts to require revolutionary forces to observe the laws of war which were framed almost exclusively for regulation of the conduct of regular forces in primarily conventional war and, marginally, for auxiliary irregular forces, co-operating with regular forces.

These difficulties suggest the necessity of developing separate or additional laws of war for the kinds of conflicts described in Chapter VII. The feasibility of such a special law of war for modern revolutionary warfare can be argued both ways. On the one hand, it does seem almost inescapable for revolutionaries to engage in behavior that has traditionally been legally and morally condemned. On the other hand, the *discipline* and *will power* characteristic of most successful revolutionary forces make the idea of rules of the game plausible. Moreover, it should not be forgotten that it has been the revolutionaries such as Mao Tse-tung and Ho Chi Minh who have utilized the device of "generous" policies toward prisoners of war, which have had their propaganda and political payoff. This is a whole new subject, which needs to be studied in the light of the practice of contemporary conflict.

Thus far I have been speaking in terms of principles that I hold to be both legal and moral. What about public opinion and the belligerent status of parties to typical modern conflicts?

As a very broad generalization, it appears to me that there is a definite split between public-opinion trends within a society torn by civil strife and foreign intervention and what is loosely referred to as world public opinion. Within the society undergoing civil war and foreign intervention, it seems to me that the public, even if it is not anamored of the incumbent regime, is quite naturally suspicious and resentful of the revolutionaries. They are causing the trouble. Their whole approach is to make life unlivable under the system, and the "average man" is not enthusiastic about having his life and that of his family made unlivable or about being personally destroyed or brutalized by any party to the conflict. But he knows that there would be no conflict if the revolutionaries ceased their activities. I make no attempt to prove this contention with behavioral evidence, but I suspect that domestic public opinion would be reluctant to dignify revolutionary and foreign subversive activity with belligerent status. Accordingly, there is a propensity to go along with the government's characterization of them as "criminals."

World opinion, on the other hand, seems to require very little in the way of apparent political, racial, or social-economic grievances, to side with the revolutionaries. Specifically, harsh treatment of large numbers of obviously politically motivated rebels will usually bring down considerable world-wide criticism, regardless of the subtleties of domestic and international law. But even this statement must be qualified because of the double—or it may be triple or more—standards prevalent in contemporary world public opinion.

The same sources of outraged public opinion which identified every repressive measure of the Diem regime with flaming headlines and anguished protest meetings looked the other way when hundreds of thousands, if not millions, of adherents (mainly Communist) of the *coup d'état* which the Indonesian military nipped in the bud were killed or imprisoned. But if a Western, "neo-colonialist" influence is detected, then both the opinion-makers in the Third World and the guilt-ridden domestic critics of so-called neo-colonialism join in support of the revolutionaries against an "unrepresentative and oppressive" regime.

Thus, in my opinion, sound legal and moral principles argue for maximum extension of belligerent status in confused revolutionary-interventionary wars. Whatever its value, this opinion tends to be supported, often for very different reasons, some of which I think are unfair, by world public opinion. If conservative interpretations of positive international law are technically correct and the policy I have proposed is not legally mandatory, sound policy as influenced particularly by intervening states such as the United States should be moving international customary international law in that direction. The implications of this issue should become clearer as we discuss the rights and duties of belligerent personnel.

Prisoners of war, henceforth *POWs,* and the sick and wounded are entitled to:

1. Quarter, the right to surrender and become POWs;
2. Protection, the right to be moved out of dangerous areas as expeditiously and safely as the military situation permits;
3. Decent Treatment, the definition of which is elaborated in the Hague Convention of 1907 and a number of specific conventions on the subject, now replaced by the Geneva Convention of 1949 on Treatment of Prisoners of War. Verification of this treatment is entrusted to the International Committee of the Red Cross, as well as by designated "Protecting Powers," which look after a belligerent's interest in its POWs;
4. Immunity from reprisals, torture, abuse from the Detaining

Power's population, and any other mistreatment not justified by reasonable requirements of security and discipline.[4]

It would appear that in practice the vast majority of POWs in most conflicts receive substantially that treatment to which they are legally entitled. At least most of them survive, a result not lightly to be assumed if we look back over the history of warfare. However, state practice has revealed the following violations of law and difficulties with the existing system established to enforce it:

1. Quarter is often denied in the heat of battle or in precarious situations, for example, that of a small patrol behind the enemy's lines, wherein prisoners are an unwanted burden or source of danger;

2. Normal standards of POW treatment can sometimes be impossible of achievement because of the level of life in the society of the Detaining Power or the condition of the forces holding the prisoners. This would be true particularly in the case of prisoners held by guerrilla forces in primitive societies. But the question of diet alone for those in captivity in Oriental countries is a serious one;

3. The International Committee of the Red Cross has not been accepted by some Communist states and revolutionary forces as a neutral body, thus eliminating the main source of objective reporting and humanitarian assistance with respect to POWs, for example, in the Korean War;

4. Most importantly, prohibitions against reprisals, torture, and other ill-treatment have been so widely violated as to raise serious question as to their continued validity. The international law "on the books" regarding these subjects is often, in some respects, generally disregarded by belligerents today, especially in revolutionary wars.

The legal and moral issues concerning protection of POWs can be divided into two categories:

1. Issues that result from inefficiency, corruption, malice, apathy,

[4] HR, Articles 4–20; GPW, Articles 3, 12–20, 39–45, 82–108.

or other reasons that do not involve a deliberate and necessary collision between reasonably perceived military necessities and the rights of POWs;

2. Issues caused by the clash of reasonably perceived military necessities and legal-moral principles. These include:

a. denial of quarter;

b. execution, torture, or mistreatment of POWs; as reprisals, to obtain vital information, or to "brainwash," "reclaim," "orient," or otherwise change the ideological and other loyalties of the POWs.

All that need be said about the first category of issues is that the Detaining Power is responsible for failure to meet the international law standards established for the protection of POWs. Under the well-established legal, moral and military principle of command responsibility, responsible officials and commanders may be held legally responsible and are morally for delinquencies that are the more reprehensible since they have no military utility. The really tough questions are in the second category and I will concentrate on them.

I fear that denial of quarter is a hopeless issue except for the legal-moral responsibility of commanders to minimize its occurrence. Systematic denial of quarter would clearly be wrong but it is uncommon except in cases of gross and continuing disparity in the contending forces. Usually fear of retaliation prevents a general policy of denying quarter. It is true, however, that localized and temporary cases of general denial of quarter occur when troops are incensed by actual or supposed atrocities by opposing units.

Execution, torture, and deliberate mistreatment of POWs cannot be sidestepped as legal and moral issues, however. Unlike denial of quarter, these practices are not limited primarily to unauthorized or insufficiently checked battlefield behavior. Moreover, the prevalence of these practices is sufficiently widespread that they constitute perhaps the most important and difficult legal and moral problem of modern war since, again, modern war usually means some kind of revolutionary war of the kind described in Chapter VII. I stated at the outset of this chapter that the laws of war should be analyzed in terms of the interaction between developing law, morality, and public opinion, in the context of belligerent behavior. These distinctions and relationships are more necessary for adequate normative analysis of the subject under discussion than any I know of with respect to war. As to execution, torture and mistreatment of POWs it can be said:

1. The law is clear and is highly restrictive;

2. The law is in conformity with basic moral principles;

3. Public opinion varies from encouragement or acceptance of violation of the law under the influences of hatred and fear to condemnation of violations of the law, particularly: (a) by others in situations wherein the critic has no stakes or is positively opposed to the cause of the delinquent party; (b) by domestic critics of a policy who join their opposition to a war policy with their opposition to seemingly illegal and/or immoral conduct of the war. Thus the opponent of the U.S. involvement in the Vietnam War who is particularly outraged by photographs of torture of Vietcong may not have objected to coercion exercised by American-Jewish intelligence interrogators against captured German S.S. troops in World War II.

4. It is the near universal practice of belligerents, and of *all* belligerents without exception in the revolutionary wars, to violate the existing laws on these subjects, regardless of moral objections and in the face of strong and very often extremely effective protests from domestic and world public opinion.

In these circumstances, a question not unlike some of those involved in nuclear deterrence is raised. Is it possible for a party to a revolutionary war to observe the morally and popularly approved laws of war and still hope to have enough hope for success in such a war as to make engagement in it reasonable? *In short, we have nuclear pacifists. Should we have revolutionary war—or torture—pacifists?*

We must now deal with the unpleasant but inescapable problems of protecting POWs from arbitrary execution, torture, and deliberate mistreatment. Some preliminary definitions must now be offered, bearing in mind that the three categories analyzed overlap and that there are subdivisions within each.

Execution would appear to consist in the killing of POWs:

1. Directly, in a single act, e.g., shooting, hanging, beheading, gassing;

2. Indirectly, but intentionally, as a result of torture or systematic mistreatment such as deliberate denial of adequate food, clothing, shelter, or medical care, or through unreasonable forced "death" marches.

Torture is more difficult to define. For the moment it will suffice to indicate the elements that go into definitions of torture:

1. Authority: What, if any responsible authority, orders acts of torture?

2. Torturers: Who inflicts torture, what is the relation between their treatment of the tortured persons and the intentions and policies of the responsible authority ordering such acts?

3. Victim: Is the victim as suspected or even a known criminal under the laws of war? Is he a person whose status ensures possession of significant information? Or is the victim a comparatively anonymous person who has been rounded up more or less indiscriminately?

4. Means: What are the means, physical and psychological, that are used? Can we distinguish means that are intrinsically immoral, *mala in se,* from those which may be disproportionate and wrong in a particular context but permissible in other situations, from those that, however regrettable, may not appear excessive even as general operating procedure *if* torture, however defined, is ever legally and morally permissible?

5. Effects: What are the physical and psychological effects of the form of torture used? How lasting are these effects? How can the element of the subjective reaction on the part of the victim or, for that matter, of the victim's race or ethnic group be evaluated?

Reflections on these questions with respect to each element immediately suggests a plurality of definitions of torture ranging from a very unpleasant or frightening experience which was nonetheless not unreasonable in legal and moral terms, e.g., "It was sheer

torture to live in that camp wondering what they might do to us,"
to torture in its most violent sense, "he was tortured to death or into
insanity."

Rather than attempt to go through the whole spectrum of combina-
tions of the elements identified, I will propose three definitions of
torture, as concerns POWs, each of which will be judged in moral
terms.

First, torture is clearly immoral when it is done without responsible authority or supervision by persons more interested in torturing than in obtaining a result of extremely great military utility,
especially when done to a victim who does not certainly possess the
information or capacity to act elicited by means which are physi-
cally and psychologically inhuman and depraved and which leave
lasting physical and psychological damage.

On the other hand, it is conceivable that torture may be moral
if it is carried out by order of responsible authority by torturers acting
in accordance with the intentions of that authority with respect to
information, capacity to act, or any other capability which it is certain or highly likely the victim possesses and which is of critical
military importance by means which are as limited and barely sufficient as possible and which do not leave inadmissible lasting
physical and psychological effects.

Finally, torture in the sense of a "standing operating procedure"
carried out with respect to all captives in a certain category which
is supervised and which does not exceed "roughing up" and temporarily frightening the POW could be morally countenanced (and
is, of course, fairly standard practice).

Rather than attempt a synthetic definition of torture I think that
I will let these examples serve as guidelines for further discussion
later in this section.

Mistreatment of POWs is the failure to provide the protections
required by the laws of war. Mistreatment includes the acts prohibited in common Article 3 of the Geneva Conventions of 1949.
It also includes deliberately inadequate food, clothing, shelter, medical attention, and unduly severe disciplinary penalties. It includes,

moreover, forced marches under severe weather conditions, as we have said in describing mistreatment as an indirect form of execution.

Having delineated more fully these acts which conventional international law condemns but which are so widely practiced as to require further analysis let us go back over them, one by one, in an attempt to find some legal-moral guidelines between the unbending but unobserved rules of the conventional law and the license so widely indulged in by belligerents.

The principal circumstances in which POWs are executed appear to be the following:

1. After conviction by due process of law for crimes committed *while* a POW, e.g., murder of another POW or of a guard;

2. After conviction by due process of law for war crimes. It is the better and moral practical view, and the prevailing practice, that this should only occur after the conclusion of hostilities. Threats to try and execute war criminals during hostilities may, on the one hand constitute a form of torture or mistreatment, and, on the other hand, they may endanger the security of the POWs of the power threatening war crimes during the continuation of hostilities;

3. As a result of torture and/or mistreatment which was calculated to lead to death, as happened to many Soviet POWs in World War II on a tragic scale;

4. As reprisals for execution or other illegal acts by the POWs' state or its allies;

5. By lynching by civilians, unchecked by military and civil authorities, as happened in some cases to downed airmen in World War II.

In the light of the fundamental principles of the laws of war, it should be clear that execution of the kind described in the first two categories is permissible if there is, indeed, due process of law. The last three categories are legally and morally wrong and are war crimes. While it is at least conceivable that some forms of torture may be condoned and some reprisals against POWs carried out as sanctions of the laws of war (the Geneva Convention of 1949 notwithstanding) such as denial of privileges, restrictions on diet, or the like may be permitted exceptionally, execution under the circumstances described in the last three categories is clearly illegal and immoral.

Torture is engaged in against POWs for three principal reasons: as retaliation for similar treatment of the Detaining Powers POWs, to obtain vital information, and to "brain wash" or drastically change the beliefs and dispositions of the POWs. From the standpoint of military necessity, the second reason, vital intelligence, is overwhelmingly *the* issue at stake. I have little evidence that retaliatory torture is a great *independent* issue. It can be a highly significant factor in shaping policies regarding the other two objectives of torture. If it is known that the enemy engages in torture on a large scale, inhibitions on torture for any reason are sure to diminish. Rather than dealing with all three reasons equally, I will concentrate on the issue of torture to obtain vital information, leaving "brainwashing" for separate treatment. In so doing I will follow the elements comprising the process of torture previously distinguished.

First, as already indicated, torture can only, if ever, be justified as an official policy for which responsible commanders must answer.

Second, the torturers must be trained to do their job with the least morally offensive means and in such a way as to do the least possible permanent physical and psychological damage to the victim. If they take advantage of their grim work to engage in gratuitous barbarism and sadism their moral guilt is manifest, and, to repeat, the legal, moral and military responsibility of their commanders is engaged.

The practical dilemmas of finding torturers with the nerves and will to do their work and still remain conscious of legal and moral restraints must surely be one of the most agonizing of modern war. The French faced it with dismal results on the armed forces and on the society. The Americans are facing it and finding that you cannot look the other way or leave the room, particularly when you have *Life* photographers recording acts of torture in living color. And, friends of the New Left please note, before the euphoria developing for a "theology of violent revolution" gets utterly out of hand, Christian advocates of violent revolution had better face the issues of torture and who is going to do it. It is reported that drafted seminarians in the French army in Algeria, when ordered to serve as interrogators, worked the "electros," which tortured through electric shocks, "gently." Will the priest-guerrillas of Latin America find "gentle" means of torturing their enemies to obtain the information which may be the difference between survival and annihilation by the counterinsurgents? Or will they take a walk and say some prayers while a tough leftist rebel does the job?

Third, if torture involving any substantial degree of physical or psychological agony can ever be justified, and we are now at the razor's edge of this question, it can only be justified with respect to victims who:

1. Are reasonably suspected of criminal behavior under the laws of war and whose knowledge of accomplices and their plans cannot be obtained without torture; e.g., in the case that the Soviets had captured a high S.S. or Gestapo leader who had been directing genocidal activities;

2. May reasonably be assumed to have absolutely vital information, the knowledge of which will almost certainly permit the captors to frustrate enemy actions which could not otherwise be anticipated much less defeated.

There must be a very high stake, involving great danger of disproportionate suffering and destruction, which justifies using the exceptional means of torture to obtain the information which in all likelihood will permit action sufficient to meet this danger. The classic and agonizing modern case is that of the captured guerrilla leader who knows the plans, the personnel, the bases and sources of external support of the revolutionaries. Or, it may be a high military or police officer on the counterinsurgent side. But only such persons should be submitted to any extreme physical or psychological torture.

Fourth, the means employed in torture must obviously be very critically and constantly scrutinized. One way to achieve this is to follow the example of French commanders in Algeria who felt obliged to order torture in certain types of interrogations, but who first insisted that *they themselves* be subjected to the standard tortures being applied in order to judge for themselves, the hard way, just how far they should permit their interrogators to go. The checks should come from basic policies and orders established in advance, frequent inspections and investigations, and from continuous and competent medical surveillance of the procedures.[5]

In summary: The legal rule prohibits any torture, but practice makes a strong case for the necessity of some forms of torture with regard to certain types of POWs. Still the legal presumption is against it. A moral case can be made for the proportionality of good resulting from torture far outweighing the evil done to the victim. If international law is what is stated in the conventions, all torture is illegal. If international law is what states and revolutionary forces are doing on a near universal basis without, apparently, great feelings of guilt, a legal-moral case can be made for torture as an exceptional measure when it involves a high degree of suffering and as a fairly routine measure if it is limited to "roughing up" and intimidating prisoners in interrogation in ways that will not have lasting effects.

Brainwashing is a term that is used here to facilitate a difficult discussion, since it is widely recognized. I realize that it is an unscientific and potentially mischievous term. The experience of totalitarian regimes with their own political prisoners and foreign POWs seems to indicate that brainwashing in the sense that it is often popularly conceived is virtually impossible. That is, crushing a human will and intellect and then rebuilding a new man—or robot—handmade to meet the requirements of his masters is an extremely difficult thing to do. As I understand it, breaking a man's will and leaving him a shambling, defenseless clod, as is often done to defendants in totalitarian political-juridical proceedings where all that is desired is a confession is not brainwashing. Brainwashing is the

[5] For a discussion of this subject by one of the most experienced, tough, and candid of the French experts on revolutionary warfare, see Roger Trinquier, *Modern Warfare,* A French View of Counterinsurgency, (New York: Praeger, 1964), pp. 21–25.

act of breaking a man's will and character and then creating a new and different man.

But since the term has such currency, it serves to identify the broad problem of coercive indoctrination, education, or "rehabilitation," which is a fairly standard feature of the treatment of POWs in modern conflicts. As will be recalled from the analyses of the models, the mystiques, both of revolutionary warfare and of counter-insurgency, there is a great deal of emphasis on winning the hearts and minds of the people, although both sides, when the going gets tough, tend to agree with Mao Tse-tung's dictum that political power ultimately comes out of the barrel of a gun. Still, ideological-political education, psychological operations, whatever it is called, is a very important element—some claim the key element—not only in the success of the antagonists in the ideological-political realm—but in the military realm wherein psychological warfare that is effective may effectively replace military actions which are necessarily counter-productive insofar as the society in which they take place is concerned.

For summary purposes the following legal-moral guidelines may be suggested (I say legal-moral rather than legal because neither the law of peace nor the law of war has really caught up with the problems of psychological warfare):

1. Coercion or manipulation in the form of rewards and punishments within the broad limits of the POW regime does not raise too much of a moral problem. Even violations of the laws of war designed to defend the POWs against brainwashing in the looser sense of the term do not raise major moral issues, although they may be both illegal and wrong.

2. Coercion in the form of extreme mistreatment, and, particularly, in the form of intense torture, physical or psychological pressures for the purposes, *not* of obtaining vital information or other immediately relevant militarily relevant co-operation, but for the broad purposes of brainwashing in the literal sense is morally wrong and ought to be legally prohibited. It is wrong for two reasons: (a) the end is immoral; (b) the means are immoral.

As to the legal aspects of the problem I would argue along two lines. First, as a prisoner of war, a person is *hors de combat,* entitled to be left alone as long as he behaves himself. Carrot-and-stick manipulation of POWs cannot go very far without exceeding the rights of the Detaining Power and denying the rights of the POWs. Second, it is fundamental to the spirit and letter of the laws of war that it is wrong to seek by coercion to force a person to betray his own side in a conflict and change over to the enemy. If he wants to, fine. But programs that approach the brainwashing technique of extreme rewards and punishments according to support for or resistance to the enemy cause are absolutely contrary to the precious and precarious concept of the POW system.

Obviously, much that has been already said about the issues raised by execution, torture, and brainwashing of POWs applied to *mistreatment* not assimilable into any of these categories. A person who has taken himself out of a conflict by surrendering is entitled not only to all the rights and benefits provided for by international law but, also, to treatment as a human being. He must not be an object of hatred, contempt, or humiliating public display. There is a real danger, if modern experience is the criterion, that a Detaining Power may manage to keep close to the minimal requirements of the international law of war respecting POWs, and, still create atmospheres and situations which deserve moral condemnation. Many of the moral and psychological problems that plague domestic racial and class conflicts arise in this regard. POWs have a moral right to be treated as human beings and honorable enemies who have surrendered in good faith—not as "Gooks," "Krauts," or "imperialist bandits," much less, "monkeys" or "swine." It is all too often the case that sub-human characterizations and stereotypes produce or encourage sub-human treatment.

It is difficult to arrive at anything more than generalities concerning the relation of public opinion and the protection of POWs. Nevertheless, these generalities, however imperfect, must be considered, for public opinion is extremely important in shaping policies concerning the treatment of POWs. The following insights, which are impressionistic rather than scientific, reflect considerable ambivalence on the part of the author. This ambivalence, in turn, is in considerable measure the result of ambivalent belligerent practice and the domestic and international reactions of public opinion to that practice.

It is my observation that, public opinion in nations not directly involved in a conflict places great importance on the protection of POWs. This is first evidenced by the fact that there is more, and more detailed, treaty law on this subject than on any other covered by the laws of war. It is also reflected by reaction to allegations of unjust and inhuman treatment of POWs. For example, there is the bitter criticism of torture in Vietnam, on the one hand, and the successful pleas to Hanoi not to hold war-crimes trials of captured U.S. pilots. The attempted manipulation of public opinion with respect to prison camp revolts and alleged atrocities by the Detaining Powers in the Korean conflict is a prime example, in which POW incidents and diplomatic and propaganda initiatives and attitudes at Panmunjom were sometimes orchestrated in incredible fashion.

Public opinion within societies directly involved in a conflict, however, appears to divide into the following attitudes:

1. Approval of execution, torture, and mistreatment of POWs as a military necessity, unquestioned by popular opinion stirred by wartime emotions;

2. Reluctant acceptance of such behavior as inevitable or justifiable—usually accompanied by a preference not to know too much about what is going on in this unpleasant realm;

3. Silent opposition to such behavior;

4. Public opposition to alleged violations of the fundamental rights of POWs.

The first three attitudes explain in part the gulf between the solemn commitments made by most governments and the near-universal practice of belligerents, particularly in the revolutionary wars dominating contemporary conflict.

Once again, we see the dichotomy: I approve the war and approve or condone the necessary methods pursued; and, I oppose the war

and cite in particular the means used to pursue it. Where the fourth
attitude, public opposition within a society at war, to means of the
extreme but seemingly necessary kind of which we have been speaking, have occurred, it appears that the main effect of such opposition
has been to increase pressures to terminate the conflict altogether
rather than to limit severely or eliminate some or all of the practices
objected to. This was true in France during the Algerian war and
is now true in the United States with respect to the war in Vietnam.
This again raises the question whether execution, torture, and mistreatment of POWs is not *unavoidable* in modern revolutionary wars
and, therefore, whether literal adherence to the laws of war is com-
patible with successful engagement in such wars, on either side, that
of the revolutionaries or that of the counterinsurgents.

Having raised but far from resolved the nasty problems of most
of the wars that are, let us turn to the wars that might be, and the
state of the laws of war insofar as the means of destruction is concerned.

We turn next to the extremely difficult question of defining realistically the *permissible means of destruction in war*. As far as the
laws of war are concerned, those regulating the means of destruction
are the least satisfactory. Indeed, there is a gaping hole in the laws
of war which has been evident since 1914. The reasons for this
state of affairs are many, and, as is often the case where law and
morality fail, reflect the complementary effect of the workings of
forces starting from almost opposite perspectives. The international
idealists have sabotaged and/or ignored the laws of war generally,
and, particularly, the laws respecting the means of destruction, because they have aspired to the elimination of war. The hard-line
proponents of *Realpolitik* and military superiority have also discouraged the development of legal restraints on the means of destruction. These attitudes have contributed to a result wherein there
continue to be wars that are increasingly destructive, and increasingly unsatisfactory or unreliable as instruments of *Realpolitik*. Accordingly, this subject is one wherein moral analysis is more important than tortured attempts to stretch antiquated or irrelevant

rules of international law, although the principles of international law, in my view, will stand up to the test.

The subjects included in normative analyses of the means of destruction are:

1. Prohibition of means causing superfluous suffering;
2. Prohibition of poison;
3. Prohibition of Chemical-Biological warfare;
4. Prohibition of attacks on noncombatants, non-military targets; and on Red Cross, i.e., medical installations, vehicles, and personnel;
5. Prohibition of widespread devastation, e.g., "city busting" air raids and "scorched earth" policies by ground forces not justified by military necessity;
6. Prohibition of pillage.

These subjects will be examined by contrasting relevant legal provisions, moral considerations, and recurring expressions of public opinion about them, the context of contemporary belligerent practice.

Under treaty provisions of international law, notably the St. Petersburg Declaration of 1868, and, more importantly, in Article 23 (e) of the 1899 and 1907 Hague Conventions Respecting the Laws and Customs of War on Land, infliction of "superfluous suffering" is prohibited. This prohibition takes the following forms:

1. It is a general principle, the definition and application of which is to be worked out by law-abiding and conscientious belligerents;
2. It is the source for specific prohibitions of means which belligerents have identified as being essentially the cause of "superfluous suffering." Such prohibitions concern, first, antiquated or only marginally effective means of which cause great suffering, such as shooting hot grape shot and chains from eighteenth- and nineteenth-century cannons—obviously no significant concession. Second, the principle is applied to *effective* military means which are thought to cause superfluous suffering. The best example is the 1899 prohibition of dum-dum or other expanding bullets, which cause hideous, gaping wounds. Unhappily, although the majority of states ac-

ceded to the 1899 convention on this subject, Great Britain and the
United States did not. Their real reason was that they were at the
time engaged in colonial wars against fanatical natives who simply
could not be stopped by ordinary firearms and they claimed that
dum-dum bullets were a military necessity. This sad case demonstrated the difference between military necessity in the sense of
military utility and what I call legitimate military necessity wherein
utility is subject to normative restriction.

Aside from specific prohibitions, it seems hard to improve on the
official U.S. position that the definition of the broad—and potentially subjective—principle prohibiting superfluous suffering. FM 27-
10, the U. S. Army Field Manual on *The Law of Land Warfare*
states:

> . . . What weapons cause "unnecessary injury" can only be deter-
> mined in the light of the practice of states in refraining from the use
> of a given weapon because it is believed to have that effect. The pro-
> hibition certainly does not extend to the use of explosives contained in
> artillery projectiles, mines, rockets, or hand grenades. Usage has, how-
> ever, established the illegality of lances with barbed heads, irregular-
> shaped bullets, and projectiles filled with glass, the use of any sub-
> stance on bullets that would tend unnecessarily to inflame a wound
> inflicted by them, and the scoring of the surface or the filing off of the
> ends of the hard cases of bullets.[6]

Note that the U.S. now accepts the prohibition of dum-dum bullets
under customary international law. Note also that many of the primitive devices used by guerrillas, such as traps with poisoned stakes
are contrary to customary international law; one more problem for
those sympathetic to revolutionary warfare.

This is the state of the subject in international law. But there is
a serious problem when moral claims and public opinion deal with
this subject. The problem is all too painfully illustrated by the current controversy over the use of napalm in Vietnam.

[6] FM 27-10. Department of the Army Field Manual, *The Law of Land Warfare* (Washington, D.C.: Department of the Army, July 1956), ⌗34, p. 18.

Napalm has been condemned as immoral and abhorrent, by vocal and often prestigious portions of American and world public opinion to such an extent that it has virtually become the main symbol against which opponents of the Vietnam War protest. In these protests it is often asserted that the use of napalm is specifically prohibited by international law. This is not true. It is also asserted that its use is contrary to the general prohibition against causing superfluous suffering. This *could* be true if the practice of states made such a judgment. But no such practice has been established. Israel used napalm against the Arabs in 1967—a decidedly counterforce war, it should be added. There is good reason to believe that napalm is as much a standard part of the armaments of modern armed forces throughout the world as high explosives. If this is the case, use of napalm is not contrary to international law except in cases of disproportionate or indiscriminate use. In such cases the essential element of illegality would be the disproportionate or indiscriminate nature of the act, not the means employed.

Napalm is a weapon, or more precisely, a munition that has been employed against specific targets since World War II. The current napalm B used since 1966 was developed by Major Brooks Harris, an Air Force officer. It is composed of 46 percent crystalline polystrene, 21 percent benzine and 33 percent gasoline. Prior to that time gasoline was jellied by the use of an aluminum soap. The name comes from naphtha which was originally mixed with gasoline to form a gel—napalm. In its cruder forms napalm can be prepared by relatively unskilled people from materials commonly available and without sophisticated equipment.

The use of thickened hydrocarbon fuel, however, has been gradually developed since ancient warfare. It was used in flame throwers in World Wars I and II.

The first use of napalm was in 1944 by the then Army Air Corps against bunkers in the Marianas in the South Pacific. At about the same time, napalm was used in Europe. Figures for the amount of napalm used in World War II are nonexistent, but in Korea 32,215 tons were employed. In Vietnam the U. S. Air Force has employed approximately 2.2 tons in 1963; 1.8 tons in 1964; 17.6 tons in 1965 and 54.6 tons in 1966. During the first six months of 1967 the Air Force employed an average of 3.6 tons a month, at an average monthly cost of almost three million dollars. Air Force figures beyond mid-1967 are unavailable, but it may be assumed the rate of use and cost increased. U. S. Army use of napalm independently of the Air Force has been so slight that no figures exist.

As a conventional weapon of war, napalm or a similar compound is used in flame throwers (man-carried and tank-mounted) in almost all armies of the world. All Air Forces are considered to have the capability. The North Vietnamese and the Vietcong have used napalm in flame throwers against U.S. troops.

Napalm is a tactical rather than a strategic weapon. U.S. doctrine requires that it can be employed against strictly military targets. It is used by the U. S. Air Force for close air support and interdiction of soft targets such as supply dumps and vehicles. Presumably there is little objection from most people to the use of napalm against such targets. It is when napalm is used against individual human beings that it seems so repugnant. Napalm is adhesive. It is not as sticky as pitch but can be likened to corn syrup: it cannot be readily brushed off. It can be extinguished by rolling a person in a blanket or covering with non-consumable material. Napalm needs oxygen to burn. Death by fire has always been abhorrent to man and may well go back to the influence of the Judaic Christian vision of hell. A lingering death from burns is even more offensive. The fact is that napalm kills by sudden and rather painless asphyxiation more than it does by burning. U.S. doctrine (and practice) precludes its deliberate employment against innocent or defenseless civilians. When employed against individual humans it is against targets that will not yield to other weapons. Many Vietcong ambush positions are built so that they have a layer of logs and earth overhead with apertures through which they can fire. When a U.S. unit encounters the ambush either by falling into it or "tripping" it ahead of time, casualties are usually taken almost immediately. In order to evacuate the casualties and continue the advance, napalm may be employed. The splash and spreading of the napalm go into the ambush positions in a way no other weapon could do. In a similar manner, napalm is used against dug-in anti-aircraft positions in North Vietnam where only a difficult to achieve direct bomb hit would otherwise neutralize the position.

While a description of this sort seems ruthless it is important to recognize that napalm is not used indiscriminately. General Earle G. Wheeler, Chairman of the Joint Chiefs of Staff says bluntly that napalm is considered to be a legitimate military necessity. Alternative weapons exist, but since they involve high amounts of explosive, they would create greater casualties. Since napalm is employed as close as twenty-five to fifty meters from friendly troops, casualties from alternate weapons could include even friendly troops.

The standard napalm bomb weighs 750 pounds and can be carried by all U.S. fighter aircraft. A napalm bomb is a cylindrical aluminum container similar to a fuel tank. It has an impact-detonated fuse which ignites a white phosphorous over the napalm mixture. Napalm is normally released from the aircraft during low-altitude flights. On rare occasions it has been the source of unintended but nonetheless tragic casualties among U.S. troops (1st Infantry Division in August 1967) and Vietnamese civilians. In addition, a few accidents have occurred during ground handling of napalm.

When employed in Vietnam, the decision to use napalm is made at the headquarters level of the 7th U. S. Air Force. Napalm has never been used to deliberately attack non-military targets in Vietnam. There are not even any claims that it was used for this purpose in World War II or Korea. Finished napalm or its ingredients have been sold by American companies to the armed forces of other countries.[7]

Perhaps napalm should be branded as immoral, but even if it

[7] The foregoing material was drawn from several official sources within the Pentagon in October 1968 by Lieutenant Colonel R. L. Schweitzer, U.S.A. and cleared for release by the Public Affairs office of the Secretary of Defense.

were to be, it would not follow that it is illegal. Given the horrible characteristics of generally accepted means of war it would appear difficult to establish that use of napalm *in itself* is morally more reprehensible than many other means of war.

Public opinion is further distorted by the foregoing considerations. Some protest against napalm because they think that it is both immoral and illegal. Some protest against napalm because its use can cause dreadful suffering, evidences of which are prominently displayed by the mass media and by opponents of the Vietnam War; it is sickening and repugnant. Others, as noted, combine a revulsion against napalm itself, with indignation against napalm as the symbol of the type of war the United States is fighting in Vietnam and the fact that Americans are in the war.

Article 23 (a) of the Hague Conventions of 1899 and 1907 provides that it is especially forbidden "to employ poison or poisoned weapons." Considerable light is cast on this rule by that which follows, 23 (b) which forbids belligerents "to kill treacherously individuals belonging to the hostile nation or army."

I consider the proper interpretation of this rule is to limit its application to the use of poisoned weapons, e.g., poison-tipped daggers, swords, lances, and the poisoning of food and drink. I reject the contention that this rule applied to gas warfare in World War I or to modern CB warfare. The legal-moral *rationale,* suggested by the positioning of Article 23 (b) immediately after 23 (a) is twofold: (1) prohibition of poison as offensive to civilized standards and as dangerous to innocent persons and to the resources of the earth (thus, revulsion from the practice of poisoning wells goes back to very early times); (2) prohibition of treacherous killing, which has often taken the form of poisoning, as Shakespeare more than adequately demonstrates in *Hamlet.*

But public opinion and some moralists have on many occasions seized on what I consider to be a rather limited rule, declaratory of past customary international law and not properly applied to means of war not anticipated in 1907, to condemn all of the so-called ACB means, i.e., atomic-chemical-biological. This is in my opinion incorrect as a matter of law, unreasonable in terms of limiting modern armed forces, and mischievous as a matter of moral analysis and the creation of public opinion on these important subjects which have not and will not be settled on the basis of an unelaborated prohibition of poison in a 1907 treaty. An astounding example of this misuse of the legal rule against poison is to be found in Clergy and Laymen Concerned About Vietnam's *In the Name of America,* a sweeping indictment of U.S. practices in Vietnam (a), (b), and (e) of the Hague rules of 1907, implying that these articles are the relevant sources of international law on the subject of chemical warfare. As will be seen in the next section, this is not the case.

Careful analysis will show that the true source of international law regulating chemical-biological, or CB, warfare is the Geneva Protocol Prohibiting the Use in War of Asphyxiating or Other Gases and of Bacteriological Methods of Warfare of June 17, 1925. This treaty prohibits "the use in war of asphyxiating, poisonous or other gases, and of all analogous liquids, materials or devices," as well as of, "bacteriological methods of warfare." Were this treaty alone the source for prohibition of what is now called CB warfare, I would not be very sanguine about the strength of the prohibition. I will not go into detail on the intricacies of attempts to deal with this subject in international law as I have done in an earlier publication.[8] Suffice it to say that the treaty suffers from a number of defects:

It starts by stating that "the use in war of asphyxiating, poisonous, or other gases, and of all analogous liquids, materials or devices *has been justly condemned* by the general opinion of the civilized world" and by treaties to which the "majority of the Powers of the World are parties." This is a difficult assumption to accept, since gas warfare was used by every World War I belligerent having the capability to use it. The Allies never protested the Germans' introduction of gas warfare in 1915 but simply copied it. The Allies condemned the *German* use of gas in Article 171 of the Versailles

[8] "Biological/Chemical Warfare and the International Law of War," *The Georgetown Law Journal,* Vol. 51, No. 1 (Fall, 1962), pp. 1–63.

Treaty but said nothing about its use by anyone else, and the only
other international agreement, other than the Hague 1907 Convention, which I consider to be not determinative of the problem, that
condemned such means was the Washington Treaty of February 5,
1922, which never went into effect because of failure of the French
to ratify it, ironically, because of its restrictive provisions concerning
submarine warfare.

Thus, in 1825 it was by no means clear that CB warfare was
legally condemned at all. Whether it was condemned morally and
by public opinion is something I cannot say. It does appear that the
reaction to gas warfare was that it was unsavory and *not militarily
decisive,* and therefore, if you will, expendable from the military
standpoint and a good object for condemnation by a generation that
specialized in condemnations and outlawries but not in building a
secure and peaceful world.

Moreover, most of the adherents to the treaty entered reservations
such as that of Great Britain which limited its application to "powers
and States which have both signed and ratified the Protocol, or
have finally acceded thereto" and declared that, "The said Protocol
shall cease to be binding on His Britannic Majesty towards any
Power at enmity with him whose armed forces, or the armed forces
of whose allies, fail to respect the prohibitions laid down in the
Protocol."[9] The Soviets entered a similar reservation.

This means that the Geneva Gas Protocol of 1925 only regulates
adherents and may be broken if any adherent, or its allies, breaks
the ban on CB. It also implies "open season" on non-adherents,
the principal two being the United States, which signed but never
ratified the Protocol, and Japan.

It also raises the interesting question whether the wording of the
Protocol is either inaccurate or internally contradictory, or, whether
the regime established by the treaty was not actually retrogressive.
For, had it been the case that this kind of warfare was *already*
illegal and immoral, an agreement to reiterate such an alleged state
of affairs *conditioned* on reciprocity of all possible enemies *and*

[9] 94 L.N.T.S. 65 (1929).

their allies, was retrogressive. It made legally permissible something that had supposedly already been legally and morally "condemned."

In any event, the Geneva Protocol of 1925 was rescued from all these legalistic problems by the practice of state. Until the Vietnam War, no belligerent used CB methods except the Italians in the Ethiopian war in incidents which I trust that they repent and would like to forget and, possibly, the Japanese in China in World War II, although the facts are very hard to pin down. More recently another exception and very bad breach in practice has occurred, namely the use of lethal gas—which the U.S. has not used in Vietnam—by the incumbent, Egyptian-supported regime in Yemen, against defenseless inhabitants of areas under control of the rebels—or loyalists, depending on your point of view. What *is* clear is that the major powers in World War II did not use CB warfare although they all prepared for it as any recruit who went through the "gas chamber" remembers. The important point is that this record of abstention from CB was not based solely on fear of retaliation in kind. Some U.S. commanders requested permission to use gas against Japanese troops holed up in inaccessible positions, but permission was denied. In any event, for whatever variety of reasons, a ban has been in effect with respect to the kinds of means prohibited by the Geneva Protocol. In my view, there is now a rule of customary international reiterating the prohibitions of the Protocol, limiting almost to negation the reservations of the great powers who adhered to it and applicable to all states, including the United States and Japan. If this analysis is correct, the use in Vietnam of non-lethal gases and, perhaps, of defoliants, constitutes a breach of international law. The breach, moreover, is a most serious one, since it crosses a threshold that was not crossed in World War II or the Korean War and, in the business of normative limitations on the means of destruction, I have come to prefer defense of thresholds to situation ethics.

The ominous subject of CB warfare is one which brings out extraordinarily well the intricate interaction of law, morality, and public opinion. In my view, the law is clear and inflexible. At the very least it prohibits first use of any CB means and would only permit retaliation in kind if such means were used. Morally and humanly, there are obviously many arguments *for* the use of some form of CB warfare which are less destructive than many of the means already condoned in war. Would it not be more humane to use chemical means to put an enemy unit on a collective LSD trip while their position was being taken than attack them with artillery, mortars, small-arms fire, and bayonets? Proponents of CB warfare have produced moving pictures showing the effects of certain agents on cats who run away in terror from mice. The mice win, and the effects wear off. What is so wrong with such gentle methods of immobilizing the enemy?

Furthermore, within the sweeping category of CB means now apparently condemned by convention and custom are moderate means such as tear gas which are universally used to maintain domestic order. The ironies, paradoxes, and dilemmas are either agonizing or ludicrous—or humorous. If a Regular or National Guard unit uses tear gas to suppress a riot in an American city, instead of shooting, they are commended. If the same unit was sent to Vietnam and used the same tear gas against suspected Vietcong strongholds the headlines would blaze with the news of recourse to gas warfare and scientists would hold protest meetings.

It all comes down to the concept of the threshold. The CB threshold has been held. Once it is breached by "gentle," generally accepted means such as tear gas, where does it stop? Does the threshold remain intact? This is the big question for which I have no answer. I do know that it was possible to defend the threshold in the Second World War and the Korean War and that it is not being held in Vietnam. It is true that there are particular necessities in Vietnam, but there were particular necessities in the Pacific in World War II.

I am aware that one may redefine the threshold and draw the line at "lethal" and non-lethal. Ironically, one may answer this argument with *the* favorite argument of the proponents of CB, namely, that there were fewer fatalities, proportionally, among victims of gas warfare in World War I than of the other means of injury. Still, public opinion, nations, and the military themselves, concluded that CB was a pandora's box better left closed. I concur with this judgment.

Whereas modern CB warfare raises problems of creating new law to meet new problems, the legal principle of noncombatant immunity, as well as related principles of immunity of long standing, all of which are now either ignored or jeopardized, raise questions of squaring old law with new realities. The principle of discrimination traditionally considered as illegal and immoral direct, intentional attacks on noncombatants, non-military targets, and on medical and other humanitarian installations, vehicles, and personnel, whether of the International Committee of the Red Cross, or of national Red Cross or similar organizations pursuing similar objectives. My earlier comments on belligerent rights to revolutionary forces obviously lead me to claim an equal immunity for insurgent individuals and groups comparable to the aforementioned categories. Once again, law, morality, and public opinion tend to differ and to splinter into conflicting interpretations of contemporary practices.

As a legal principle, the principle of discrimination arises out of the fortunate coincidence of the character of warfare and the dictates of morality and humanity. Until at least the war engendered by the French Revolution of 1789, modern war, that is, since 1648, was fought mainly by professional forces using means that permitted discrimination. Broadly speaking, there was little or no military reason to attack noncombatants and non-military objectives. Exceptions, when they occurred, were deplored. With the evolution of "total war," beginning with the mass armies, ideological causes, and extension of objectives of the wars resulting from the French Revolution of 1789, the situation changed. The purposes of war became more profound, the forces were larger and less professional, and, noticeably in the American Civil War, the means of war, the capabilities of communication and rapid movement produced by the Industrial Revolution, became so devastating that the principle of discrimination was increasingly difficult to apply in purely military, utilitarian terms. Obviously, by the end of World War I the principle in its original form was technically impossible, and its demise was recorded, in part because of the demise of the original principal of discrimination, along with the hope that war would be outlawed. The only exception was the continued immunity of Red Cross installations, vehicles, and personnel, and even this was subject both to violation and abuse, the two interacting.

As a moral principle, the principle of discrimination has always been closely linked with its legal counterpart and, therefore, subject to the same vulnerabilities arising out of the changes in the character of war as the international law of war. The absolute immunity of noncombatants from intentional direct attack cannot be justified as a moral imperative if the right of legitimate recourse to armed force is conceded. Insistence on such principles as absolute immunity under modern conditions of war, ranging from revolutionary to nuclear, leads logically to pacifism, a position obviously rejected in this book.

However, as a matter of international law as well as of morality, the following may be said:

1. Deliberate attacks on noncombatants and on targets that are of no apparent, or only extremely marginal, military importance, are immoral and violative of the principle of legitimate military necessity, for example, deliberate or random attacks on small villages because of some allegation that it is "friendly" to enemy forces;

2. Attacks involving a high degree of danger and/or death and destruction to noncombatants and/or non-military targets are contrary to the principle of legitimate military necessity and the dictates of morality when such attacks are disproportionate to the military utility claimed for them.

I see no need to elaborate on the first point. As to the second, I will concede that it is a difficult one to work out in practice. The problem is raised at all levels, nuclear, conventional, sub-conventional. Legitimate nuclear targets, as well as proper targets for conventional aerial or artillery attack, may often be placed, very possibly by design, in otherwise non-military areas in which large numbers of noncombatants are to be found. The attacker must weigh the considerations for military necessity and for immunity of noncombatants and non-military targets. I have already indicated a choice in favor of the latter with respect to first use of countercity warfare, nuclear or conventional. I was thinking then in primarily strategic-missile and bomber-strike terms. But what about ground defense of or attack against a city, or a densely populated area likc Western Europe? Before Hiroshima, Hamburg, and London, there was Verdun, back in the old days of conventional warfare. Noncombatants and non-military targets "on the battlefield," and modern "battle-fields" can stretch across hundreds of miles, are simply caught in the cross fire, as the small number of persons and targets in earlier types were caught when they had the misfortune to be located at Waterloo or Gettysburg.

As to sub-conventional, revolutionary, or guerrilla warfare, *since* it is a characteristic policy of the guerrillas to come from the people, hide among the people, manipulate the people—and their real and other property—it is evident that the concept of immunity of non-combatants and non-military targets is, in a very real sense, too much to ask of the revolutionaries. If they really observed it, would they have a chance? Counterinsurgency forces have more options in this matter and ought to be held more closely accountable for their be-havior, but when "combatants" include children and old women who throw grenades, when "peaceful hamlets" are fortified strongholds, when the rebels make it a practice of indiscriminately attacking cafes, restaurants, movie theaters, and, with rockets and mortars, towns and cities, what are the counterinsurgents to do? All that I can see that can be required of them that they "do their best" to minimize death and destruction to noncombatants and non-military targets, as legal and moral obligations, and as good counterinsur-gency policy.

Across the board, then, if you insist on noncombatant immunity you insist on pacifism and nonviolence, a perfectly rational, and per-haps more moral position, which I am unable to take.

Widespread devastation not required by legitimate military neces-sity violates the general principles of proportionality and discrimina-tion, and the specific provisions of Article 23 (g) of the 1907 Hague Rules, as well as the Nuremberg principles concerning war crimes.

The law is clear, but its interpretation is very difficult and in a state of disarray. Recourse to general principles of international law and/or morality, will be necessary to correct the widespread and *wrong* (legally, morally, in terms of public opinion, militarily) practices of virtually all contemporary belligerents in this regard. The crux of the problem, a product of the neglect of the laws of war in the inter-war period, is that all the laws and precedents concern actions by *ground* forces, whereas, despite the continuing importance of ground forces, we have been in the air age, much less the space and nuclear age, for some time.

The Hague Rules and the Nuremberg principles refer to devastation wrought by ground forces, for example, as part of a scorched-earth defense by a retreating force wherein all shelter facilities and material potentially of value to the enemy are systematically destroyed and the inhabitants driven from their homes. Neither source of international law applies to aerial bombardment, insufficiently anticipated in 1907, and quite simply avoided at Nuremberg and in the other war crimes trials by nations which had overtaken and exceeded their Axis enemies in their "city busting" practices.

Every modern belligerent having the capability of doing so has attacked or is likely to attack major population centers through strategic bombing policies, employing such dreadful methods and expressions as "city busting," "fire bombing," or, in the nuclear vernacular, "taking out a city." This raises issues closely related to but not synonymous with those of nuclear deterrence. For, strategic bombing of population centers occurs or threatens to occur quite independently of retaliation in kind and, conceivably, with little relation to deterrence.

If this is the case, there should be little difficulty in applying vigorously the condemnation of countercity warfare by modern popes, Vatican II, and many other sources of authoritative moral judgment. Absent the deterrent dilemma, there are no adequate grounds for violation of the prohibition against countercity warfare. This prohibition should be strictly construed to include not only "area bombing" but also attacks against military targets in heavily populated areas. Specifically, U.S. air strikes in or near Hanoi and Haiphong in December 1966 and March 1968 violated this principle. The undoubted military character of the specific targets, and the considerable advantages derived from these attacks, did not justify violation of the prohibition against countercity warfare. Other air raids over North Vietnam would have to be judged on a case-by-case basis. It is admittedly difficult to weigh the military requirements for interdicting and destroying enemy forces and supplies with the foreseeable death and destruction that raids for such purposes will cause among noncombatant individuals and habitations adjacent to the military targets.

Insofar as counter*force* strikes, by air, sea, or ground forces, there is no limit. The Israeli devastation of the Egyptian air force is the model.

Public opinion is perhaps more variable, going in the direction of limitation as well as of permissiveness on the subject of widespread devastation is concerned. This is the case, I believe, with respect to countercity warfare, more than on any other issue raised here. Perhaps the heart of the problem is that many people, ranging from military experts, who should by now have learned better, to supporters or opponents of particular wars, tend to overestimate the effectiveness of large-scale aerial countercity warfare. To the military involved in a conflict, the hope that "escalation" to maximum strategic bombing will markedly reduce the sacrifices required on the ground is eternal. It is shared by proponents of the war within the belligerent state who want to "win" and who also want to "get it over with." Domestic opponents of the war seem to rally particularly around the issue of "stopping the bombing" as a major part of their anti-war protests. The same is true of foreign critics.

The fact is that no modern war has been won *primarily* by strategic bombing, specifically, by countercity warfare. No contemporary state has been bombed into submissiveness and demanded that its government surrender. On the contrary, the record is almost universally that of proud and stubborn acceptance of the horrors and hardships of continued bombing—whether in Britain, Germany, or North Vietnam. Yet the pressures of public opinion within any state at war or threatened by war are always heavily in the direction of increasing the strategic air capability or of escalating the air war. Thus, many nations, for example in the Middle East, which denounce U.S. bombing in North Vietnam engage in senseless arms races in the field of air power, would probably not adhere to any international restrictions on recourse to air power, and seem ready to use it when they think they can. They have been known to miscalculate.

The upshot? The prospects for formal international legal limitations in this field are poor. This is a field that calls for enlightened application of sound general legal and (in my view) moral and military principles, all enjoining restraint and warning against reliance on mass destruction as an easy route to victory.

Pillage was once a rampant and greatly feared feature of warfare. It still exists, but the law of war is clear in condemning pillage. Indeed, this is virtually the only unqualified prohibition of the 1907 Hague Rules (Hague Rules, Article 28). Pillage is, of course, likewise morally condemned, involving as it does wanton destruction, arson, theft, and rape. As usual, public opinion tends to be variable on this subject, as on the others treated. There is, for example, a tendency to condone pillage in the conquest of a much-hated aggressor such as Nazi Germany. Responsible molders of opinion, must, like responsible military commanders, constantly combat the mentality that would condone or even encourage such vengeful and immoral behavior.

One of the cornerstones of the laws of war is the *concept of communication between belligerents*. Since war ought not to be an orgy of hatred or destruction—no matter how much hatred and destruction result from war, the dreaded but last and necessary arbiter of international conflict—there is both a legal and moral obligation to enter into communication with the enemy with respect to subjects such as:

1. Truces: to care for or evacuate the sick and wounded, as well as noncombatants, to observe religious or nation feast days or

seasons, to discuss terms of temporary truce, or of surrender at the tactical level;

2. Agreements to exchange prisoners of war;

3. Armistice agreements leading to temporary or long-term, indefinite cessation of hostilities, or to formal peace.

Such communication requires protection of messengers under flags of truce, as well as of medical personnel and chaplains. The Hague Rules of 1907 and the Geneva Conventions of 1949 specifically prohibit perfidious behavior which violates express or implied indications of the willingness of a belligerent to communicate with its opponents. The U. S. Army's Field Manual 27-10 states:

49. *Good Faith*

Absolute good faith with the enemy must be observed as a rule of conduct; but this does not prevent measures such as using spies and secret agents, encouraging defection or insurrection among the enemy civilian population, corrupting enemy civilians or soldiers by bribes, or inducing the enemy's soldiers to desert, surrender, or rebel. In general, a belligerent may resort to those measures for mystifying or misleading the enemy against which the enemy ought to take measures to protect himself.

50. *Treachery or Perfidy*

Ruses of war are legitimate so long as they do not involve treachery or perfidy on the part of the belligerent resorting to them. They are, however, forbidden if they contravene any generally accepted rule.

The line of demarcation between legitimate ruses and forbidden acts of perfidy is sometimes indistinct, but the following examples indicate the correct principles. It would be an improper practice to secure an advantage of the enemy by deliberately lying or misleading conduct which involves a breach of faith, or when there is a moral obligation to speak the truth. For example, it is improper to feign surrender so as to secure an advantage over the opposing belligerent thereby. So similarly, to broadcast to the enemy that an armistice has been agreed upon when such is not the case would be treacherous. On the other hand, it is a perfectly proper ruse to summon a force to surrender on the ground that it is surrounded and thereby induce such surrender with a small force.

> *Treacherous or perfidious conduct in war is forbidden because it destroys the basis for a restoration of peace short of the complete annihilation of one belligerent by the other.*[10]

This is sufficiently clear not to require elaboration. What is more difficult is the modern phenomenon of "fighting and negotiating," as in the Korean conflict and in that in Vietnam. In such situations, talks concerning cessation of hostilities, prisoner exchanges, and other subjects, are held concurrently with the continuation of hostilities. There is, in general, no legal obligation to negotiate in any particular way, unless one is under constraints imposed by the UN Security Council or General Assembly—and these can be handled, as Israel has demonstrated. Morally, the question of negotiations is a part of the basic question of the permissibility, particularly the proportionality, of the conflict. It is also a question of good faith in bargaining, always a difficult question, whether in the realm of labor-management relations or of international law and diplomacy.

Domestic and international public opinion play a heavy role in this regard. Desire for peace places heavy pressures on the party which seems to be blocking a settlement. In assessing these pressures it is important to distinguish—insofar as possible—moral pressures from emotional or humanitarian pressures which are expressed in moralistic terms.

Current negotiations over Vietnam provide the focus for this kind of pressure. Similar pressures, likewise complicated, are brought to bear on Israel and her Arab adversaries. I would like to propose the following moral principle. It will no doubt anger those for whom peace is always the priority and it will very likely appear "out of season." So be it. *Proposition:* If a nation's reasons for waging a war are reasonable or plausible, its obligation to negotiate an end to such a war is inextricably linked with the attainment or protection of the purposes for which the war has been fought, insofar as the outcome of the conflict and the disposition of the negotiating parties permits. If it is morally wrong to fight an unreasonable war it seems

[10] FM 27-10, ※49 & 50, p. 22. [Emphasis added]

to me to be also morally wrong to fight a reasonable war—one
that can be reasonably justified, not that everyone will agree with
the justification—and then throw away much that one has been
fighting for out of a desire to end the conflict or under the always
formidable pressures of public opinion.

International law, under the Hague Conventions of 1899 and
the 1949 Geneva Convention Relative to the Protection of Civilian
Persons in Time of War, provides in some detail for the *protection
of societies occupied in the course of international conflict*. Under the
traditional law the occupying power was entitled to reasonable use
of the resources of the occupied territory, but could not permanently
alter or exhaust those resources, human and material. The occupant
was obliged to provide the fundamental protection and governmental
services no longer operative because of the retreat of the defeated
sovereign. The traditional law emphasized the temporary, "precarious," character of belligerent occupation and, accordingly, an
obligation not to incorporate the occupied area into the occupant's
domain or substantially to alter its political, economic, and social
institutions. Finally, these duties of the occupant were balanced by
a legal presumption of obedience to reasonable and lawful measures
and laws of the occupying power.

A number of problems of modern conflict make continued adherence to the international law of belligerent occupation difficult
if not impossible.

First, modern conflict often emphasizes rapid and fluid engagement with enemy forces rather than occupation of territory. It is
often difficult to know what, if any, belligerent force is or ought
to be the responsible belligerent occupant or responsible ruler of an
area.

Second, modern ideological warfare, fought for great stakes, often
originating in a manner that constitutes indirect aggression, works
against any concept of "temporary allegiance," loyalty or, at least
docility, on the part of the occupied or disrupted society.

Linked to the two former points, the development of guerrilla
warfare has made it difficult for an occupant to retain substantial

control of occupied territory. It has encouraged resistance and has left the general populations in occupied or disrupted areas caught in a cross fire of pressures and hostilities, objects of acts of terrorism and reprisal originating from two—or more (e.g., Yugoslavia in World War II)—contending parties.

Particularly in guerrilla warfare, whether as part of a larger conventional war or in a revolutionary war in the sense of Chapter VII, the population is used, pressured, coerced, terrorized—ultimately by all sides. The war is fought *through* rather than in and around the society (e.g. rather indiscriminate U.S.-RVN sweeps in "VC" zones in Vietnam, the Tet offensive of 1968). Thus, the problem of warfare directed against population centers, condemned by the Church and by enlightened public opinion, is in point of fact more of a problem in existing revolutionary conflicts than in the much-feared nuclear or general wars, the specter of which produced this teaching.

Moreover, a belligerent, whether a poor nation or an insurgent force, may not be able to provide the protection and governmental functions usually required of a belligerent occupant. Introduction of outside assistance from the International Committee of the Red Cross, other nations, and other sources of aid, may be difficult. In such cases a society may be as badly harmed by starvation, disease, and the collapse of organized government as by hostilities waged within it. As these lines are written the plight of the inhabitants of Biafra presents an all too clear example.

Finally, there is a very real problem, raised by the Biafran tragedy, of a *rebel* force which may, in effect, be considered a belligerent occupant. The same could be said of Vietcong or North Vietnamese-controlled areas of South Vietnam. The Vietcong are not "recognized" belligerents and, until very recently, the North Vietnamese did not even admit that they were in South Vietnam. But, if these forces are to benefit, as I have argued, by qualification as belligerent beneficiaries of the laws of war, they most certainly are responsible for extending to peoples under their control the maximum number of rights required by the laws of war that can reasonably be expected of them. Unfortunately, as often as not, such forces live off the country and take rather than give, except when it comes to discipline. International law has no answer for this problem, nor do I. Once again, enthusiasts for revolution have some thinking to do. Who looks after the people once the government is chased out? Sometimes the rebels do, very well in some cases, better than the old government. If the going is tough they cannot, and the people, as is always the case in revolutionary war, end up in the middle, suffering.

The moral dilemmas of belligerent generally parallel those of the POW regime. They are:

1. Does a party to a modern war which really observes the international law protecting occupied societies have a fair chance of success?

2. If not—on either side, occupant or resistance—is there a moral obligation to observe the law and probably lose, or to break with the law and have a better chance of winning?

Underlying these general questions is the illusive issue of the true utility of violating the law. Experience and legal precedent, for example, the U. S. War Crimes Tribunal's decisions in the "high command" and "hostages" cases at Nuremberg condoned some practices by the German occupants of the Balkans and other parts of Europe which are now prohibited by the 1949 Geneva Convention Relative to the Protection of Civilian Persons in Time of War. The positive law is up for re-examination both in the light of moral and military considerations.

I have already stated that I favor maximal extension of the rights and duties of international law to unrecognized actual participants in revolutionary wars. This, of course, means that such participants must undertake as far as possible responsibility for area under their more or less continuous control. Often they do, for their own ultimate ideological-political purposes. If they do not, and are in physical control of certain areas, they are deliquents under international law. One cannot have it both ways. One either is in control, at least most of the time, and therefore responsible for what happens, under international law, or one is not in control, and is neither responsible for nor can legitimately take credit for, behavior within an area.

In summary, this survey has demonstrated that, in terms of positive international law, the laws of war are elaborately codified in widely accepted treaties, primarily governing what Hugo Grotius called the *temperamenta belli*. The positive law does not, with the exception of CB warfare, deal explicitly and adequately with the means of destruction in wars. Thus the U. S. Army's Field Manual on *The Law of Land Warfare* can say laconically in 1956: "The use of explosive 'atomic weapons' whether by air, sea, or land forces, cannot as such be regarded as violative of international law in the absence of any customary rule of international law or international convention restricting their employment."[11] In other words, short of arms-control and disarmament agreements, nuclear weapons are permitted.

From the moral standpoint we see a number of dilemmas. Neither nuclear war in general nor countercity war is clearly condemned by international law, but at least some forms of both, and perhaps both categories, ought to be. Some things at the other end of the spectrum of military coercion, on the other hand, are clearly contrary to international law, and may well be immoral, but they are commonly practiced by belligerents, such as certain forms of torture which appear to be destined for continuation as seemingly necessary if revolutionary war, from the perspectives of both sides, is to be countenanced.

We see, further, that public opinion, both within warring societies and in unengaged nations, fluctuates greatly. Domestic public opinion tends to be quick to defend that which appears necessary for success in a war that is generally approved. If there is strong opposition to a particular war, public opinion tends to impute violations of international law and morality in the process of protest. Public opinion at all levels is further influenced by a natural re-

11 ⌗35, p. 19.

vulsion against the terrible suffering of war, ranging from the victims of bombing to those of terrorist guerrilla attacks, all of which are thrown into view by the communications media daily. There is a great tendency to embrace slogans such as, "Stop the killing." Such slogans beg the whole political, military, legal, and moral question of war. There is either reasonable justification and proportionality of ends and means for war or not. One might as well ask the surgeon to "stop the bleeding," or the psychiatrist to bring a halt to insanity. The war is either, generally speaking, right and permissible or wrong and impermissible, and a great deal of human suffering will be involved in either case.

What seems necessary is a candid confrontation by responsible decision-makers and citizens with the following propositions:

1. War is a fact. Attempts at prevention of war are not enough. There must be laws of war as long as man is sinful and attacks his neighbor, a possibility that I not only anticipate but accept on authority from a very internationalist pope, Paul VI, before the General Assembly of the UN.

2. Adhesion to international agreements regulating war may be generally desirable, but a careful, constant watch should be kept on the relationship between written law, actual practice, moral values widely held, and public opinion.

3. The laws of war are improved by facing the practical and moral dilemmas of war, not by pretending that they are covered by existing law when they are not—or ought not to be—or, by total war—or total peace approaches—unfortunately held in both cases by many Americans.

There are basically two kinds of sanctions for the laws of war: (1) those imposed by enemy belligerents or by bodies purporting to speak for the international community; (2) self-imposed restraints and sanctions.

Under international law the two principal sanctions of the laws of war are reprisals and war-crimes trials.

Reprisals are acts which technically violate international law but which are justified as retaliatory reactions to *prior* violations of the law by the enemy. They must be proportionate to the need to punish the violators and to deter continuation of lawless behavior. We have seen that reprisals should not be made against POWs and protected noncombatants, even as retaliation in kind. Reprisals represent both the strength and weakness of the laws of war. Fear of reprisals is probably the greatest sanction, aside from acceptance based on reason, of the laws of war. On the other hand, reprisals have notoriously served as as excuse for almost every violation of international law and morality in war. Just as the definition and application of "self-defense" is the key to the legal/moral question of recourse to armed force in international relations, reprisals are the key to the legal and moral dilemmas of establishing and main-forces of field manuals on the principles and laws of war;

War-crimes trials may by instituted either by individual belligerents at the end of a conflict or, as in the case of the Nuremberg Trial of Major War Criminals, by a number of belligerents who may or may not purport to represent the majority of the international community.

It is true that these trials represent "victor's justice." They have to, since there is no international war-crimes tribunal in the sense that the International Court of Justice is an international tribunal. The war-crimes trials following World War II established or reiterated a substantial body of international law, procedural and substantive. However, contemporary conflicts seldom produce situations akin to that of 1945. War-crimes trials are usually either not possible or desirable as a sanction for the laws of war. Accordingly, greater attention should be given to *self-imposed* restraints by belligerents.

Belligerents should *demonstrate* self-restraint:

1. Through the distribution and enforcement within the armed forces of field manuals on the principles and laws of war;

2. Through court martials and other disciplinary dispositions of violations of the laws of war by members of their own armed forces;

3. Through explicit and implicit adoption of "rules of engagement," such as the limitation on UN bombing north of the Yalu

River in the Korean conflict, various limitations on areas of attack in Vietnam and its neighboring states, and the restrictions imposed on their troops for fighting in historic and religiously important parts of Jerusalem by the Israelites (e.g. use of small-arms fire and the bayonet rather than artillery which would destroy historic or sacred buildings).

It should be recognized that military discipline makes self-restraint possible. Civilian control of the military ought to shape the form and magnitude of such self-restraint, although this has not always been the case. Sometimes the military are more sensitive to the need for self-restraint than civilian superiors and civilians in other agencies of government, and, certainly, than the bellicose gentlemen who tend to dominate legislative committees concerned with military matters. But only the collaboration of a responsible and disciplined military establishment, a firm and understanding civilian government, and an enlightened public opinion represented by real statesmen and not demagogues, can make military restraint, limited war, the laws of war—and, ultimately, arms control and disarmament—possible.

IX   War and the Christian Conscience

War, deterrence, and revolution must be confronted by "the Church" in many ways. I will not attempt to define "the Church," even in Catholic terms. There is enough controversy over the definition of "the Church" and the distribution of authority within it today. Without attempting technical distinctions, I write of "the Church," as the Church to which I belong, the Roman Catholic Church. When I refer to "the Church," I refer both to the teaching authority, the *magisterium,* of the hierarchy of the Church, and to its members, "the people of God." I have no wish to exclude from this discussion, or offend, other Christians or Jews. On the contrary, I address myself to all men of good will, in the spirit of Pope John's *Pacem in Terris.*

But I do not want to seem to speak for other traditions, for which I have neither the knowledge nor the right. This then is a discussion of war and the Christian conscience in the sense that I have defined "Christian," with all men of good will invited to join in—and to help, because the Christian conscience on war is not very good and help from any source will be appreciated.

In closing this consideration of war and/or survival I would like to discuss four voices and consciences of the Church:

1. The institutional Church speaking officially through the pope and the hierarchy;

2. Authoritative Catholic moralists and scholars;

3. "Peace organization";

4. Responsible Christian citizens.

The first question that must be faced squarely by all four voices and consciences of the Church, which is appropriately raised immediately in discussing the institutional Church, is the question of the relation of God and the theological truths handed down by Him to the issues of war, deterrence, and violent revolution.

The first published version of Fr. John Courtney Murray's 1958 address to the Catholic Association of International Peace was entitled "Theology and Modern War."[1] Other versions did not use the term, "theology." Thus, the version which was issued as a pamphlet by the Church Peace Union, now the Council on Religion and International Affairs, was entitled, *Morality and Modern War*.[2] The version that Fr. Murray included in a chapter of his book, *We Hold These Truths* has the interesting title, "The Uses of a Doctrine on the Uses of Force, War as a Moral Problem."[3] Most books on the subject speak of the "doctrine," or "theory" of "just war"; or of the "thought" or "teaching" of the Church on that subject. Many books emphasize the word "problem," for example, René Coste's, *Le Problème du droit de guerre dans la pensée de Pie XII*.[4] Quite frequently "ethics" is the rubrics for discussions on this subject as in its consideration by Johannes Messner.[5]

Thus we have theology and war, morality and war, the moral problem of war, the "doctrine," "theory," "thought," "teaching," of the Church of Scholasticism or of a particular tradition, on war, and "ethics" and war.

Today one hears demands for a theology of violent revolution, ironically, sometimes from some of the same sources that also demand the abandonment of any moral toleration of war and the development of a theology of peace. Yet most of the principles that

[1] *10 Theological Studies* (1959) 4061.

[2] (1959.)

[3] New York: Sheed and Ward (1960), pp. 249–73.

[4] Paris: Aubier (1961).

[5] *Social Ethics*, trans. by J. H. Doherty, rev. ed.; St. Louis: Herder (1965), Chapters 105 (pp. 510–15) and 146 (pp. 665–69).

come down to us in the "official" just war doctrine, a modified version of which still is, as we have seen, the starting point for the Church's teaching on war, appears to be rather more dependent on scholastic natural law philosophy and ethics than on explicitly theological bases. This would appear to be particularly the case as the doctrine moved from St. Augustine's emphasis on war as the scourge of God punishing the unjust to modern modified just war concepts of war as an unfortunate and exceptional social necessity wherein offensive wars against injustice are expressly prohibited.

It seems to me that Christ's messages to us and personal example tell us very little about public or corporate ethics and least of all about the ethics of war and revolution. The Old Testament seems capable of many interpretations, some of them closer to St. Augustine's attitude than that of Pius XII, and some of them fairly blood-curdling. As a known friend of Israel I have heard "just war" interpretations from learned American Jewish rabbis which would give pause to a devotee of General LeMay or Dr. Teller.

But I believe that the Church Christ founded through Peter has the authority to expand and elaborate His teaching and has, indeed, done so in many fields of social ethics that were not and could not have been treated in Sacred Scripture. (Contrast modern social teaching of the Church on labor-management relations with the admonition to *slaves* to be obedient to their masters, even the bad masters!) I take it to be a tenable Christian position that I may look to the teachings of Christ's Church, rather than to His own teaching and example as described in the New Testament, for guidance on the moral problems of war.

Christ, after all, did not come down from heaven to be the Messiah ruling over a triumphant, liberated, Jewish nation or to be a partisan leader of a Jewish resistance movement. He came to offer Himself as a sacrifice to redeem sinful mankind. Regardless of the possible implications of His words in Gethsemane, "all those who take the sword will perish by the sword," it is clear that the Divine Plan for Christ's sacrifice did not permit self-defense measures by His followers—which might otherwise have been quite appropriate. In other instances, before the time for His sacrifice for us had come, when Jesus was threatened, He managed to extricate Himself, sometimes apparently by miraculous means not available to those of us who are mere mortals and not saints. Accordingly, it does not seem helpful to enjoin men and nations to "act as Christ would have acted" in situations of war or violent revolution.

If we did we would all be pacifists. Indeed, it would be interesting to see a community of any size, much less something that purported to be a nation, acting on honest pacifists principles. Even neutralized nations have armies, or at least internal security forces. Even the Vatican has Swiss guards who bar your way if you attempt to enter the wrong door at the wrong time. But perhaps the Vatican is corrupted by an unsavory history of meddling in power politics. What about a pacifist community? Would it call the local or neighboring police if it were viciously attacked by people who do not like pacifists? Since I have taken on more than enough problems already I will leave that one for the pacifists, some of whom I greatly admire.

But the Roman Catholic Church is not a pacifist Church and as recently as Vatican II it was necessary to clarify the rights of Catholics to take a pacifist position. Indeed, the institutional Church has not only condoned and supported wars and revolutions, it has initiated a goodly number, some of which we regard in retrospect with penitent dismay. Thus favorite questions of pacifists and opponents of a particular war, "Would Christ submit to the Draft?" "What would Christ do about Vietnam?" seem to me extremely irrelevant. Christ was a man, but a man with an utterly unique purpose, the sacrifice of His life as God-Man for the redemption of mankind. The fact that the core of Christianity is to be found in the teaching and example of Jesus Christ seems to me to render difficult a moral analysis of war than can be termed *theological*.

Certainly many basic theological concepts condition our moral analyses of war. We must recognize every enemy as a man born in the image and likeness of God, a man for whom Christ died. This should surely influence our attitudes and acts, even in the heat of war. But I prefer to leave theology, whether of war, peace, or revolution, to others. As stated in the beginning of this book, I prefer to discuss the moral problem of war on an ethical rather than a theological level.

Once one has moved from a claim to theological grounding for normative principles to the realm of ethic, considerable room for discussion and disagreement obviously exists, not that theology is free from either. Moreover, as we turn from the science that deals with the ultimate truths about God to that which deals in less authoritative and dogmatic fashion with detailed questions of human behavior, often quite removed from any relevant authoritative theological precepts, to ethics, we move to a discipline that is subject to constant reconsideration and revision in the light of historical experience and the development of relevant secular disciplines.

For example, contemporary Catholic social teaching is now emphatic on the issues of racial equality and justice. But there was a time, not so long ago, when it condoned slavery and, later, manifest racial discrimination. Thus, for years Catholics in the United States were not encouraged or coerced into acceptance of racial equality. It was enough if they contributed generously to collections for the "Negro and Indian Missions." There came a time when changes occurred in American society and the place of the Catholic Church within that society became more assured. Meanwhile the social sciences conclusively demonstrated the humanly degrading and indefensible character of racial discrimination. Ethical theory, practice, and emphasis changed, even in the South, and Catholics who had grown up in a segregated Catholic Church were excommunicated by their bishop when they violently resisted his pronouncements requiring integration and racial justice.

The distinction between moral analyses of war that claim to be theologically grounded and those that are ethical is particularly well demonstrated in the debate over the absolute principle of noncombatant immunity from direct intentional attack discussed earlier. Acceptance of this as an absolute principle derived from theology drives one logically into a pacifist position with regard to modern war. But if, as I have argued, the principle is at best an ethical principle, based on *a* natural-law approach, not on "the universal natural law," resulting from historical circumstances, which have now been decisively altered, and that adherence to the principle as an absolute principle, rather than as a guideline or preferred goal, is incompatible with the modern application of the right of self-defense or community enforcement action, then modification of the principle is justified.[6]

In short, ethical theory must be faithful to genuine first principles —of which there are few—but it is properly elastic and subject to development in the light of relevant secular sciences and historical circumstances. Ethical theory which unjustifiably freezes or treats as immutable, principles which are not really entitled to such immutable inviolability, and which neglects the knowledge and techniques of the relevant secular sciences, and which is unresponsive to the historical context in which it is advanced, is subject to criticism and rejection and is likely to be ignored.

This book has argued that the contemporary ethical teaching of the Church on war, deterrence, and revolution is insufficiently responsive to the real problems of nations, statesmen, and citizens in a world of conflict. Moreover, it displays a very uneven acquaintance with the theory and practice of modern war, deterrence, and revolution. As earlier noted, the basic deficiency in the Churches teaching on these subjects is derived from an unwarranted belief in the possibility of early, fundamental change in the international system, leading to world government, the elimination of armaments and war, and a sufficient amelioration of the social-economic-racial-political conditions which seem to contribute to the outbreak of war and violent revolution. The desirable or ideal has been proposed as the possible and necessary in terms of human behavior. This technical and prudential judgment is then made a moral imperative, the impact of which is only mitigated by vagueness as to the time-frame during

[6] I have argued this point in more detail and with more documentation that I believe to be warranted in this book in *Nuclear War, Deterrence and Morality* (New York: Newman Press, 1967).

which this fundamental systemic change is to be effected. I should reiterate that the same can be said about similar religious and humanist idealist views of international relations.

This moral imperative is given to men and nations at a time when quite obviously both the theory and practice of international relations and of domestic politics throughout the world offer little or no reason to believe that the changes necessary to make an adequate response to the teaching of the Church—of the admonitions of idealists of all persuasions—are anywhere on the horizon. If the Church and so many other authorities are right in saying that the world cannot survive *with* war, it will not survive, for "elimination" of war means elimination and replacement of the present international system, and that is not in prospect. We must cope with war within the present international system, which we will try to improve in order to survive.

Moreover, since the social teaching of the Church continues, however reluctantly, to condone limited war and, by inference, violent revolution, it is both permissible and responsible for the realist to delve into the moral and material problems of limiting war as long as the present system continues. For if limited war, especially when waged for causes consonant with international law, order, and justice, is necessary in the international system here and now, survival requires immediate attention to the problems of limiting war. This, of course, does not preclude support for efforts to change the system. But, from the realist's standpoint, even if the system is replaced by a new system, the problem of limiting war will remain. It will only change the formulation of the issues and the terms used, such as limiting a "world police force," of limiting the means of deterring "revolution" against a new, better world order. The practical problems will remain similar to those arising from war deterrence and revolution in the present international system.

The task of limiting war now, in the system that exists now, and also, thereby, of improving the prospects for limiting recourse to permissible force under a different international system in the future, has not been adequately faced by the institutional church or by other organizations of the international idealist persuasion. Indeed, in its pleas for peace, in its moral imperative demands for international systemic change, the Church has probably obstructed some of the necessary work required to limit war so that we may survive.

How has the Church obstructed the work of limiting war? It has done so by consistently begging the question of war and peace, as well as the savage dilemmas of violent revolution. It has done so by reiteration of Pope Pius XII's theme: *Nothing is lost with peace; all may be lost with war.*[7] This is simply not true. A great deal may be lost by peace, perhaps values of such importance and on such a scale as to render the decision for avoidance of war disproportionate and irresponsible. For there can be disproportionate, unjust peace as well as disproportionate, unjust war. There would have been peace in Europe in 1940 if the British had made a deal with the Nazis. As the Holy Father would have looked out on a peaceful Europe under such a regime he would have seen some things that would have been every bit as wrong and inhuman as the dreadful suffering brought about by the Second World War. Granted, a great deal is always lost with war, particularly modern war. But great evil on a stupendous scale exists in the world because of war which was *not* fought or which was fought and lost.

To be sure, the Church and most idealists do not argue for "peace at any price." The Church specifically rejects this concept. But its pronouncements on war-peace issues, whether by popes, council, bishops, moralists, or peace organizations purporting to rely upon these pronouncements, implicitly encourage belief in and action in the direction of "peace at any price." Moreover, the words that followed Pius XII's August 1939 appeal further begged the question of war and peace: *"Let men return to mutual understanding! Let them begin negotiations anew, conferring with good-will and with respect for reciprocal rights."* (Emphasis added.) In other words, back to Munich! Ponder those well-meant words by the Vicar of Christ on Earth, addressed to, among others, two totalitarian powers which

[7] Radio Address to the Whole World and Its Leaders, August 24, 1939. [Emphasis added]

were both practicing genocide as standard operating procedure and plotting a new and terrible conquestion and division of Poland. Nineteen thirty-nine was a time for just war—not even for permissible war, as I have preferred to call it, but just war. Justice was at stake. Sadly, neither the Church nor the secular proponents of international idealism had prepared men for a modern just war *that was limited*. There ensued a war that was unlimited, in part because insufficient thought had been given to the contingency of a modern just war.

So the institutional Church (excluding, usually, the hierarchies of nations in which war is threatened or in course, who generally rally around the flag, which they should not do automatically and uncritically), concedes the continuing right of defensive war in the abstract. But in virtually every concrete case of threat or recourse to war the admonition is for parties whose differences are so great that they consciously accept the terrible, well-known costs of modern war or revolution, to solve the problems peaceably. In many cases this advice is no more relevant or adequate than advice in other fields, such as that of birth control and the population explosion, wherein the essence of the advice is to discount the problem. There *are,* manifestly, the more so since the issuance of the encyclical *Humanae Vitae,* profound problems created by the Church's traditional teaching on birth control. It is no longer tenable to say that there is really no world population problem but only a problem of reallocation of the world's food and other resources—or of self-control.

References to Pope Pius XII's 1939 peace appeal bring us to the dual function of such appeals. They are both source materials for the social teaching of Church and diplomatic initiatives. The modern Church has increasingly thrown the weight of Vatican diplomacy into the cause of peace, whether in direct papal appeals to the parties, as in the Vietnam conflict, or in such interventions as that of the Papal Nuncio in Santo Domingo during the 1965 revolution. Similar but different functions are of course performed by the pronouncements of organizations such as the World Council of Churches. The seemingly enhanced influence of the Catholic Church and of the popes in particular, as well as of the World Council of Churches and similar bodies, can be a great force for good in international relations. But this force can be exploited, sometimes by parties who would quickly eliminate or silence these religious voices if given the opportunity, to the disadvantage of those men and nations who most respect the Church's authority and the fundamental rights of human dignity respected by all men of good will.

If we turn from the popes to the hierarchies within individual nations and to Vatican II, we note related obstacles to moral and practical efforts to maintain the option of morally permissible war but to keep such wars limited. Here the subject becomes even more complicated, because there are trends in the direction of peace at any price and other trends toward "My Country Right or Wrong." There is also a tendency to avoid the issues of war and revolution altogether. Several observations appear relevant:

First, national hierarchies seem to be divided on the issue of patriotism and presumptions in favor of one's nation in time of war, or of incumbent governments in cases of threat or outbreak of violent revolution. Liberal elements tend to be haunted by the historic record of uncritical patriotism, symbolized by bishops and chaplains blessing troops, flags, and battle trophies. Whatever religious background or instinct moved Joe Louis to say that America would win the Second World War because, "God is on our side," the effect is much the same as the "Gott mit Uns" mentality of World War I Germany or parallel beliefs in most of the parties to the two world wars. The natural reaction of the liberal churchman is to be skeptical about religious endorsement of war and alert to occasions where it appears appropriate to question or condemn his nation's recourse to and/or conduct of war.

Conservative elements remain staunchly patriotic, symbolized by the late Cardinal Spellman. In our times these elements have seldom gone so far as to tell troops in the field that they were "fighting for Christ." More likely, they ally with those who would prefer to shun these issues and ensure that episcopal statements will be few, rather general, and seldom explicitly critical.

Second, national hierarchies are also divided on their attitudes toward communism, Communist states, individual Communists, and Communist and fellow-traveling participation in domestic revolutionary activity. Thus, whereas the Vatican has gone quite far in a *détente* policy toward communism and Communist states, national hierarchies operate in a variety of nations, ranging from those wherein communism is outlawed to those where it is tolerated to those where it exercises great but not controlling power, to states that are Communist and in which the Church survives from day to day perilously. Generalizations are, therefore, difficult and of limited value.

However, it seems clear that throughout the majority of the nations in which Christianity dominates the religious scene there is a great and continued reaction against communism that is inflexible, sterile, and doctrinaire. But, increasingly, there blooms a reaction which seeks communication and understanding with domestic Communist and foreign Communist states, groups, and individuals. This is good. As we have said about the laws of war, communication with "the enemy" is the starting point of reasonable, limited conflict, hot or cold. But there are risks to "dialogue" with Communists, a very "in" concept among liberal Christians. One cannot discount the problem, so painfully manifested in the 1930s and so cruelly muckraked in the McCarthy era of the late 1940s and early 1950s in the United States, of the well-intentioned people who were taken in by nice, reasonable Communists, who later on did unpleasant things like joining the Nazis in aggression and genocidal actions against Poland —or holding the Soviet armies outside of Warsaw to permit the Nazis to finish off the elite of the Polish resistance.

Churchmen of this liberal, let's-have-dialogue tendency naturally discount the need for wars with Communist states or interventions in Communist-controlled revolutionary wars. They also tend to be optimistic about "talks," leading to "coalition" governments, the models for which have not been too reassuring. One recalls Czechoslovakia in 1948. The quick answer then comes, "under strick international inspection." Experience in Vietnam, Laos, and Cambodia, and the swift demise of UNEF in 1967 do not encourage enthusiasm over this attempted reassurance.

On the other hand, the hard-line, anti-Communist elements in national hierarchies hamper efforts to prevent and limit war, particularly revolutionary wars and interventions into such conflicts, by their outdated formulations of *"the* Red menace" (there are either *many* Red menaces or a few or none, but there certainly is not *one*), and, by their inclination to identify as "Communist" radical non-Communist individuals, groups, and ideas which might contribute positively toward amelioration of conditions leading to violent revolution.

Third, many national hierarchies are influenced strongly, at times too much so, and, again, in contradictory ways, by racial issues. This applies both to the issue of race in the Third World and to the American Civil Rights Movement which seems to have a world-wide influence. These attitudes, on colonialism, race, poverty, and on the means needed to combat them have, particularly in the United States tended to create an assumption that the basic problems, attitudes, and tactics, of "the civil rights movement," and, "the peace movement," are substantially identical or very closely related. This is such an important point that I will discuss it only in terms of the liberal elements in the hierarchies concerned, especially in the United States. Obviously, conservative or apathetic elements do not agree with their liberal colleagues on most of these points.

I would single out three points of identity between the movement for racial justice and the peace movement:

1. A feeling of guilt, shame, self-doubt, on the part of the advantaged toward the disadvantaged, of the great power toward the small power of the revolutionary opposition;

2. Tolerance and/or support for and participation in civil disobedience and revolutionary behavior on the grounds that the past and present injustices of the system justify and require such behavior;

3. A feeling of the necessity for commitment, involvement, social action, in order to be positively Christian and to avoid the worst of all stigmas, "irrelevance."

These historical phenomena have combined to develop a mentality within liberal elements in the Church which emphasizes opposition to virtually everything that exists: to the System as a whole and in its parts—the political system, the economic system, the social system, the racial system. It links domestic and international issues of many diverse types in its condemnation of "the war-system," meaning the international system as we have described it *and* the so-called "war-state." The presumptions are overwhelmingly against things as they are. The morally responsible thing to do is to join in action *against* "the system," *against,* indeed, virtually *all* "systems" that exist. As concerns the war-system, the place where the action is in the peace movement and the war-resisters movement.

But war-peace issues are distinct from, although obviously related to, racial issues, particularly racial issues over the denial of the clear constitutional rights of citizens on the grounds of color alone. Moreover, it remains to be seen whether all the "victories" of the civil rights movement will be as practically significant in the long run as they were psychologically and morally satisfying to some when they were achieved.

In any event, the departure of an articulate and effective elite minority within the American Catholic hierarchy, as among many Protestant and Jewish churchmen, from traditional patriotic or laissez-faire attitudes on war, deterrence, and revolution, and their active criticism of, and resistance to, war and compulsory military service, underscores the grave need for a thorough rethinking of Catholic thought on war, deterrence, revolution, and peace. One can welcome the new attitudes and involvements of the hierarchy in long-neglected areas of intense moral controversy. But if these attitudes and involvements are to be little more than imitations of, endorsement of, or exploitation by, other traditions, institutions, and viewpoints, then the significance of the intervention of bishops, clergymen, and nuns into war debates depends on the individual credentials of the person, notwithstanding the attempt of those who are anxious to brandish the power and prestige of the individual on letterheads and lists of signatories to letters and telegrams.

I have the impression that most "Catholic" supporters of strong positions on war-peace issues who take a position critical of a particular war add very little to the debate except their prestige. This is made possible by the fact of the optimistic, idealistic, vaguely pro-peace, anti-war character of contemporary Catholic teaching. For the pacifist or war-resister there is no tension between a possible need for war, or certain methods of war, and the need for peace with justice. He is against war. There *is* such a tension in official Catholic thought, not as much as there should be, but it exists. I do not sense enough of this tension, enough of this agonizing indecision, in some of the hierarchical support for opposition to the Vietnam War. I hope that I am wrong. I would like to see less of a dichotomy between, "My Country Right or Wrong," and "anti-communism," on the one hand, and "Clergy concerned," bishops on the other. (Just imagine, they are "concerned," they are not alone.) I would like to see some "limited war," members in the hierarchy who upheld the right to go to war when necessary but who sought to influence the conduct of war so that it would be at all times as limited as possible.

In any event, in most instances the intervention of representatives of the American Catholic hierarchy in the peace movement and in anti-war organizations does not represent the intervention of an expert on morality and war or of a high official of the Church who is expertly briefed on the material *or* the moral issues of war, deterrence, and revolution. These interventions represent the witness of holy, intelligent, concerned members of the hierarchy whose comparatively simplistic and human reactions *against* war (one would expect that, all things being equal, of a man of God) are, of course, for them, more than supported by the idealistic and humanitarian words and initiatives that emanate from Rome.

This raises a very difficult question, that of the authority of the intervention into peace debates by persons high in the hierarchy. The question might be answered with the familiar statement that a particular bishop is speaking and acting only as a "concerned" individual, and, certainly not in his episcopal role. But there is no way, at least in a church organized as is the Catholic Church, to maintain this distinction. Moreover, despite the disclaimers both of sponsoring organizations and of their supporters from the hierarchy, it is obviously the case that those who agree with a particular bishop's intervention will attribute much greater weight to it than would be accorded to lesser members of the hierarchy or to prestigious lay persons.

Fortunately, it is increasingly the case that liberal bishops, and, indeed, members of the hierarchy of various points of view, are seeking informed guidance. This has been a hallmark of the new U. S. Bishops' Secretariat on Justice and Peace, an approach pioneered by Monsignor George Higgins when his Social Action Department handled international problems for the U. S. Catholic Conference. But this still leaves problems. There is not enough relevant doctrine. The paucity of "experts" on the morality of war, deterrence, and revolution—persons comparable in competence to, say, Monsignor Higgins or Father John Cronin on economic and social problems, or Father Andrew M. Greeley on the sociology of American Catholicism, is a very serious problem.

For popes, bishops, priests (especially those who claim special competence as theologians), cannot be universal or instant experts on all moral problems. They need expert advice as to the technical facts and issues and as to moral analyses of the implications of such facts and issues. To be sure, not all subjects admit of the same degree of expertise, and, even the most technical and scientific experts are prone to error. Doctors lose patients unexpectedly. Space ships suffer malfunctions and even destruction. In the realm of social problems both the empirical social scientist and the moralist are working with relatively new and tentative tools. Miscalculation, error, and bad luck are normal in attempts to "solve" social problems. But there are persons who are comparatively expert in the social and moral sciences. Clearly those with competence relevant to war, deterrence, and revolution should be consulted, through careful reading of their works, and, where possible, through direct exchanges. In my view, a review of official statements by the American hierarchy on war, deterrence, revolution, and peace fail to reveal an adequate awareness of the need to consult secular empirical disciplines when grappling with extremely difficult problems. A member of the hierarchy is, of course, free to reject the views of the so-called experts, to be skeptical as to the extent of their expertise, or to prefer some experts over others. But he should reflect *exposure* to the principal findings and perspectives of the experts.

Moreover, the member of the hierarchy needs more than the advice of technical experts. He needs moralists who are competent to sift that advice and to provide moral analyses of the implications. Such moralists are to be found in a number of fields, ranging from birth control to the dynamics of parish life in different environments. But there are very few moralists to help with questions of war, deterrence, revolution, and peace. Most of those who have wrestled with these questions are irrelevant to the existing international system and to the domestic societies in which most of us have to work out our problems. They tend to be alienated, desirous of removing themselves from society, desirous of removing themselves from things as they are. This is their personal right. But popes and bishops have to concern themselves with nations, statesmen, citizens, who are not alienated and removed from society. What is to be said to them? If the institutional Church is to speak authoritatively and competently, it needs some technically competent, well-thought-through social theory about deterrence, revolution, and peace with justice, and it needs such theory now.

All that has been said thus far can be summed up insofar as the universal Church and the American Catholic Church is concerned, is that the Church needs moralists and scholars, studying the material and moral problems of war, deterrence, revolution, and peace. What should be the prerequisites for Catholic moralists and scholars equal to the difficult task the Church faces, as it works for the control of war and the establishment of peace with justice? Competence in the following fields seems necessary:

1. Theology;
2. Ethics;

3. Political and legal theory; domestic and international;

4. International relations theory and contemporary history, including peace research;

5. Military history and science, including modern war and deterrence theory and practice and their relation to arms control;

6. The psychology and sociology of political violence.

One could add such subjects as economics, the interdisciplinary study of development, race, and international relations. One could go on and on. In any event, it is clear that few moralists presently possess competence in more than a few of these subjects. I assume that the experts will have to be developed, not discovered.

I can see two basic models for the moralists and scholars needed to help advise the Church on war, deterrence, revolution, and peace.

One model could be called the John Courtney Murray model. Father Murray possessed great competence in the first three of the fields just listed. He came to possess impressive familiarity with a number of the others. But even this eminent model underscores the difficulty of the problem. For Father Murray was, at a critical time for the subject, a truly outstanding authority on Church-State relations, and, in the end, it was to this subject that he was obliged to devote the major part of his attention. But the war-peace problems with which he had been grappling in the late 1950s were subject to great change—ideological, military, technical. Whoever undertakes to specialize in war, deterrence, revolution, peace—and morality—must make a total commitment to this problem area. So the model must be John Courtney Murray as a specialist in Church-State matters, not Father Murray as a brilliant but intermittent commentator on moral aspects of war and international relations.

The alternative model would be a specialist in some of the empirical subjects relative to war, deterrence, revolution, and peace, who would be willing to master sufficiently the normative subjects of theology, ethics, and legal and political theory. I find it difficult to judge the possibilities and difficulties of such an undertaking. Theology and ethics are in revolutionary turmoil. Leading biblical scholars are accused of heresy by bishops and the present occupants of seminaries where "immutable" principles once reigned unchallenged seem to be rushing to the nearest exponent of situation ethics. To complete the crisis, Pope Paul VI has found it necessary to unleash his encyclical *Humanae Vitae* on a divided Church and a shaken world.

It seems to be the mode to pick one's own preferred moralists and ethicists and head, without further ado, into social arenas, where the action is. Since "relevance" is the highest of virtues, except for the conservatives for whom "orthodoxy" remains number one, and since, for the kinds of people who concern themselves with war, deterrence, revolution, and peace, all outstanding problems should have been solved yesterday, there is little time or patience for extended research, study, and contemplation.

But these problems which should have been solved yesterday, especially those of war, deterrence, and revolution, will still be here tomorrow. While immediate judgments and actions are necessary in the face of contemporary conflict, continuing research and study, empirical and moral, of these problems are needed to judge the efficacy and moral quality of past judgments and actions and to provide guidelines for the future. The necessity for study and analysis side by side with social action will, in my judgment, remain until the end of the world. It cannot be arbitrarily delimited in terms of substance, methodology, or time. It will take whatever proves necessary, and it will last as long as the problems remain, in one form or another. Moreover, such studies must always be undertaken with the humble realization that not all problems will be "solved" on this earth, even though there will always be a moral obligation to keep trying to solve them.

As to the alternative models, normative expert turned social scientist, social scientist turned normative expert, it is almost certain that the model which emerges depends on who volunteers for this necessary but unpleasant work. As a legalist and social scientist, I would be very chary about purporting to speak in theological terms, less so in ethical terms, even though I would hope to be inspired and informed by theological and ethical truths and perspectives. I would like to see professional theologians and ethicists turn seriously and on a long-term basis to the problems of war and revolution. Eminent Protestant thinkers have shown that it can be done—Reinhold Niebuhr, John C. Bennett, Paul Ramsey—Catholics should benefit from their work, example, and counsel.

At the same time, I would hope that other legalists and social scientists will increase their awareness of the profound moral implications of their studies relevant to war, deterrence, revolution, and peace. I would hope also that my legal and social science colleagues would be a trifle less clinical in their studies of human conflict and that they would realize that more than occasionally they are playing God. That being the case, they would do well to check in from time to time with men whose calling it is to study, proclaim, interpret, and apply the word of God.

Research and study commensurate with the magnitude of the problems of war, deterrence, revolution, and peace, requires continuing, devoted, teamwork. They call for coherent, co-ordinated, adequately supported programs of research, writing, education, and, ultimately, mass education. The Christian churches have a great and challenging role to play in contributing to this effort. They have, as well, and especially in the case of the Roman Catholic Church, a great debt to make up for the centuries of neglect which have contributed to the present world of conflict wherein weapons systems and social systems, following dynamic processes that at times seem virtually out of control, dictate man's fate, rather than human intelligence and will, informed by religious and human perspectives.

Happily, the Roman Catholic Church is beginning to improve its efforts to devote adequate human and material resources to the study of peace and development, on the one hand, and to war, deterrence, and revolution, on the other. Vatican II was explicit on the necessity of such efforts. In concert with the efforts of other Christians and men of good will, teamwork in the study both of peace and development, and of war, deterrence, and revolution, must be pressed. But, in the end, such efforts depend upon individual human beings with the talents and the will to study international problems instead of turning their back on them or wishing them out of existence.

The "peace movement," like the "civil rights movement," in the United States is difficult to define. It suffers from periodic announcements that it is "dead," or "captured," or had "sold out," or, "taken over by the Commies," which reflect differing views as to what it is or ought to be. The peace movement also suffers from a malady apparently endemic to humanitarian movements, internal strife. The anger of a jilted woman is nothing compared to that of individuals or factions within the peace movement who disagree on ends, means, or both. It takes thick skin, good nerves, and a strong heart to survive in the peace movement. It also requires great tolerance. Since there are many paths to peace, and since peace is illusive, recriminations within the peace movement are understandable, but they should be mitigated by charity.

Needless to say, a realist finds work in the peace movement frustrating at times. With Paul Ramsey, I deplore the tendency throughout much of its elements to take strong positions on difficult foreign policy issues without adequate study, reflection, knowledge, or realism.[8] Moreover, I find it hard to tolerate the moralistic tone taken by many activists in the peace movement, those with explicit religious identifications and those for whom the quest for peace is, in effect, a religion. Too many people in the peace movement are quick to say, "I condemn as immoral," rather than, "I strongly disagree."

It would help those of us who are less prone to optimism and to moral indignation if the leaders of prominent peace movement organizations would do two things; first, they should endeavor to study foreign-policy issues on their merits within the realm of the possible and re-examine their own policy positions periodically; second, they should recognize the limits of peace organizations as forces for political action and broad public education.

As to the first, it is a disservice to the legitimate goals of peace

[8] Paul Ramsey, *Who Speaks for the Church?* (Nashville & New York: Abingdon, 1967).

organizations to remain locked in fixed positions and slogans, as is so often the case. For example, most of the peace movement is deeply committed to foreign aid and international development. Aid and development are among the best hopes for eliminating the causes of war. Therefore they are good. The more aid and international development there is, the more the causes of war will be diminished. Every year such positions are reiterated in statements submitted to hardhearted members of congressional committees.

Some of this testimony is informed, responsible, and imaginative. Much of it, I fear, is not. Foreign aid is not just a matter of figures and percentages of GNP. It involves complex questions of techniques, timing, assessment of attitudes, and behavior of recipients, and the like. Some of the most experienced practitioners and students of foreign aid, who are also dedicated to international social justice, have serious reservations about U.S. and other aid programs.[9]

It is not enough for a peace organization to go through the annual ritual of supporting foreign aid and to preach the gospel of aid and development to its constituents and anyone else who listens to it. Within reasonable limits, according to its resources, such an organization should be "studying the question" of aid and development, just as it should be studying the questions of war, deterrence, revolution, and peace. This involves a seriousness of practical commitment that surpasses blind adhesion to something that sounds like a good idea.

In the case of Catholic peace organizations, the need for independent and sometimes sharply critical thinking applies to reactions to official Church pronouncements on aid, development, war, deterrence, revolution, peace, and related issues. For example, many American Catholics with enormous practical experience in aid and development do not share the euphoria with the encyclical which *Populorum Progressio* has been met in the peace movement. In the long run, it would be better for the quality and influence of papal

[9] See, for example, Victor C. Ferkiss, *Foreign Aid: Moral and Political Aspects* (New York: Council on Religion and International Affairs, 1965).

encyclicals, development, and the peace movement, if such critical reactions were openly and charitably voiced and debated.

Concerning my second proposition, peace organizations should re-examine their actual power and influence with their constituencies and with society generally. They should from time to time ask themselves:

1. What attention do our constituencies pay to our opinions on foreign-policy matters?

2. What attention does the government pay to these opinions? Further, what *kind* of attention does the government accord them? Are they part of serious dialogues? Are they treated as informed sources of support, opposition, new ideas? Or are these opinions considered uninformed, unduly simplistic, not worth noting, or only silly views to be coped with by better PR and, if necessary, stern lecturing? Honestly, what attention *should* the government pay to our opinions?

3. What attention does the general public pay to peace organizations and with what effect? We know that foreign-policy issues rarely play a large role in voting and in voters' attitudes. The exception is provided by an unpopular war, and virtually all extended wars today soon become unpopular. Yet any veteran of the peace movement has heard sweeping claims to political influence or aspirations to the attainment of such influence, that seem exaggerated on their face, by peace activists.

Peace organizations should ask themselves not only whether they can achieve major immediate political influence on the climate of opinion but whether they really see intervention in politics as their proper role. For my part, I would prefer the role of long-range education and influence on the climate of opinion in a nation than that of lobbyist, or participant in political coalitions, or in competition with those who judge effectiveness in terms of the number of thousands of telegrams dumped at the White House or in the mailrooms on Capitol Hill.

The point may well be made in rebuttal to my line of thinking that the peace movement has played a major role in changing political situations, notably in its crusade against the Vietnam War. Some peace activists claim that they toppled the most effective American politician of recent years, Lyndon B. Johnson, and are changing history. Even in this case, I persist in my contention that the peace movement has only modest political muscle and that this may be all to the good. Among the reasons for my estimate are the following:

In the first place, all modern wars have been accepted as necessary evils by the American people. The only modern war to which the nation was clearly committed was World War II, which resulted from an attack on Pearl Harbor. Subsequent wars and threats have seldom, except the Cuban Missile Crisis, involved clear and present dangers to the United States. There is always pressure to end these wars. For example, the Korean War presented extraordinarily clear-cut legal-moral issues favoring American participation. It was, in a very real sense the first international "police action," and was the subject of some of the most indefensible Communist negotiation tactics and propaganda. Yet, it was an unpopular, ultimately unsupported war, from which the United States extricated itself as rapidly as it could.

Thus, one reason for public support of the U.S. war effort in World War II, aside from Pearl Harbor, and the immoral character of the Nazi regime, which, however, had not been sufficiently opposed to bring America into the war before Pearl Harbor, was the great quantity of government propaganda arousing the nation. This element tended to become internally contradictory and self-defeating in the Korean War, when some had too much war spirit to go along with the limited-war policies of the Truman administration. In the Vietnam War, the government has deliberately sought, in Mr. Rusk's words, to avoid creation of a "war spirit," for fear that an aroused public might demand measures which responsible statesmen in a nuclear nation could not take.

To complicate matters, a sizable portion of the American electorate, and an extremely influential element in Congress, as well as some corners of the Pentagon, are unreconstructed *air power* "true believers." They believe that unlimited war, based primarily on air power, using, if necessary, weapons of "mass destruction," can *win* "victory." All problems will then be solved, under Pax Americana. This, of course, requires an endless spiral of scientific and technological development as advocated by Dr. Teller and, in effect, substantially a blank check for this purpose permanently deposited in the Pentagon. If this great power is not developed or used, if total victory is not an attainable goal, this important element in the American society and government tends to join forces with those who oppose wars generally, or who oppose a particular war that is lagging, such as that in Vietnam. This combination of super-hawks and doves, *not* the imagined power of the peace movement, seems to explain most adequately the Johnson administration's difficulties over Vietnam.

Of incalcuable importance has been the intervention of other movements into war-peace debates—particularly the civil rights and the various Negro or Black movements, and the Poor People's campaign. They brought not only numbers, but talent, courage, and, at times, frightening powers of coercion, as well as prestigious sympathizers, into the movement to end the war in Vietnam.

Finally, revolution on college campuses has put anti-war and anti-draft activism at the top of the goals of student dissidents. It has given them an ideal issue, justifying on moralistic grounds conduct that would normally be generally condemned as self-evidently lawless and outrageous. This has occurred in part as a result of the revolt of the professors in the "teach-ins," giving a variety and depth of expertise to the peace movement which it normally does not possess. In the process, it was often overlooked that temporary teach-in reinforcements to peace movement protests against a particular war were not necessarily supporters of the peace movement, or of its several idealistic or pacifist approaches to war-peace problems. Thus, the paradox of the role of Hans Morgenthau, whose anguish has already been alluded to.

My point is not to denigrate the peace movement, to discount its very real role in debates on Vietnam and other foreign policy issues. Nor is it to criticize that role because I often disagreed with the policies and techniques of prominent individuals and organizations in the peace movement. My point is that the peace movement is headed for catastrophic euphoria, catastrophic for the movement and for the cause of peace—with justice. The activist in the peace movement with any experience beyond contemporary melodramas should remember the normal days of the movement.

He should remember that his activities usually cannot draw and retain the attention, much less the support, of most of the temporary allies who poured into the fray protesting the Vietnam War. End the war in Vietnam, find new issues to engage the attention of advocates of Black Power, Poor People's Power, Student Power, Faculty Power, and all the other Powers, and the peace-organization leader and his faithful flock will once again meet in modest circumstances, generally ignored, mentioned in the press only occasionally, and then on the Saturday Religion page. Opposing an unpopular war and toppling a harassed administration is news. Working to prevent and mitigate war and to build peace the hard way is not news and does not draw large crowds looking for "relevance," and "action."

What, then should be the proper goals of peace organizations? I think that their role should be primarily in the realm of thought and discussion, rather than action. They should provide the audiences and readers for the discussions and writings of the moralists and scholars who write on morality, war, deterrence, revolution, and peace. They should debate the approaches and degree of progress of these moralists and scholars, as well as of initiatives of their own government and of international organizations. In the light of their own individual and organizational views, members of peace organizations should try to influence the society in which they live, in whatever way is appropriate to their organization. They should try to influence opinion and opinion-making institutions and individuals, but on a quiet, patient, continuing basis, not in a series of desperate "either-or" forays into a world where the making and manipulation of opinion is a profession and advanced art that should be approached with caution by amateurs.

As already indicated, peace organizations should mix criticism with approval with respect both to subjects that seem to lead to "peace" and subjects that involve "war." By constructive criticism they should try to keep internationalists honest and realistic. As to those who have to deal with war and preparations for war, they should support and encourage enlightened efforts to limit war as well as protect preparations for war they consider unjustified. They should support reasonable recourse to armed force as well as opposing recourse to it that they think is unreasonable. Thus the efficacy of a peace organization should not, as is the current vogue, be judged in terms of frequency and noise level of its protests against war and its demands for peace. It should be judged on the merits of its stands on the real, not the ideal or rhetoric or illusory issues of war, deterrence, revolution, and peace. This appraisal should be a matter of practical appreciation of the problems and contributions, not of the fervor or moral commitment with which peace organizations take their stand.

War, deterrence, revolution, and peace are fundamental problems for every morally responsible human being. The nature of the individual's moral responsibility with regard to these problems is established by his station in life and the events of his lifetime. For the responsible Christian, for the responsible human being, war is an acute and constant moral problem from which he cannot escape. The attitudes and actions, as well as the failures to act, of the Christian citizen, or of any other morally responsible citizen contribute to the totality of attitudes, acts, and omissions that make up human history in his lifetime and greatly affect the future. There is no place to hide from the moral dilemmas of war, deterrence, and revolution, nor from the positive requirements for peace with justice.

There are no other individuals or institutions to whom the responsible individual's moral responsibilities in these matters can properly be transferred. Lack of adequate moral guidance, or conflicts of views as to the moral guidelines to be followed in judging the issues of war, deterrence, revolution, and peace, do not absolve the individual from responsibility to study and make judgments about these questions. Absence of clear doctrine and leadership, disagreement

among authoritative leaders and experts, mitigate the degree of individual moral responsibility, but they do not remove it. Even lack
of freedom from fear or punishment cannot provide a total excuse
for avoiding individual judgments on the issues of war, deterrence,
revolution, and peace.

One other, often cited, excuse properly ought to be denied to the
individual who would shun the moral dilemmas of war, deterrence,
and revolution. This is the plea of lack of adequate information. Certainly, as this book has stressed, thought and action based on inadequate knowledge or lack of understanding of relevant normative
principles and material facts, are to be discouraged. But there is a
continuing obligation to learn more, always more, about the principles
and about the facts relative to the problems of war, deterrence,
revolution, and peace. This obligation increases in proportion to the
astonishing increase in available sources of information concerning
both issues and facts.

In the advanced and free nations, the news media, news magazines, journals of opinion, and magazines directed to almost every
conceivable audience, ultimately get most of the issues and most of
the facts to the individual who is looking for them. This is the case,
notwithstanding the inadequacies and biases of these sources. Books,
especially paperbacks, deal with all of the problems we have dealt
with and are widely available. Moreover, the impact of the transistor
radio and, in the future of television and other means of mass communication, as well as rising literacy, will increasingly make possible
a more informed and responsible response to the issues of war, deterrence, revolution, and peace, in the developing nations. In some
of these countries, as in some of the advanced nations, political
control severely limits recourse to sources of information, and much
misinformation is propagated. But the trend is toward a gradual
increase in knowledge throughout the world which, it is to be hoped,
will increase the number of human beings who can become more
informed and responsible citizens of the world, as well as of the
nation in which they live. Perhaps the day will even come when
some of the developing nations drop the attitude that the material

and moral problems of war, deterrence, and revolution, are almost exclusively the problems of the older, affluent nations, who are presumably rightly stuck with the results of their own past mistakes and sins, and acknowledge that these problems are everybody's problems.

In any event, there is no excuse for contemporary man, in an advanced, open society, to say that he does not know enough about the relevant moral principles, the issues, and the facts, concerning war, deterrence, revolution, and peace, or of the causes of international conflict and their possible remedies, to have some responsible opinions, or at least questions, which he should persist in arguing and/or raising.

Since this book was written from a Christian perspective, I will end it on a specifically Christian note. Christianity, as faith, as society, must face the issue of war and/or survival. The subject can no longer be begged or finessed. This means that the individual Christian has to inform himself, question the adequacy of the teaching of his Church on war, deterrence, revolution, and peace, and *press* for competent, realistic answers. We are not children—would that we were—so we cannot settle back and yearn for "world authority" with peace and disarmament based on sincerity and mutual trust. We are adults in a divided and extremely dangerous world—dangerous to life and property, and also to fundamental values and human dignity —and we have to cope with it, if necessary by some form of war.

Accordingly, for the individual Christian conscience the question is not, "What would Christ do about war, deterrence, revolution, and peace, if He returned on earth?" The question is, "What does Christ require *me* to do, given my station in life, about these problems?" Just as Donne's bell tolls for all of us, the call to confront the hard facts of war, deterrence, and revolution—and the illusiveness of peace with justice—goes out to all of us.